ALSO BY DICK MORRIS AND EILEEN MCGANN

Rewriting History
Because He Could
Condi v Hillary
Outrage
Fleeced
Catastrophe
Revolt
Screwed
2010: Take Back America
Here Come the Black Helicopters
Power Grab
Armageddon: How Trump Can Beat Hillary
Rogue Spooks

ALSO BY DICK MORRIS

Bum Rap on American Cities
Behind the Oval Office
The New Prince
Vote.com
Power Plays
Off with Their Heads

50 Shades of Politics

50 Shades of Politics

DICK MORRIS
with EILEEN MCGANN

Triangulation Publishing

50 Shades of Politics

FIRST EDITION

Library of Congress Cataloging-in-Publication Data has been applied for.

ISBN: 978-1-79-087722-5

To our dear late friends, Jorge Estrada and Miguel Sal,
who are still in our hearts.

50 Shades of Politics

Contents

INTRODUCTION

I've seen it all.

For the past fifty years, I've been immersed in the thrilling kaleidoscope of American politics.

It's been an amazing journey and unexpected evolution as I passed through the shades of political coloration from blue through purple to bright red.

I've changed along the way. As a student in the 1960s, I began my career on the left side of the political spectrum—embedded in the darkest shade of radical blue Democratic party politics.

From there, as a political consultant, I progressed to another shade—purple, the result of combining blue and red to form a new color. That's when I worked with both parties, sometimes in that extinct arena of politics formerly known as bipartisan cooperation. It was clothed in purple that I helped Bill Clinton pass landmark legislation like welfare reform, with bipartisan support.

The rest of my journey—from purple to red—was largely involuntary. As Ronald Reagan once said, "I didn't leave the Democratic Party. It left me."[1] Bipartisanship stopped working as the Democrats lurched so far to the left that I didn't recognize them or support their agenda. So, ultimately, I became a bright red Republican.

Fifty years of laboring through the labyrinth of competing shades and hues of party politics gave me a unique vantage point and understanding of the perspectives and workings of both the right and the left.

I understood them both and I also understood that—at that time—things were not always so black and white.

Instead, there seemed to be at least 50 shades of politics.

I've advised Democrats and Republicans, men and women, conservatives and liberals. And I've helped elect 19 senators and governors (11 Republicans and 8 Democrats) and the presidents or prime ministers of 12 foreign countries.

I wrote this book to share some of the wonderful experiences I've had—the fun, the people I've met, the places I've traveled to, and the memories that stand out.

It's not a typical political memoir or an accounting of the most serious and important things I've ever done.

Instead, this is a compilation of about one hundred stories telling what happened along the way. Some are autobiographic, others are funny examples of working in this quirky business and traveling in foreign countries. Some are controversial. Some reveal exactly what-it-was-like.

This book isn't finished yet—and neither am I. I'm still living new chapters, even as I pause to write up the old.

Any story about my life would be incomplete without including a view of my wife Eileen, so there are glimpses of our lives together and our decades of collaboration and adventures. I hope you get to know her as I do. She changed my life from dull to vibrant, from flat to textured, and from black and white to brilliant color.

Eileen's contributions to this book (as well as in all our others) makes it a bit like the famous: *Autobiography of Alice B. Toklas* by Gertrude Stein.

The chapters skip around. So has my life and career. I hope you enjoy reading them as much as we have loved living them.

1. Dreams Really Do Come True

I understood just how important dreams are when my biggest one was realized on a freezing night in January 1995.

I was working alone in the handsome Treaty Room that served as President Bill Clinton's version of a home office in the White House Residence.

The beauty of the room was distracting. It was perfect—in its proportions, in the balance of brilliant colors, and in the collection of historical memorabilia and furniture. But it was also surprisingly warm and inviting.

And I definitely wanted to stay.

Looking around, I found it hard to believe that I was actually there, really working in the White House…for the President of the United States.

I sat down in a comfortable chair near the fireplace for a moment, gazing around the room and considering its history.

I knew it had been used as a Cabinet Room by Presidents Andrew Johnson and Ulysses Grant. And a large painting over a leather couch depicted President McKinley signing the Peace Treaty that ended the Spanish American War in this very room.

I wanted to linger, to savor the moment and think about the ghosts of Presidents past. But it was time to get back to work, so I walked over to the typing table that had been installed for me, topped by an old IBM Selectric typewriter.

I was thrilled about what I was doing. For several months, I had been privately advising the President, trying to help him develop a strategy to turn around his dismal approval numbers. After the Democrats resoundingly lost both houses of Congress in 1994, Clinton's popularity plummeted. Now only 41% of the voters approved of him, while 47% didn't.

He'd been vanquished, and he was devastated. But he was determined to turn things around.

Less than a year before, he maintained a 63% approval rating and believed he was invincible. But now he was suddenly in free fall and his own party blamed him—and Hillary—for its staggering defeat.

Clinton was profoundly shaken and already deeply worried about his own reelection in two years. The midterm elections had been nothing less than a massacre of historical proportions.

For the first time since 1952, the Democrats were not in control of the House. Thirty-four democratic incumbents were defeated and another eighteen open seats were picked up by Republicans, resulting in a monumental shift of fifty-four seats to the Republicans.

The news media called the cataclysmic change "The Gingrich Revolution" because it vaulted the charismatic and brilliant Newt Gingrich into the Speakership of the House. It was going to a whole new ball game.

I had seen the rumblings of a growing party shift, but I never expected the magnitude of the tsunami-like hatred of the Democratic Party and the unmistakable anti-Clinton fervor that swept the country.

In October 1994, weeks before the election, I tried to warn the President when he surprised me with a call to discuss the mid-term elections. I cautioned him that it looked like a massive rout was coming.

He seemed bewildered when I reported polling results in several states that showed a clear Republican trend in the Senate and a possibility of a game changer in the House, too.

"Those are old polls," he countered, noting that he had just returned from signing the Israel-Jordan Peace Agreement. "My ratings are better now. I can turn things around."

As he campaigned all over the country, he basked in the glow of his strongest supporters. Based on the cheering crowds, he was convinced that the House was definitely not in play and that the Democrats would hold on to the Senate.

But, of course, he was only preaching to the Democratic choir, those core voters who would never abandon the party—no matter what! Those who disagreed would never come near him.

When I told him that he was living in an echo chamber of Democratic partisans and needed to prepare for the Republicans taking over at least the Senate, he brushed the idea aside.

I suggested that his highly-publicized campaigning for Democratic candidates was actually hurting him—that he was eroding his hard-earned "presidential" image and was beginning to be viewed as just another party hack, not a presidential leader.

"Here's my advice: Stop campaigning and go back to the White House or go on a foreign trip. Focus on your role as President, as the leader, not as a politician," I told him.

He resisted and described his plans to double down and barnstorm from coast to coast.

I tried again. "Remember Nixon's Rose Garden strategy?" I asked. "It was a good one. Try it."

But he didn't—or wouldn't—get it. He was still confident of a Democratic triumph and nothing would convince him otherwise. So I put it to him in the starkest terms I could.

"You don't want to hear this, but you are going to lose the Senate and the House, too," I told him.

But it was obvious that he never considered that to be a serious possibility.

And then came the humiliating across the board defeats.

Hillary immediately understood what was happening. On the day after the election, she called and asked me to come to the White House right away to meet with her and Bill.

As Yogi Berra would say, this was déjà vu all over again. This same thing had happened once before when Bill lost the Arkansas Governor's race in 1980.

Some background: After I worked to help him get elected Governor in 1978, Bill Clinton fired me. He resented my advice and disagreements with him over tax issues. We didn't speak for almost two years. Then, two weeks before the 1980 election, Hillary called and told, Eileen, that Bill was in trouble and needed me to come to Arkansas right away.

I was busy working on other elections and, anyway, it was much too late to reverse Bill's fortunes. On election day, the Arkansas voters soundly defeated him after only one two-year term.

But the Clintons didn't miss a beat. Starting only one week after election day, they and I worked closely together for the next ten years. Bill regained the governorship in 1982 and got re-elected in 1984, 1986, and 1990. We became estranged after a serious altercation in the Governor's Mansion in Little Rock in 1990. We spoke only occasionally for the next few years.

But now, history was repeating itself.

That's how I ended up in the Treaty Room that night.

Except for the President, First Lady, and several discreet ushers, no one had any inkling that I was there that night, quietly drafting the 1995 State of the Union address. (That's why I was using the IBM Selectric and not the White House computer system.)

5

Neither Bill nor Hillary wanted the White House staff to know that there was a new kid on the block. If a draft appeared the next morning on the computer system, his people would know that someone else had written it. Neither Bill nor Hillary knew how to type.

So the president wanted me to type the draft on the old IBM Selectric. He took each page from me as I finished it and copied it out in his left-handed writing.

I hadn't been typing for very long when I heard footsteps. President Clinton had entered the room. I started to stand up and he quickly motioned for me to sit back down.

I nodded and resumed typing. For a while, he sat at his desk, reading through papers. Then I heard him get up and move directly behind me to look over my shoulder at what I was writing. When I looked up, he was looming over me like a giant sequoia.

We had worked together like this for many years when he was Governor. But tonight was very different.

Now Bill Clinton was no longer the governor of a small southern state. He was the President of the United States. The magnitude of that reality sank in, very deeply.

I got emotional. I choked up.

I turned fully around in my chair to look up at him, way up, and said, "Mr. President, you know, I've dreamed of doing exactly this—in exactly this way—ever since I was eight years old."

The President smiled back: "Me, too."

And it was true. My lifelong obsession with American history and U.S. Presidents began with the first chapter book I ever read when I was eight years old—a biography of Thomas Jefferson. That was the beginning of a habit that continues to this day. I consume history and biographies, often staying up late into the night and enjoying quiet time reading my books—with the sounds of the ocean or a snapping fire in the background.

My parents prepared me for a career in politics that might involve advising a President. Not consciously, of course. But they encouraged my interest in history and Presidents.

We took family trips to Washington, Mount Vernon, Hyde Park, Charlottesville, Sagamore Hill, and Gettysburg. And my library books were all about American history.

I started seriously concentrating on the presidents when I was nine. That's when my Aunt Florence gave me a set of presidential statues that I adored. I spent endless hours each week carefully organizing them into different categories: chronological order, one-termers, political parties, war presidents, former generals, bearded presidents (Lincoln, Grant, Hayes, Garfield, and Harrison). I would constantly move them around, reshuffling them into the categories. I was like a kid playing with a Lego set. My final category was a ranking in order of greatness.

Almost forty years later, I discussed those rankings with the President of the United States—something I never expected to happen—even in my wildest dreams.

I am still amazed—and grateful—that I was blessed to be able to achieve my childhood goal of working with a President precisely as I dreamt it.

I *did* advise the President and turn around his dismal poll numbers, I actually *did* work in the White House. And I *did* work with the President to pass seminal legislation like the Welfare Reform Bill. These dreams actually happened!

Sometimes, it felt like I had come to bat in the bottom of the ninth in the last game of the World Series and hit the winning home run. (Combining my two great fantasies: baseball and politics.) But this daydream became my reality and, ultimately, an unforgettable memory.

Yours can, too.

So, don't give up on your special dreams—even if they often seem impossible. Hold on to them and do whatever it takes to achieve them. Prepare for the day when that dream suddenly seems attainable. They really can come true.

2. Getting Started

Whenever I speak to a group and meet new people, I'm always asked: "How did you get into politics?" The answer is simple: I was born into it.

Politics is all I've ever known, all I've ever done.

There was one minor exception—a short stint at a neighborhood pharmacy when I was twelve. I delivered perfume on Saturdays. It wasn't inspiring, but I managed to save enough money to buy posters for my candidates for the school elections.

Other than that, I've worked on political campaigns or public policy issues for my entire life.

It's in my blood.

My father came from a Democratic political family in the Bronx. He was raised by "Uncle Al," his mother's brother and a New York State Supreme Court Judge, who was a leading Jewish political boss and Mr. Fix-it. Uncle Al dispensed patronage and named judges and candidates. What my father learned from Uncle Al, he passed on to me.

On Saturday mornings, I would accompany my father on the forty-minute walk from our apartment on West 85th Street to his office in midtown. I loved that time with him.

Along the way, he would pick a topic and teach me all about it. On several Saturdays, he taught me about the "favor" system in politics, always using examples of Uncle Al's political style that was based on building a constituency by providing help for tenants, the elderly, and local politicians in dealing with the bureaucracy. I never forgot that.

"Whenever any politician gets a job or a contract or a grant from the government," he told me, "he should always look for how to use his power to do favors for other politicians and, of course, for voters. It's how the system works. Everybody has a memory of the favors he granted and those he received. You have to give in order to get. Nothing is more important than to balance out your favor account."

That's often still true in politics. But, in politics and in life generally, I've come to believe that there are givers and takers. The former give without thought of any return. The latter receive with no notion of gratitude or obligation. You just have to know with which one you are dealing.

My father frequently reminisced about growing up in his grandmother's house and watching Uncle Al meet with local politicians to decide who would be the judges and the legislators.

Uncle Al ruled the family. He found jobs, apartments , and did various other favors. It's part of the family folklore that he eventually intervened somehow to help a particularly unpopular law graduate who had married into the family. That man had failed the Bar Exam four times, but somehow he passed on the fifth try and got a civil service job with city government.

It was Uncle Al who strongly advised my father to leave his position teaching art history at City College and go to law school. When Uncle Al spoke, his relatives listened. My father dutifully enrolled in St. John's Law School, leaving behind a potentially successful career in academia. But he moved on to law, and practiced for more than sixty years.

Uncle Al was famous for another reason, too.

His son was Roy Cohn, the bad boy of the legal establishment who became Donald Trump's lawyer, and some say his mentor.

Roy rose to fame—and infamy—as the majority counsel for the famed McCarthy Committee, hunting down communists real and imagined. Later, he became one of the world's most successful lawyers, representing everyone from Donald Trump to Aristotle Onassis.

Like most liberals at the time, my mother despised Roy and his tactic of portraying innocent people as communists.

His subsequent representation of mobsters did nothing to improve her opinion of him. That's probably why I met him only a few times, even though he worked for my father's law firm for a while.

On those walks, my Dad described, in great detail, the political machinations that were necessary to get the necessary zoning and other controversial approvals for his many projects. Lincoln Center for the Performing Arts, on 63rd street and Broadway in Manhattan, was one of them. It took years to clear the property and relocate the tenants who lived on or near the site. But he got it done.

My father took me to the groundbreaking ceremony in 1959. That was the first time I actually saw a real president. I was thrilled to be up close to President Eisenhower as he walked into the tent to the tunes of *Hail to The Chief.*

After the ceremony, we strolled through the property that would eventually become one of the most beautiful cultural centers in the world. It was certainly not beautiful at that point. It was a mess. The slums had been razed but there was debris and dirt everywhere. That didn't interfere with my Dad's vision.

He pointed out where the Metropolitan Opera House, the New York State Theatre, the New York Philharmonic, and the fountain would eventually be located. It was very hard to imagine at the time.

Years later, Eileen and I lived right across the street from the finished Lincoln Center. As we'd walk through the square on our way to a concert or the Opera, I could still recall the muddy mess that was transformed into that glorious space and remember that day with my Dad.

9

He was quite an attorney. He represented all the top real estate developers in New York City: Harry Helmsley, Bob Tishman, and Sam Lefrak.

One of my father's major clients was Fred Trump and then his son Donald. My father, Roy, and Donald worked closely together with my Dad doing the legal heavy lifting, Roy the politics and Donald the financing. I remember that the future president came to my parents' house for dinner with his then wife Ivana, who, I think, had a broken leg. Eileen and I stopped by to meet them. They were a stunning couple.

When I ran into Donald Trump over the years, he would always say that my father was "the best lawyer I ever had." Then he'd point at me and say "nothing like you. He wasn't political."

3. I Am Nearly Silenced by Cancer

"You've got cancer."

Three words that are truly game changers.

I heard them in November 2017 from my friend and dentist in Florida, Dr. Larry Kawa, as he reviewed the results of my tongue biopsy.

Cancer! Of the tongue! Frightening thoughts immediately swirled through my mind. Would I live? If I made it, would I be able to speak? Was this the end of my career? Of my life? Cancer!

I was blessed in my choice of doctors. After several consultations in various cities, I went to see Dr. Clarence Sasaki of Yale-New Haven Hospital. Several years earlier, I had been referred to him when a pre-cancerous growth was found on the bottom of my tongue. Two or three people we trusted had highly recommended him.

And they were right—he saved my life.

He was honest about what I was facing. Before the surgery, he couldn't assure me that the cancer hadn't spread or that he would be able to leave enough of the tongue to let me continue to speak. No guarantees.

In 1997, on my fiftieth birthday, I converted from atheist/Jewish to Catholic. I was able to take refuge in prayer. I also found inspiration in a song by Leonard Cohen, *If It Be Your Will,* that he composed after he had throat problems of his own. Like him, I understand that whether I ever spoke

10

again was something I couldn't control. It was in God's hands. And, like Cohen, I prayed for his mercy and tried to accept the possibility of the worst.

Cohen's poem/song/prayer was my constant companion. I quietly sang it to myself as I was having an MRI and a CT-Scan. On the way into surgery and when I woke up from the operation. As I was trying to breathe during recovery, God was always there in this song. With me. Right there.

So was Eileen.

Fortunately, very few husbands ever have to answer the ultimate question: When the chips are down, will my wife be there for me?

The chips have been down for me twice: the scandal that forced me out of the White House in 1996 and my cancer in 2017. And Eileen was there for me both times. I wouldn't have made it without her. I truly believe that.

Eileen is a warm, loving person. But, when necessary, she is also a combative lawyer/gladiator. And did I ever need her! Her work was cut out for her.

My surgery was on December 15, 2017, performed by a team of thirteen led by Dr. Sasaki. It took about 8 hours.

I am particularly indebted to Dr. Saral Mehra, who took over after Dr. Sasaki excised the cancer by removing a large piece of my tongue. It was Dr. Mehra who then reconstructed my tongue. It was an amazing procedure. From my wrist (where the skin was thinner and more malleable), he cut a square and grafted it onto the right side of my tongue, along with nerves and capillaries. (The scar runs all the way up my arm to my elbow.) The nerves and blood vessels were connected to veins in my neck through my mouth. Finally, six lymph nodes were removed from my neck.

It was miraculous. In two weeks, I could speak almost normally. Almost. I was back on TV in three weeks. But I recently saw my first post-surgery interview and realized that I was not talking quite as normally as I thought I was. I sounded a bit froggy.

It took about two weeks before I learned that the cancer definitely had not spread. Suddenly, I had a future. I am so very grateful.

But during those ten days in the hospital following the surgery, I wondered if I would make it. So did Eileen.

The complications started almost immediately. Instead of sitting up and moving the day after surgery, as I was told I would be able to do, I couldn't even lift my head. It would be eight more days before I could sit in a chair for ten minutes. I couldn't breathe and I felt like I was drowning. Eileen

11

watched over me and fought incessantly for the attention of the medical and nursing staffs. But for her, I might not have made it.

A tracheal tube for breathing had been inserted before the surgery because the swelling of the tongue made it impossible to breathe normally. But over the weekend, my breathing and oxygen levels kept getting worse and worse. Late Sunday night, while the rest of the hospital was quiet, Eileen was frantically calling the resident. She was worried that I had a stroke because I couldn't lift my arm (as I had been doing for the previous three days to signal her). I kept trying, but I couldn't pick it up. I didn't respond to questions and was very confused and sleepy. My oxygen level was plummeting.

Apparently, I had an "idiosyncratic" trachea, which was not obvious at first. As a result, the tracheal tube didn't fit right and kept moving and blocking my airway. That's why I couldn't breathe.

I went back to the OR early that Monday morning for an emergency procedure to replace the original tracheal tube with a smaller one. Afterwards, Dr. Sazaki called Eileen and said I was clear and coherent. We thought I was finally going to begin to recover.

But another complication immediately intervened. When Eileen saw me an hour later in the ICU, she was once again alarmed. I wasn't clear headed at all. In fact, I was in a deep sleep, confused, and not responsive at all—even worse than before I went to the OR. She found the physician in charge and he immediately came in with a team. They spoke in whispers at one end of the room.

Eileen's cousin Tom gestured to her to listen to them. "You know where I'm going with this," one doctor said to the group. They all nodded—without saying where it was they were going.

Eileen was frightened. "Could we speak in English and not in code, please. What's going on here?" Eileen asked them.

"Well," said the physician in charge, "I think he's overdosed."

Eileen was shocked, but the ICU doctor's very dramatic explanation did not mean that I was overdosed in the way we would normally think.

He explained that it wasn't any single dose that caused the problem; it was the cumulative effect of five days of round-the-clock opioids, anti-anxiety/sleeping medications, and two rounds of anesthesia. My breathing and oxygen levels were dangerously suppressed and I was not responding.

12

I had too much of the narcotics and anesthesia in my system. Combined with the airway blockage, I had critical breathing problems. My pulse, heart rate, and oxygen levels were at dangerous levels.

They needed to give me Narcan to bring me back to the land of the living. The same drug that cops give to street junkies who overdose is sometimes administered in hospitals because it immediately reverses the effect of the opioids and restores breathing. It worked for me—for a while.

It was a terrifying experience lying there, unable to speak or even make a sound. And it was right before Christmas. One night, Eileen left for a half hour to go take a shower. I had trouble breathing again and frantically tried to ring the ICU nurses assigned to me. No one responded. I was separated from the nursing station by a glass wall. I panicked! I wanted to yell "help!" as loud as I could, but I could make no sound at all.

I looked around for things to make noise and attract attention. But the only things I could reach were gauze or bandages My left arm was immobilized so that the skin graft would not move. And I had very little strength in my right arm, which was connected to various tubes. Then I noticed that I was connected to an ultrasound monitor at my bedside table that was tracking my arteries. Summoning all my strength—which wasn't much by them—I shoved the machine forward on the table until it fell to the ground, making the requisite racket.

When the nurses finally arrived, I scribbled on a chalk board "WIFE, FAST." It was the first time I was without her in seven days and nights. I was in a panic. She ran back.

But I was still not recovering as I should. Three nights later, Eileen and my brother-in-law Andy were in the room when a male night nurse named Chris in the ICU came in to give me a sponge bath. They left for about a half hour. Apparently, when I was moved a bit during the process, my blood pressure shot up to 260 and I turned purple. Chris' quick reaction saved me. The tube had moved again and I could not breathe. He saw what was happening and immediately connected me to a respirator. I couldn't breathe on my own for several hours. I felt like I was dying and about to meet the Lord.

That's when I went back to the OR for the third time. While we were waiting, Dr. Sazaki's resident, Dr. Castle, came down and manually jiggered the trachea tube so my airways would not be blocked until I went to surgery again in a few hours. That third surgery—with a new smaller tracheal tube—eliminated the problem and I could finally both breathe and speak. I was jubilant. Later that day, I sat in a chair for the first time.

The next day, Christmas Eve, I left for a rehab near our home.

There were many other complications, but I got through all of them. Each time, it was Eileen who spotted my trouble and insisted on immediate attention. Sometimes, that wasn't so easy. She was there 24/7, sleeping on the couch in my room for ten days, so she could watch over me. She was my advocate, fighting for me, while soothing me back to health.

Many days and nights, she was joined by my sisters-in-law Maureen, Mary, and Jean, brothers-in-law Andy, Paul, and Joe and cousin Tom. I felt the love of my family all around me. God how I needed that large Irish family just then!

And my close friend Dr. Don Gordon kept in constant touch with Eileen and spoke to the doctors when necessary. He guided us through the storm.

I am more grateful than I can say to the staff doctors and nurses at Yale.

Now, a year later, I speak like I did before. I still taste food. No trouble swallowing. God saved me. For what purpose? To do what? I hope He reveals it to me.

4. From the Dinner Table to TV

The debates at the dinner table proved to be excellent practice for my ultimate career as a pundit.

I became so conversant with politics that I frequently appeared on the children's TV show, *Dorothy Gordon's Youth Forum*—a sort of junior version of the O'Reilly Factor sponsored by *The New York Times.*

With reporter (and Moscow Bureau Chief) Harrison J. Salisbury as the adult moderator, I appeared in one show that featured a mock summit meeting in May 1960, a week before the actual Eisenhower-Khrushchev encounter in Paris. The show was aired one week after the Soviets shot down a U.S. spy plane over Russia. I was twelve.

On the show, I chose to represent Russia while the other kids chose the U.S., Britain, or France. Although expectations for the summit were clouded by the U-2 incident, Salisbury predicted that Moscow would try to mend fences.

I disagreed. I didn't quite bang my shoe on the table (as the real Khrushchev did in a later appearance at the United Nations) but I made my view quite clear. The *New York Times* story about the show reported that I said—acting as Khrushchev—that the U-2 flight was "the most outrageous blunder in the history of espionage" and predicted that Khrushchev would walk out of the summit.[2]

I was right. That's just what happened.

The afternoon after the Sunday morning broadcast, my parents and I were walking in Riverside Park when we overheard a couple behind us discussing the show. When they recognized me, they said, "Hey, that's the kid we just saw!"

My parents were thrilled.

So was I.

More prized, though, was a nice letter from Salisbury himself commending my prescience.

5. My First Candidate: The Kid Upstairs

I got my first taste of politics when I helped the kid who lived two floors above me in our apartment building get elected president of PS 9, the local public school I attended.

My "client" was named Mark Zurrow and I seized on the slogan "the Z that stands for Zurrow,"—a takeoff from Disney's Zorro TV Show, featuring a masked man who left his mark with a dramatic Z. I can't recall what that had to do with student council, but, at the least, it built up his name recognition.

On election day, Mark won!

I made a decision very early in my life that I never wanted to run for office myself. The only time I tried, when I was in the seventh grade, I lost badly.

I was prepared to fund my own campaign. Anticipating the age of big money politics, I saved money from my birthday presents, allowance, and the nickels I got returning empty soda bottles. I amassed the munificent sum of forty dollars (in 1960 dollars—it seemed like a million).

I was flush.

Armed with my war chest, I ran for student council president. I had all of the accoutrements of a serious campaign. I put up posters featuring my

15

picture, taken by Bobby Rifkin, my best friend who was an amateur photographer. I had buttons, flyers. Everything.

But I don't think I had any kind of message or any organizing plan—it was all process.

I didn't even get nominated.

My parents were worried that the defeat would deflate me and perhaps end my interest in politics. But, to their surprise, it didn't. In fact, I cheerfully announced a few days later that I was going to run the campaign of the kid that beat me.

My career path was quickly set in stone—it would be behind the scenes.

That was the beginning of more than 50 years of a career as a political consultant.

I began to write about politics when I was nine! My first visit to a political organization was to cover a meeting of the neighborhood West Side Democratic Club for my elementary school newspaper. I interviewed the leaders of the local club and its State Assemblyman Bentley Kassal. (As we write this, Bentley, a former judge, is alive, well, and alert at the age of 106. I recently had fun calling him and reminiscing about our political work together.)

When I was eleven, I got a volunteer job writing a weekly column "For Young Interests" in *The West Side News*, a neighborhood weekly. I would write about exhibits at the nearby New York Historical Society, trips to famous historic homes in the New York area, and other geeky topics. I loved doing it and never missed a deadline. Forty years later, I became a columnist for *The New York Post.* I wished that my mother had lived to see me on those pages that she had so loved. I kept thinking I could call her and tell her—and then I would sadly remember she was gone.

6. Getting JFK's Autograph

Like many of my generation, I was obsessed with John F. Kennedy. I wanted to talk like him, look like him, be him. I avidly watched his 1960 debates with Nixon, proudly telling my parents that I marveled at his skill with "cliches." Clichés? I had no idea what the word meant and when my folks explained it to me—boring, lacking originality and overused—I was embarrassed.

Maybe I meant sound bites? In any event, I memorized his signature phrases, like "in the last analysis" and always put my hands absently in my jacket's side pockets just the way he did.

At 12, I was ready to get serious about campaigning. I got dressed up in a newly purchased jacket and tie and canvassed my 64-unit apartment building at 515 West End Avenue, pushing for JFK at each door.

I slavishly studied Kennedy's foreign policy proposals. I read *The Ugly American* by Eugene Burdick and William J. Lederer, criticizing U.S. foreign policy for ignoring the Third World.

And my Mom had written a children's biography of Tom Dooley, the American missionary, about his time in Laos. Both books stirred my interest in public policy.

As I visited each apartment in my building, I would proselytize (and perhaps amuse) my neighbors by talking about how we had to fight communism by relating the newly learned problems of the Third World.

My campaigning was not restricted to my apartment building. My mother recalls rounding the corner of Broadway and 86th Street one afternoon to find me speaking, atop a stool (I was very short) on a sound truck supplied by the local Democratic club, campaigning for Kennedy.

Several weeks later, I had a chance to actually see him. On October 27, 1960—just days before the election—Kennedy appeared with the Amalgamated Clothing Workers at Union Square in New York City, just a few subway stops away from our apartment. I went to the rally.

I advanced easily through the huge crowd. I was very small and while I couldn't elbow anyone aside, I could stealthily move underneath.

At first, I couldn't see the podium, but I could hear Mayor Wagner's distinctive voice as he introduced Kennedy.

As I inched closer to the front, I heard Senator Kennedy compare his vision to Nixon's. He offered the audience a dramatic choice for the future. Contrasting the philosophies of the two parties, he reminded everyone that the Democrats had supported the Social Security Act, while the Republicans had opposed it. Which one did they want?

It was my first lesson in negative campaigning by using true comparatives. I never forgot it.

I kept moving through the excited crowd and soon found myself inside the cordon of guards right next to my idol. He had finished speaking and was moving across the front row of the crowd. Now I had seen a second

President! There he was - dressed in a long navy overcoat and looking very, very tall. But on top was the familiar coppery head of hair. I whipped out the only paper I had with me—my student council card—and he signed it.

I still have it. Right next to the 1954 baseball hand signed by all the New York Yankees (that, I got at a garage sale).

7. A Rough Beginning

My parents had been married for thirteen years before I was born. And my birth was a difficult one for my mother—physically and emotionally.
So, it was a rough beginning for everyone.

I arrived on Thanksgiving night, although I wasn't due until late January. Every year on that holiday, my Mom retold the parable of my birth. Apparently my mother thought she had indigestion after the holiday dinner. But it was not a turkey. It was me!

On arrival I weighed only two pounds, eleven ounces—almost two full months premature. At that time, there weren't the amazing high tech pre-natal care units that are standard now. But, fortunately for me, there had been another baby who had just left the New Rochelle Hospital and an incubator remained behind. I was immediately ushered into it and lived there for many months.

My mother described those early, fearful hospital days in a McCall's Magazine article *"Faith, It's a Boy"*: "I pressed close to the glass partition and looked at my baby, lying in his womb of glass and tubes and dials. Scarcely the size of a broiling chicken, he was concentrating all his tiny might on drawing the next breath."

My mother was even advised not to name me or get too attached. My parents were heartbroken. Mom wrote me a letter on the day after I was born.

"I write to you now, little son, when all you have of life is a set of odds and a sparrow's strength for allies. Each breath you draw is an heroic offensive and each thrust of your arms and legs is a giant stab at the enemy: Death. Fight, fight, little one."

My mother would spend her days in the nursery, although it was a while before she could even hold me.

A month later, on Christmas Eve, while I was still struggling in the hospital, the famous blizzard of 1947 was raging outside. An unexpected twenty-six inches of snow fell, with drifts of 10-12 feet.

My Dad took out his cross-country skis and went through the neighborhood to look for people who needed help. A few blocks away, he saw a disabled car. Inside was a young couple with a newborn infant. Without hesitating, he invited them home, offering them a safe haven from the storm.

My parents had already prepared a nursery for me and my father, the artist, had painted toys and teddy bears on the walls. The crib was already made up and waiting for me.

When the strangers arrived, my mother had very mixed feelings. Her innate kindness wanted to protect the baby and his parents. But she wanted *her* baby to be in the crib, not some stranger. She made them comfortable, but felt stricken, worried that I would never see that room.

My Mom wrote an article for *McCall's* magazine entitled *Room at The Inn*, describing the emotional events of that Christmas Eve.

The baby's mother boasted about her son's progress, much to my mother's discomfort. "He's three months old and can you imagine, he's nearly doubled his birth weight already! A regular little blockbuster, this one. Seven pounds, two ounces at birth and now he's about twelve pounds."

My mother wrote: "If she was pre-occupied with statistics, so was I. I thought of the telephone bulletin I received that morning from the hospital nursery: 'three pounds, eight ounces today.' Richard was coming along, although they carefully avoided any mention of when he might be expected to reach the magic weight of five pounds."

With that, may parents showed their guests to my, as yet unoccupied, room.

My parents left me a legacy of gifts and helped me in so many ways to develop the skills I needed for some kind of work in politics. I am so grateful to them.

But like most people, growing up was not all good times. I was often alone and sad. My parents sent me to sleep-away camp for eight weeks every summer for five years starting when I was six-and-a-half years old. I was undersized for my age—attributable to my early birth. And I was shy and not too good with social skills.

To get to the camp, I took an overnight train with the counsellors from Grand Central to Tenant's Harbor, Maine, where the camp was nestled along the shore.

Some summers, I saw my parents only on the visiting weekend. Others, not at all, because they were traveling. Then, I had to make do with a visit from my Aunt Florence, who hugged me warmly, but it was not enough.

The camp in Maine was frightening and unknown. But the decision had been made—my folks wanted me in camp to toughen me up. So to Maine I went, hating it, while my parents traveled extensively in Europe, Africa, Asia, and South America.

Looking back as an adult, I understand that it was an important respite for them.

But as a young child, it was a devastating time for me.

I was miserable. I hated swimming in the freezing Maine water and didn't like to play organized games. I did like collecting blueberries—1 cup for a muffin, 1 quart for a pie.

The happiest day of the year was the day I got on the train to go home. My parents would then take me to a rented lake house in Northern Westchester for the rest of the summer. We'd spend a week or two swimming, canoeing, barbecuing, and reading together. I played ping pong with my father. He always beat me, but I kept meticulous track and would announce my record: "won three, lost one hundred and nine."

That time together always helped erase the loneliness I had felt earlier in the summer and things were good until it was time to go back to Maine again the next June.

Years later, I took Eileen to see the camp on the coast of rural mid-Maine. She was horrified and described it as looking like an Ethiopian prisoner of war camp. It was certainly primitive and desolate.

One of the camp owners, Henry Haskill, was still there and clearly remembered me. A former Vassar child psychologist and a loving, warm, and wise man, he recalled my small size and homesickness. Henry reminded me that he and his late wife Bess used to take me to their cabin to soothe me that first summer when I was so lost. He even pulled out my files, which included letters back and forth to my parents as they toured European capitals.

20

There was one high point of every day at camp. By the second year, my parents had arranged for the delivery of *The New York Times*!

I read it intently. A scrapbook compiled by my mother for my 21st birthday contains a letter I wrote from camp about the Suez Canal War in 1956. I was nine.

"Boy, the British and the French really made Ike mad. They better watch out for Ike. He's pulling the rug out from under them at the UN. Eden might have to resign. But I hope Israel really smashes Nasser. Hard."

If it isn't obvious, I was a certified geek—well before I was ten years old.

Until their dying days, both of my parents insisted that sending me to camp was the best thing they could have done for me.

I vehemently disagreed,

But we got past it.

My parents had different hopes for my future.

My mother, who abhorred practical politics, was a firmly committed liberal intellectual and one of the leading magazine writers of the day.

Quite well known and unusually well-liked even in the rarified world of New York authors, she was one of the founders and early presidents of the American Society of Authors and Journalists (originally called the Society of Magazine Writers).

She was a pioneer for woman who worked as freelance writers, contributing articles to all the top magazines—including McCall's, Redbook, Good Housekeeping, Life, Look, and all the others. Her capstone was her then exclusive chronicle of why and how Svetlana Allenueva, Stalin's daughter, defected to the U.S.

But she shuddered whenever my father would discuss practical politics. She wanted me to be like historian Arthur Schlesinger Jr., part of politics, but above it.

I finally met Schlesinger after my days with Clinton. We had lunch at the Harvard Club in New York on his eightieth birthday. As we were being served, a waiter spilled a martini into the historian's lap. I quipped, "It's OK, Arthur, it was a dry martini."

21

8. The Stuyvesant High School Debating Team: My Formative Experience

It was at Stuyvesant High School in Manhattan that I really began my political career. Stuyvesant was the most challenging and competitive environment I've ever been in—including the White House.

It wasn't the courses that interested me. It was the debating team. (The school was focused on science and math and I wasn't.)

At Stuyvesant, an all-boys school back then, I worked with a number of extraordinary young men including Jerry Nadler, now a Congressman and Chairman of the powerful House Judiciary Committee, Dick Gottfried who is in his fiftieth year in the State Assembly (a record), and my close friend Simon Barsky, who went on to become the general counsel to a major national trade organization. Teammates Sandy Zabell became a university mathematics professor and Neal Arluck a successful actor.

Historically, Stuyvesant had not had much of a debating team and our "faculty advisor" was a bio lab assistant who agreed to lend her name so we could meet the school's rule that every club have a faculty overseer.

We were required to bring an adult to each inter-scholastic debate—to judge the other teams (never our own). Most schools brought their coach. But, because we didn't have one, my Mom or Dad would often fill in.

I was the captain and de facto coach. I had developed my own ideas about debating and argument from the dinner table and I proceeded to coach my fellow teammates according to my lights. To refine my delivery, I listened to recordings of speeches and fireside chats by FDR. From my television appearances and street corner speaking for Kennedy, I had developed a polished public speaking style – unusual for a fourteen year old.

Our team was damn good.

The Catholic schools in New York, particularly those staffed by Jesuits, dominated debating. Few public schools even had teams and none were much good. To get real competition I went to meet with the Monsignor who ran the Catholic Forensic League and begged to be included. Taking pity on a public school waif, they admitted us into their league with the agreement that we could never be the champions, - an unlikely event given our absence of resources, coaches, or experience.

But, as it turned out, we won all the debates, finishing at 11-0 for the season. We would have won the championship had we been allowed.

It was one of the most exciting times in my life.

From there, we went to tournaments throughout the northeast. Every weekend we would win, vanquishing all the Catholic, private, and the few public schools that competed.

It was the first time in my life that I felt that maybe I had a gift. In the tournaments, you would do two debates in the morning and two after lunch. But they didn't announce the winners until it was all over. I would typically worry all day that I had lost the debates until I heard my school announced as the winner and I learned that I was often rated the top speaker.

It was a bit of a shock. But as we won a dozen tournaments that year, losing none, I began to build self-confidence.

Part of the reason for our team's success was our unique strategy. Our topic that year was Medicare and,\ my teammate Gottfried and I usually took the negative.

The job of the negative—as with the defense counsel at a trial—is not to prove its case, but to stop the affirmative from proving its side.

Every one of our affirmative opponents said more or less the same thing: a) The elderly are poor. b) They are disproportionately sick. c) There is no government program to help them. And, therefore, we needed Medicare.

But rather than push back on these obviously accurate points, as other negative teams did, we would challenge our opponents by saying "if they are poor and if they are sick and if they aren't getting care, then why does their life expectancy keep increasing? Can you prove that they are not getting care? Where are the statistics to show that they are being left out in the cold?" Nobody had any. We kept winning.

I called the argument "correlation" and it stumped our opponents every time. It was then that I learned that an intellectual construct can prevail in any rhetorical or political contest. During my time with President Clinton, I developed the idea of "triangulation"—taking the best parts of the left and the right, combining them at the apex of the triangle, and leaving the spurious parts behind.

I used triangulation to help Clinton win the 1996 election, just as I had used correlation to win my high school debates. But the tactic of looking at the same arguments from a new perspective was one I had learned on my high school debating team.

23

9. A Summer in Washington and My Love Affair with Thomas Jefferson

In the summer of 1995, when I was17 years old, I was thrilled to spend the summer living in Washington with Simon Barsky. We both had found summer jobs in politics—I worked for a Congressman and he for the Democratic National Committee.

Filled with youthful idealism, we would make pilgrimages each weekend to the Jefferson Memorial, which we treated as a shrine in our own secular religion. We would both memorize the quotations on the monument walls and stand staring at the tall, flawlessly erect statue. We bonded with our role model.

(How unfortunate that modern political correctness has besmirched the images of all of our national heroes. Yes, Jefferson owned slaves and had children with them. But he founded the idea of equality and brought democratic thought into actual politics for the first time in human history. He still deserves our profound admiration.)

I worked in the House Office Building. I loved the excitement of Washington, working as a volunteer in the office of Maryland's sole at-large Congressman, Carlton Sickles. I had no special hook to use in getting the job. I just went door-to-door until I found a taker.

It was thrilling to work in the Capital. Whenever I could, I watched the House in session—I was mesmerized.

I was very proud of the work I did for Sickles, assisting (or at least watching) the many steps involved in the passing of Public Law 89-195 (1965), the legislation designating the Assateague Island off the Eastern Shore of Maryland as a National Seashore and Park. As a result of the legislation, the unparalleled beauty of the thirty-seven mile barrier island was preserved and has been protected for more than fifty years.

Investors and a development group had been all set to build roads, homes, and hotels on the island when a devastating storm struck the Maryland coast in March 1962. *The Baltimore Sun*[3] named it "the storm of the century" and it ravished Assateague Island, depositing over four feet of water and destroying buildings and beaches. Only sixteen cottages remained. State and local government planners concluded that the island could not support the proposed vast development and roads.

That led to the legislation to establish a national seashore park to offer a beautiful recreation area to the public with swimming and hunting and a mandated protection of the unique environment.

I learned first-hand about the long and tedious process of finalizing a comprehensive piece of legislation. It had to be legally sound, and the bill's co-sponsors had to be kept informed and approve of any changes. In addition, Sickles' office consulted with local advocates and protagonists and tamed the special interests in the area. We had to satisfy the federal and state bureaucracies that would regulate the new park. Finally, we had to negotiate payment with the investors and developers whose property would be taken in eminent domain for the project. It was complicated.

Mark Twain's comments about law making suddenly made sense:

"Those that respect the law and love sausage should watch neither being made."[4]

The bill had passed the Senate by a voice vote in June, but Congressman Sickles had to work all summer—as I watched—to get it passed in the House. Finally, the House, too, approved by a voice vote, on September 7, 1965, the first legislative day after the Labor Day break. Two weeks later, President Johnson signed it into law

Later, after the bill became law, I visited the island and marveled at its pristine beaches and dramatic views. I hated to imagine what developers might have done to :improve" it.

When Sickles' bill passed, I was filled with a joyous sense of accomplishment. My very small contribution helped lead to the permanent protection of this beautiful island.

10. Forming a Political Team

John F. Kennedy was asked how he became a war hero. "It was purely involuntary," he explained. "They sank my boat."[5]

My transition from debating to politics was also motivated by necessity of a sort.

Because for years, the Stuyvesant debating team had been an afterthought and its budget came to only $90 a year. To even attend the tournaments in upstate New York, we had to spring for bus fare out-of-pocket.

So my teammates and I entered school politics, in part, to get more money for our team. (And my team had some pretty good politicians on it: a future Congressman, State Assemblyman, political advisor, and so forth.)

We organized each class in the school and ran outstanding candidates: Jerry Nadler for school president and Simon Barsky for VP.

Surprisingly, our campaign was not about the debating team. Nobody would have cared about our budget problems. So I found another issue to run on: the class ranking system. We wanted it eliminated. Stuyvesant was a special high school that required scoring well on a competitive test to get in. The best students in the city went there. This meant that a student who ranked midway in his class would be at the top in any other high school. We wanted the administration to stop compiling class rank because it was so prejudicial in college admissions. And the whole school agreed.

We elected an entire slate of our candidates.

The enduring lesson here is: Always run on an issue.

After winning, we managed to increase the debating team budget to $500. Now we could get to all our debates.

In electing Jerry and Simon, we built an excellent political machine that came to include the brightest and most articulate kids at that exceptional school.

But now Stuyvesant's academic excellence is in jeopardy. To his everlasting shame, New York City's nutty radical mayor, Bill de Blasio is trying to dumb-down Stuyvesant by admitting the top seven percent of all public junior high schools in the city. No test required.

Back then, Stuyvesant was largely Jewish. Now it's overwhelmingly Asian. But, regardless of the ethnic composition, Mayor de Blasio will destroy its academic quality. He favors equality—make every high school equally bad.

Meanwhile, while I was working on my politics and debating at Stuyvesant, I volunteered to lick envelopes for anyone running for office. I wanted to be noticed. Make contacts. Get my own career started.

11. Senator Pat Moynihan Meets the Beatles

It was August 1965. Future U.S. Senator Daniel Patrick Moynihan stood at the window of New York City's Warwick Hotel on Sixth Avenue and Fifty-Fourth street and gazed out at the mob scene in the streets below. Hundreds of thousands of teenagers gathered yelling, pushing, jostling, vying for a view. Girls screamed and squealed. Boys shouted. It was Beatlemania live, loud, and in person.

Paul, John, George, and Ringo—the Beatles—were staying at the Warwick on their U.S. tour and held a press conference there. That's what started the frenzy. The next night, they would perform to a crowd of 55,000 fans at Shea Stadium.

Also in the hotel was the campaign headquarters of the brilliant and often droll Pat Moynihan, running for the obscure post of President of the City Council. The election was about a month away.

The Beatles had been introduced to America a year and a half earlier when they appeared on the Ed Sullivan Show and electrified the country.

After a long battle with various recording companies, the group had finally arranged for their music to be released on the American market. The British Invasion had started. The effect was not electric; it was nuclear.

Meanwhile, candidate Moynihan faced a triple whammy. Nobody knew who he was and nobody knew the job he was running for even existed… and nobody even cared. But Pat was enthusiastic, running his best.

He had been pressured into the race by New York's newly elected U.S. Senator—Bobby Kennedy—who wanted to flex his political muscle by electing Moynihan.

Now, Pat was adrift with little money and less support. And I was volunteering to lick envelopes at his headquarters. (For the benefit of younger readers, people back then used "envelopes" as containers into which they put letters—written e-mails—that the post office would proceed to deliver.)

But, as he gazed down at the huge crowd the Beatles had attracted, an amused look came over Moynihan's face.

"Look at that crowd! Look at that enthusiasm! The young people, especially the young people" he exclaimed. Of course he knew that they were there for the Beatles, but he pretended not to. "Our campaign is really catching on. Look at all the young people" he kept repeating.

I left it to others to break the news to him that they were there for the Fab Four not for him!

Moynihan was always an intellectual, gifted with an ability to strip away the veneer and get to the vulnerable essence of his political opponents.

The gist was on display when he ran for the Senate.in 1976 against Connecticut patrician James Buckley, then serving as Senator from New York. His campaign strategy called for emphasizing Buckley's upper class snobbism and his Connecticut roots. Moynihan captured both in his television ad, which he wrote himself:

"New York is one of only seven states that doesn't have a Democratic Senator. Not a Democrat to work for us. Not a Democrat to fight for us. Buckley doesn't fight for us. Sometimes you get the feeling he doesn't even *like* us! I'll fight for New York in the Senate like I fought for America in the U.N. and you'll know I'm there."

A truly original force in our politics!

12. Taking Over West Side Politics

It was June 1969. I was 22.

That's when lightning struck.

My former debating team and the growing political organization of young people it spawned had soundly and surprisingly defeated all seven of the Democratic Party district leaders who we challenged on Manhattan's West Side in primary battles.

We quickly became known as "The West Side Kids." First time voters who wanted to reform the system and change politics had taken over the process and elected people who were not political insiders, not soldiers in the ruling class of establishment liberal West Side politics. There was an irony to it: the old reformers who had been elected to change the system were now perceived as self-perpetuating dinosaurs who needed to go and were replaced by new reformers with a different agenda.

In district after district, our 22-year-old candidates—and a few slightly older allies—beat the "old" entrenched Democratic Party establishment— the men and women in their 30s, 40s, 50s, and 60s who, in some cases, had held the positions, virtually unopposed, for years.

Our sweeping victory was totally unexpected and even made its way into *The New York Times* under the headline *"Tammany Tiger Finds That Its Cubs Can Bite."*

It was David vs. Goliath. A bunch of inexperienced "kids" had slowly and steadily developed a momentum that was a game changer. The party establishment had not taken us seriously—until we trounced them.

Our voters wanted local elected officials to be accountable to the community, representative of the community, advocates for the community, and part of the community. Jeffrey Brand, one of the newly elected leaders told *The Times* that he "walked the streets of the West 80s at least once a week and stopped people to ask what he could do for them." Brand articulated the difference between the old and new reformers. The new breed wasn't interested in "patronage," like "fixing parking tickets," or "getting people out of jury duty."[6] Instead, they wanted to create block associations to promote and police safe neighborhoods, help tenants, and educate people on the draft.

It was a big difference..

We now controlled most of the Democratic Party on the upper West Side—from 60th street to 100th street, Central Park West to Riverside Drive. That meant our new district leaders were the officially recognized local representatives of the State Democratic Party. Among the new district leaders were Nadler, Dick Gottfried. And Barsky.

It had taken several years of hard work and organization to build up to this amazing crescendo. We worked tirelessly to identify our supporters, encourage them to join us, meet with them, and take on the local issues that were important to them.

Throughout the process, I continued my lifelong policy of working behind the scenes, running the campaigns. While I was the leader of the group, I never put my name out front in public.

Here's how it started: Our years at Stuyvesant High School had been so wonderful, warm, affirming, and collegial that a number of us involved in debating and student government wanted to try to continue to work together in politics and do our best to keep our focus in New York City. It began when Simon and I were accepted at Columbia University on Manhattan's West Side. Nadler followed a year later. We weren't sure exactly what we would be doing, but we assumed it would have something to do with politics.

Stuyvesant's students came from all over the. time, I was the only one in our political group who lived on the West Side. But after several of us enrolled in Columbia, it became the natural base for our political activity. Eventually Nadler, Gottfried, Barsky and many others gravitated to my neighborhood to launch their political careers as local politicians and eventually elected officials.

I was sixteen years old when I graduated from Stuyvesant. (I would turn seventeen in November of my freshman year at Columbia.) As I entered college, American politics was fraught with crisis, unrest, and widespread protests. President John F. Kennedy had been assassinated less than two years before, a blow that fell so heavily on each of us personally that it could only be compared to the death of a close friend or parent.

Something was changing. In New York—and throughout the country—young people began flocking to national politics, driven, initially, by the civil rights movement.

In the early '60s, college students and teenagers boarded Freedom Rider buses to travel throughout the South to integrate rest rooms, lunch counters, and waiting rooms. Using civil disobedience, putting themselves on the line in the face of racist Southern cops, courts, and jails, they challenged segregation. Later, kids led boisterous—and dangerous—voter registration marches in the South.

Then, when the Vietnam War began, college students were at the core of the protests against it—with good reason. For it was those young people, for the most part, who would be sent to fight in the jungle and rice paddies of Vietnam.

At first, the protests were strictly idealistic, but soon they became intensely personal as the draft brought the war closer and closer to home.

At 17—one year before draft eligibility— I understood that completely. While I was personally 4-F (physically unfit for service) due to recurring dislocations of both shoulders, my friends all had to duck and dodge to stay out of the army. In college, they were deferred. But in 1967, Johnson ended deferments for graduate school and many had to find jobs teaching to stay out.

One friend, in particular, was a very good student at Columbia— except that he could not, for the life of him, master Spanish. He kept flunking and, in the end, could not satisfy the two-year foreign language requirement for graduation. He had to beg to get a waiver.

Eager to stay out of the army, he was hired as a high school teacher. But the only opening was teaching Spanish in a largely Puerto Rican school in lower Manhattan! He figured even that was better than Vietnam.

Vietnam was largely a stealth war; the government didn't tell us the truth about what was going on and how bad it was. As I entered Columbia in September 1964, the bombings of North Vietnam had escalated and the huge military buildup required more and more troops on the ground.

The call came quickly. The very next year, the military drafted an astounding 230,991 young men. Another 300,000 were called up in each of the next four years.

Suddenly, the lives of all young American men were in jeopardy, facing interruption and possibly death for a cause that was obviously seriously flawed.

While, as yet, there was no national outcry about the injustice of the war, only an idiot could contend that the South Vietnam government was a real democracy.

It was not at all like 1941 or 1949, when the nation came together in the wake of foreign aggression and resolved to defeat Germany, Japan, and then North Korea. Now, dissent flared rampantly and each night's news testified to how worthless this war was.

As soon as we started college, my friends and I enthusiastically joined the movement to end the war . We all went to the peace marches in Washington, often inhaling tear gas and dodging cops.

And it was not just men who opposed the war for personal reasons. Women were horrified that their sons, brothers, husbands, boyfriends, classmates, and neighbors were at risk for a war that had not been declared and that threatened so many young people. Women's peace groups protested in major cities. I remember often seeing Bella Abzug, who became a close friend, speaking out against the war on a sound truck at Broadway and 72nd Street .

In 1965, given what was going on, we all decided that it was imperative to begin our careers in regular, adult politics. Forget Young Democrats or student government politics. That was like a play group. We were ready for the big time.

31

And the country was ready to listen. Of course, none of us could vote for several more years—the voting age was still 21 then—but we were focused on working to persuade people who could vote to oppose the war. (How unjust that we were old enough to be drafted and sent to Vietnam, but not old enough to vote!) When the voting age was finally lowered to eighteen in 1971, we were able to be even more effective.

But until then, we tried to make a difference. Back in 1964, when I was seventeen, Simon and I experimented with how best to influence voters to elect anti-war candidates.

Our target was Congressman Leonard Farbstein, a political hack who loyally followed the Democratic Party line wherever it led, even into the jungles of Vietnam.

We worked for the ultimately unsuccessful anti-war insurgent Bill Haddad. We focused our efforts on the 100th election district—about one square block in Manhattan—where I lived with my parents. We visited each voter attacking Farbstein and extolling Haddad at every door.

Two years earlier, in 1962, the left had also tried to oust Farbstein, nominating Assemblyman Bentley Kassal against him.

Kassal lost, in part, because he couldn't carry the West Side part of the district by enough to offset Farbstein's huge margins on the boss-controlled Lower East Side.

My own election district, for example, went for Kassal by only 65-33—a good margin, but a low turnout. After Simon and I visited each voter in person and hand wrote letters to them afterward, we carried it for Haddad by 162-28. We wrote a report describing our efforts that became a blueprint for our group's subsequent work in politics.

Who made up the group?

Our Stuyvesant alumni channeled our generational obsession with politics and issues by recruiting young people from the top high schools in the New York area—Stuyvesant, Hunter, New Lincoln, Bronx Science, Horace Mann, Fieldstone, Music and Art, Brooklyn Tech. Those recruits formed a political "strike force" to mobilize against the war starting in 1965.

One of our first projects was to provide draft counseling to help young men understand the Selective Service rules and figure out what might keep them from being shipped to Vietnam.

We also worked to elect anti-war candidates on Manhattan's West Side. Our legions of young activists worked to help elect liberals like William Fitts Ryan, Paul O'Dwyer, and the indomitable Bella Abzug.

We would follow the model Simon and I had pioneered in the Haddad-Farbstein race—canvass all the buildings up and down the West Side, visit each apartment, ring every doorbell, work to persuade voters to support our candidates, and follow up with a hand written letter.

Over the years of campaigning, we students became professionals, warriors in the political anti-war, pro-civil rights movements.

In 1964, '65, '66, and '67, we battled to defeat pro-war Democrats (everybody on the West Side was a Democrat) and elect peace candidates. But it was in 1968, that things reached an apogee—when Minnesota Senator Eugene McCarthy challenged Lyndon Johnson in a quixotic bid to end the war in Vietnam.

Professional politicians all scoffed at his chances and stayed away. They asked, "How could you ever defeat an incumbent president for re-nomination in his own party?" But that's exactly what we wanted to do. Many of the supposedly liberal politicians we had supported weren't willing to even try.

Our youth organization flocked to McCarthy's banner. We filled buses to New Hampshire, Connecticut, Massachusetts, Wisconsin, and Indiana to battle in the Democratic primaries. Those with beards and long hair first stopped at the barber to "get clean for Gene."

And then McCarthy scored a first round knockout! Defying all predictions, he won a more than respectable 42% of the vote, and held Johnson to only 49%. The results reverberated throughout the nation.

Then, another shock! Suddenly, Lyndon Johnson was gone. On March 31, 1968, he pulled out of the race. One punch and he was out! There seemed a real chance that our political work and similar efforts around the country could actually end the war!

I remember how incredulous we were that night. Had the anti-war movement really forced a sitting president out of the race? We began to believe that we really could make a difference, that we really could change the country.

But then a complication: Another anti-war candidate entered the fray. A very special one.

From the time of his brother's murder, Robert F. Kennedy had cast a long shadow over the Johnson Presidency.

As the Vietnam War intensified, his lonely, eloquent voice spoke out against our growing involvement. But when the real test came, Kennedy copped out and refused to challenge Johnson for the nomination, leaving it to McCarthy. His decision was certainly understandable given the tragedy he and his family had experienced.

But now, after McCarthy did so well in New Hampshire, Kennedy tried to push the courageous senator aside and to jump into the race himself.

We all loved "Bobby" Kennedy—and had worked hard to elect him as New York Senator in 1964—but our commitment was to McCarthy who had the guts to challenge Johnson while Kennedy fretted on the sidelines.

We were angry and felt betrayed when most of the older and supposedly anti-war politicians we had backed over the years in New York refused to come out for McCarthy. Because they did not face the danger of the draft, they could afford to put old-time party politics ahead of ending the war. Many initially supported Johnson and then some switched to Kennedy, but very few joined us in the trenches for McCarthy, except for a few principled people like Congresswoman Bella Abzug.

We were shocked to see the people we had so admired turn out to be nothing more than insider political hacks. Their conduct sowed the earliest seeds of my later aversion to the bureaucratic insiders who dominated the Democratic party.

Meanwhile, the year's politics continued to dramatically unfold. Vice President Hubert H. Humphrey, Johnson's lapdog, jumped into the race as his surrogate, refusing to enter any of the primaries, knowing he would get creamed.

Then tragedy struck again and Bobby Kennedy was assassinated. Once again, the nation was heartbroken. Kennedy's death, combined with the murder of Dr. Martin Luther King Jr. two months earlier, made us feel the good guys were being cut down while the bad ones waltzed into the White House. After Kennedy's death in June 1968, it became clear that the political bosses that ran the Democratic Party were determined to nominate Humphrey, who had not won a single vote in any primary.

Regardless, the Democratic party leadership was going to jam Humphrey down our throats, believing that our aversion to the Republican nominee—

34

Richard M. Nixon—would assure that we would have no choice but to fall in line behind them.

We went on to Chicago, the site of the Democratic convention, still fighting for McCarthy.

There we met the real Democratic Party. They were embodied by the Chicago police who used their billy clubs and tear gas outside the convention hall to silence any who disagreed.

That was their idea of party unity.

We were instantly as alienated as anyone could possibly be from the Democratic Party and its despicable leaders.

When the year's politics, with all its hopes, ended in ashes, we were all determined to take over the local Democratic Party and oust the "adult" professionals, many of whom who had not had the guts to back McCarthy when it counted.

Back then, Jerry Nadler spoke for us all when he told *The New York Times* that the Democratic establishment that had failed to back the Dump Johnson Movement to end the Vietnam war was "jaded." He attacked the Democrats who boycotted the anti-war candidacy of Senator Eugene McCarthy and then flocked to Kennedy as "generals who ride after their troops instead of leading them."

So, in 1969, we were ready to break away from the Democrats then in power and challenge them for leadership of the Party. We were 22. They were in their 30s, 40s, and 50s.

We set up rival political clubs all over the West Side to challenge the organizations that had let us down by refusing to join the McCarthy campaign the year before. The apparatus of the Democratic Party was controlled by district leaders in each neighborhood elected by the Democratic voters who lived there. District leader was a vestigial position, left over from the days when they—and they alone—determined who was nominated to run for public office. But with the advent of direct primaries in the 1950s, district leaders lost their clout as voters decided for themselves who to nominate. But the position of district leader remained and, every two years, registered Democrats (80% of the West Side's voters) chose their district leaders—one male and one female.

We sought to re-invent the post of district leader saying: "District leaders should be community leaders."

And we became active in the community. In addition to draft counseling clinics, we organized and supported tenant rent strikes when absentee landlords neglected their tenants, painted park benches to beautify the neighborhood, and even began to recycle cans and bottles decades before the environmental movement. We formed the Housing and Neighborhood Development Service (HANDS), to help tenants and kids from poor families.

Every night, after our day jobs, Simon, Dick, Jerry and I—among many others—would fan out on the West Side speaking to tenants groups and block associations, many of which we had helped to organize.

Long before Facebook, we developed a list of "friends." After the night's meetings I would de-brief each of the others by phone with a voter list in my lap, marking off the "friends" they had recruited to our cause at that evening's meetings. Then, each morning, on my way to work, I would drop off the previous night's list of "friends" with Myron Bassman, a computer expert who introduced me to the possibilities of interfacing politics and technology. He would carefully type out each voter's name on the IBM cards that he used back then to program his computer. After my workday ended, I would stop by Myron's office on my way home to pick up the updated printout to give out to that night's speakers at our West Side events. And so the cycle went. I would update the friend list every night and Myron would record them each day. No matter how amateurish this process sounds today, we were at the cutting edge of political technology. At that time, there was no such thing as a personal computer (PC) or a laptop. Microsoft and Apple were only founded almost ten years later. Our process was really a precursor of the modern emphasis on targeting and ongoing one-on-one contact with voters through social media. But we didn't have the Internet. We had to do it on foot—or phone—each night.

We kept in touch with the "friends" and invited them to meetings, rallies, and candidate forums. As our connection to the neighborhood grew, our political influence expanded in tandem. We soon developed enough clout to run some of our own candidates for district leader. And, just in time, we all turned 21.

We were ready. In 1969, Stuyvesant alumni Nadler, Gottfried, Barsky, and our friend Frank Baraff, and others challenged the incumbent leaders in seven contests.

That's when we won all seven!

In 1970, we continued our advance, electing Gottfried to the State Assembly at the age of twenty-two. In 1976, Nadler followed him into the state legislature and advanced to Congress in 1992, taking the seat formerly held by Bella Abzug.

As we won these contests, we attracted attention from the powers in New York politics. I remember meeting New York City Mayor John V. Lindsay for the first time. In 1969, after we won our district leaderships, Lindsay invited us to Gracie Mansion, the official residence of New York's mayors. I had never been there before and its beauty, perched on a hill with a panoramic view of the East River and its bridges, blew me away.

We sat in a circle with the mayor for an hour or two talking politics. I remember being awed by how handsome and charismatic he was. Nothing of any consequence happened, but we all felt excited to be recognized.

But the discontents of 1968 still burned and the hypocrisy of our former allies in the Democratic Party left a sour taste in my mouth. My friends chose to stay in the Democratic Party, hoping to change it.

Eventually, I went in a different direction.

13. My Father Comes to My Rescue

In the cutthroat world of West Side politics, candidates often use the arcane technicalities of the election law to knock their opponents off the ballot. A legal cottage industry sprung up litigating against and defending candidates who sought to run.

In 1971, as my friends and I tried to win yet more district leaderships on the West Side, our opponents mounted just such a challenge to the petitions that we submitted to get our candidates on the ballot. Citing inane technicalities (like when voters didn't use their middle initials in signing) they sought to disqualify thousands of signatures.

The Board of Elections, scrupulously following the exact letter of the law, ruled against us and struck our candidate for district leader—Ed Rogoff—from the ballot. We appealed to the state court, with little hope of reversing their ruling.

My father handled the appeal, coming to our rescue.

Arguing on Ed's behalf, he made the point that the state appellate court could look beyond the letter of the law to the equities and the fairness of the situation. Since Rogoff had collected many more than the legal number of signatures that were needed, (before the clerks at the Board of Election knocked some off), he argued that Rogoff should be allowed on the ballot.

Ed had just turned 18 and the 26th amendment to the Constitution that lowered the voting age, had just been passed that year. Indeed, Rogoff may have been one of the first 18-year-olds to run for office after the passage of the amendment, so the case had special significance.

My father thought that the court might want to bend the letter of the law and he tried to give it a peg to hang its decision on. That's why he argued that the case should be decided in equity rather than strictly following the law, as election law attorneys habitually did.

We won! It was quite a legal tour-de-force!

Unfortunately, Ed Rogoff did not win.

14. A Narrow Escape from Law School

One summer I worked at my Dad's firm, Demov and Morris, which employed about sixty lawyers at its peak.

It wasn't a really good fit!

Research on arcane issues in real estate law didn't excite me. And he was a tough task master.)to put it mildly)

Understandably, he wanted me to join his profession and become a lawyer. That's not what I really wanted to do. But to please him, I dutifully enrolled in NYU Law School—not once, but twice.

Eileen describes me as a "narrow escapee" from the legal profession. Because for two years in a row, I registered for classes. Both times, I stopped going after about a week. After the second drop-out, my father—who paid the bill—gave up on his dream of a legal career for me and grew reconciled to my career in politics. He was completely supportive of me until the day he died.

A lot of the preparation for my political career was done at home. Public policy discussions were a big part of my family life. From the time that I was old enough to listen, I heard my parents' passionate views on political issues, parties, and candidates.

It wasn't always pretty. But it was always interesting.

I grew up on the West Side of Manhattan, where everyone is a politician. Our apartment, on the ninth floor of a seventeen-story building, fit the stereotype. Every night at the dinner table, the important news of the day was dished out alongside the meat loaf or chicken.

Each weekday, I looked forward to six o'clock when my parents, Gene and Terry Morris, would stop their work and convene in our living room for a cocktail. The seminar they called dinnertime would begin at 6:30. I am an only child, so I had no brothers or sisters to share the spotlight.

My parents were intelligent and sophisticated. I adored them. But they were also quite serious, and, at times, quite intimidating.

My mother was a beautiful woman and a very successful magazine writer—one of the few women freelance writers in the country at that time. Both parents loved teaching and mentoring me. But I was always worried. I understood fully, even at seven or eight, that they didn't appreciate ill-informed chit-chat—even from little kids. That's why I desperately wanted to contribute something both provocative and pleasing to those evening conversations. Actually, what I really wanted to do was to impress them!

So, I worked overtime to do just that. In grammar school, as soon as I came home from school in the afternoon, I would have a coke with my mother and tell her about my day. Then she'd go back to writing in her study and I would read *The New York Times* (the Bible in our household) and focus on the issues that my parents frequently mentioned. They might include the Suez Canal crisis, Adlai Stevenson (they loved him), John F. Kennedy, (they suspected his links to the Vatican), desegregation (they approved), low-income housing (that was a yes), Israel, Eisenhower's military-industrial complex (fascinating), Tammany Hall (badly needed reform).

After that, I'd open the *New York Post* and read my mother's favorite columnists: Jimmy Breslin, Pete Hamill, Murray Kempton, Mary McGrory, Max Lerner, and sometimes Jack Andersen. After digesting their opinions, I was ready for dinner.

Sometimes I would go deeper. Books would supplement *The Times*. I was a regular visitor at the local New York City public library and developed an obsession with history books—especially about the Presidents. By the time I was 9, I had memorized our nation's chief executives in chronological order. I thought about the presidents all the time.

Our family trips to historic sites—Hyde Park, Mount Vernon, Monticello—gave us plenty of future dinner conversation. I loved analyzing FDR's governorship of New York, and discussing Al Smith's ill-fated presidential candidacy and whether a Catholic could be president.

It was after dinner every night that I dreaded. My parents would 'help' me with my homework. I was always nervous during those sessions—afraid that I would disappoint them. As we moved from the dining room to the living room, I would shuttle back and forth between my parents who sat on opposite ends of the large grey sectional couch.

They each had their own homework specialty, which unfortunately correlated with my weaknesses. First, my father would work with me on my penmanship. That usually ended in his quite explicit verbal exasperation at my illegible scribble. His own handwriting was elegant, neat, and proportionate (as befitted an art professor). When he signed "Eugene J. Morris," his signature was perfect. He tried various exercises with me, but I never improved. To this day, no one can ever decipher my writing. Fortunately, God invented typewriters and computers, so I escaped total failure!

My mother, who typed all her own manuscripts, didn't share my father's obsession with handwriting. Her focus was on spelling—"the mark of an educated person," she would say.

I wasn't any better at spelling than at penmanship. But, I would joke that my handwriting was so bad, nobody would notice the misspellings.

My Mom had been a high school English teacher and was a whiz at both spelling and grammar. She did the *New York Times* crossword puzzle every day—including Sunday's daunting one—in ink! Naturally, she was exasperated by my poor spelling skills. (They never really improved, either) After Spellcheck was invented, I pointed out the wisdom of my feelings about the relative unimportance of knowing how to spell. She was not convinced…or even amused!!!

After these two horrible subjects were over with, we'd move onto safer ground—history, literature, social studies, and math.

My mother spent a lot of time guiding me in writing. I can still hear her tips as I write my columns and books. In my head, I hear her saying: "now is the time to hit them with a really good metaphor," "look for a better adjective." She searched for what she called, in French, "le mot juste." The right word.

During those nightly sessions, I frequently imagined myself as a Prime Minister coming before Parliament to face a vote of confidence. If the motion could attract a majority (two parents), I was safe. But if it was voted down—signifying "no confidence"—I would have to resign. Some nights it felt like the prospects for the motion's passage were dim, but it always passed. Despite that, I lived with the constant fear that my parents would despair of me and send me to a boarding school. I always felt my fate was in play as I met my parents each night. Every night, when it was over, I'd quietly sigh in relief and curl up in bed with a great book. On the other hand, I always found that my parents were my biggest cheerleaders. They supported me in school politics. on the debating team, and, later, in local politics. My parents taught me how to research, write, and make a compelling argument for a point of view. That's why I was able to carefully build my case on those rare occasions when I disagreed with them and got up the nerve to articulate my reasoning.

I also learned firsthand how to tear down a weak argument. I had a lot of experience with that!

15. How I Became A Political Consultant

A young friend, Don Skelley, sagely observed that it is only in the modern era of cable television that political consultants and chefs have become famous.

My path to political consulting was a tortuous one.

I was working tirelessly at night and on weekends on West Side politics—always without pay. During the day, I earned a living as a research analyst for the New York Citizens Budget Commission, a civic watchdog group set up in the thirties to monitor the New York City government's finances.

I got the job in 1967, right after I graduated from Columbia at nineteen.

With the City's budget descending into chaos and balanced by chicanery in the late '60s and early '70s—leading it to the brink of bankruptcy—we had a lot of work to do and much to criticize. My training and work at the Citizens Budget Commission gave me an invaluable preparation for political consulting.

After several years of studying the details of municipal finance, the Police Department, City bonds, utility rates, transportation systems, and management issues, I became something of an expert on public policy issues, which gave me a big advantage in political consulting.

Very few of my competitors knew their way around a city or state budget. But I did. This experience gave me the opportunity to transcend the line between process and policy and use my knowledge of issues to help elect candidates.

My political work put me in close touch with the major elected officials in New York (all Democrats). So, in 1974, I left the Citizens Budget Commission and combined my political contacts with my substantive expertise to create a consulting business to advise New York's Democratic political leaders on issues and policy. At one time or another, I worked for every important Democrat in the state: Herman Badillo, Percy Sutton, Ed Koch, Eliot Spitzer, Bob Abrams, Bella Abzug, Carol, Elizabeth Holtzman, Stanley Steingut, Jay Golden, and so on.

Meanwhile, one of my associates in the West Side Kids, (as we became known) Dick Dresner, had received his graduate degree in public opinion research at the City University and went to work for Lou Harris, the premier political polling company in the country.

Dresner had not known any of us in high school, but he lived a quiet life in a brownstone on West 89th street. When he learned of our political club—the Community Free—he was intrigued and immediately joined. He later a top political consultants for decades.

After working for a number of years in our separate fields, Dick and I decided to combine his polling expertise with my political relationships. We would now offer advice based on polling data, which we would use to help develop themes, messages, and advertisements.

In 1974, I put my heart and soul into the New York State gubernatorial campaign of Democrat Howard Samuels. I served as a volunteer coordinating his policy and issue positions. During the campaign, I drafted a comprehensive program of reform for the state government on issues ranging from the budget to environmental concerns and ethics reforms. I was lining myself up to be Howard's political advisor as a full-time job. But Howard lost the primary to Congressman Hugh Carey, who ultimately became governor.

Crushed, my dreams destroyed, I was disconsolate. My mother, seeing my distress, asked why I was confining myself to New York. "Go national," she urged. "There's a big world out there."

Back then, in 1977, when I first decided to be a political consultant, there was no such profession. My Mom was always trying to understand exactly what it was that I did.

She knew exactly what I wasn't. I wasn't a lawyer, an accountant, or an economist, but she knew I worked for campaigns. She'd met many of the candidates. I wasn't a statistician or a filmmaker, but she knew I worked with polls and advertising. She couldn't understand my role and used to ask: "how can I describe to my friends what you do when they ask about what kind of a job you have?" So, I gave her an answer to use: "political consultant."

It was a brand new field.

Historically, the pollsters and media creators who consulted with election campaigns worked mainly for commercial clients, and only occasionally—during the election season—handled political candidates. Most of the strategy and advice came directly from the political parties and their staffs.

And the firms that handled political campaigns categorized themselves as either survey research organizations or advertising agencies.

Most candidates relied on their friends and local associates for political advice, politicians who ran campaigns in their local bailiwicks, often as a sideline from their regular commercial advertising or lobbying work. There were few, if any, general strategic consultants. In fact, I knew of only one: the amazing Joe Napolitan.

Joe achieved fame when he collaborated with media guru Tony Schwartz to produce the iconic TV ad that Lyndon Johnson used to defeat Goldwater in the 1964 election—one of the first political commercials in television history and one of the best.

The ad featured an innocent little girl slowly pulling the petals off a daisy and counting them, in her small voice. She sounded cute as she mixed the numbers up: "one, two, three, seven, six, ten." When all the petals were gone, the announcer interrupted in a somber metallic voice with a real countdown: "ten, nine, eight, etc." The ad culminated with an atomic mushroom cloud explosion as President Johnson said: "These are the stakes."

Ironically, the ad only ran on TV once, but it is probably the best known political ad ever made. Even after just one airing—and without mentioning the name of Barry Goldwater, LBJ's opponent—it ended the race then and there.

Goldwater had opened the door for the ad by advocating the use of "tactical" nuclear weapons in Vietnam to defoliate the jungle to permit us to spot enemy troops. But nobody was interested in the explanation: "He's going to drop the bomb!" everyone said and Johnson won in a landslide.

But, it wasn't just creative thinking that distinguished Napolitan. His methods and style led *The New York Times* to dub him as "that newest American phenomenon, the professional campaign manager."[7]

I had the privilege of learning at the master's knee from both Napolitan and Tony in Schwartz' 56th street office on Manhattan's West Side.

Joe was deeply involved with clients throughout the third world. I remember one day, he got a phone call while we were at Tony's office. After he hung up, he said to us all "I just lost my African client. There was a coup d'etat."

Both Joe and Tony focused on the "message." They weren't concerned about rallies, leafleting, or voter lists. They brought American politics into the electronic age. They preached that a candidate's message had to grow out of an idea that the voters already had in their heads that could be tapped for a campaign, almost like a chord plugged into an electric socket.

The dogma was strict: If the idea is not there already on the voter's radar, you can't put it there. You must play the hand you're dealt; use what is already in the voters' minds to persuade them.

They used polling and survey research to find out exactly what voters thought and which messages would resonate with what they already knew.

Tony and Joe called this process "presearch."

For example, while working for Hubert Humphrey in his unsuccessful race against Richard Nixon in 1968, Schwartz and Napolitan came up with a simple ad.

Polling had shown that voters considered Spiro Agnew, Nixon's candidate for vice-president, to be an ineffective fool, an idiot. So the ad played into that widespread sentiment. The simple words "President Spiro Agnew" appeared on the screen with a sound track of a growing chorus of hysterical laughter behind it.

The books *The Election Game* by Joe Napolitan in 1972 and *The Responsive Chord* by Tony Schwartz in 1973 transformed American politics and became my bibles. Both men were highly influenced by Marshal McLuhan's classic *The Medium Is The Message,* written in 1971.

I learned so much from Tony and Joe. I often brought clients to Tony's office—including Bill Clinton, New Hampshire Senator Warren Rudman, and New Mexico Senator Jeff Bingaman. They each ended up hiring Tony and me to do their campaigns.

Tony, who had designed patriotic posters during World War II had quite a wit and proudly had two toilet seats in his bathroom side by side, one labelled "Democrats" and the other "Republicans."

Tony labored under the burden of intense agoraphobia. He panicked when he found himself among strangers or out in public. He had to limit sharply his trips outside his Manhattan brownstone. Candidates had to come to him. And come they did: Jimmy Carter, Walter Mondale, Hubert Humphrey, and, of course, Bill Clinton all made the journey to his 56th street brownstone to film their campaign ads.

Sitting around Tony's office, learning his theories about media, shaped my whole understanding of politics and communication. Now it was time to put it to good use.
(I was deeply honored and moved to receive the first annual Joe Napolitan Victory Award from the Washington Academy Hall of Fame as the outstanding consultant in Latin America.)

16. How I Met Eileen

Eileen and I first met in 1973 (I was twenty-five, she twenty-four) when we both worked on the New York gubernatorial campaign for Howard J. Samuels, a moderate Democrat.

At the time, she was a nationally known consumer advocate and I was a political operative coordinating issues for the Samuels campaign. In that role, I assembled a kind of shadow cabinet of experts in all key areas and asked Eileen to be our go-to person on consumer matters.

I'd seen her on TV, excoriating Con Ed's latest rate hike. She had lobbied for laws to permit the substitution of low cost generic drugs for the first time, and to require unit prices to be displayed on grocery shelves, so people could actually compare the prices between packages of different sizes and weights. It's hard to imagine that wasn't available., but it wasn't! She pushed for laws to require full disclosure of credit terms when selling cars and houses and to amend laws that favored creditors in lawsuits. That wasn't done then. And when universal product codes, readable by scanners, first made their way onto supermarket shelves, she met with the major grocers and then worked to get a law passed requiring the market to post the price tag in numbers as well so you—not just the scanner—could still see them. We take those things for granted now, but they were big issues back then— especially with the elderly.

She frequently testified on consumer matters at hearings in New York and Washington and was one of the first to call attention to the illegal and unethical "no show" job practices in the New York State Legislature.

I had seen her in action and was impressed.

Throughout the campaign, we never met or spoke socially, but I was attracted to her. I was going through a divorce at the time. I hadn't seen her since the election and she had gone on to a position in the new Carey Administration.

Then fate intervened in the form of former Miss America Bess Myerson. The first Jewish Miss America (elected in 1945 as the holocaust was being uncovered), she was a combination of the girl next door and a glamorous star. She served as Consumer Affairs Commissioner in New York City and knew Eileen well In fact, she had asked then Mayor Abe Beame to appoint Eileen to the New York City Consumer Advisory Board. Bess and I had become acquainted when she flirted with running for Mayor of New York and asked me to brief her on local issues.

About this time, the federal courts began to consider breaking up the telephone monopoly to enable digital communication. Bess had to prepare a statement for a public hearing on the subject and she asked Eileen to do it over a weekend. "It's a lot of work," Bess apologized, "but how about if I asked Dick Morris to help you?"

"Oh God, not him," Eileen replied. "I'll end up doing all the work and he'll take all the credit."

"I think you have him wrong," Bess answered. "He's really very nice and very smart. I think you'll enjoy working with him."

Because of her affection for Bess, Eileen agreed.

For my part, I was thrilled. One day at brunch with my parents after my divorce, they asked me what kind of woman I would like to marry. I described Eileen. "Someone who is political, involved, pretty, articulate, fun, and you can talk with." But I never acted on it. Never asked her out.

When Bess suggested I meet with Eileen, I immediately set a date for that afternoon. I ran out to get a haircut.

But that made me a half hour late for our meeting. Eileen wasn't happy. It turned out that she had cancelled her own haircut appointment in order to get to the meeting on a rainy Friday afternoon! And she was having a big party the next day. She was about to leave when I showed up.

I apologized and when we sat down to divide the work for Bess' project, I acted swiftly to defuse the situation. After we discussed the specific issues, I said, "I think I know what Bess wants. Why don't I prepare a draft and get it to you over the weekend?"

That disarmed her.

Then, at the end of the meeting, I decided to take a chance and asked her to have dinner the next week. Amazingly, she said yes. I suggested we go to Hizzoner, a City Hall bar near my office. But she had other ideas and, instead, we went to Chelsea Place, a stylish piano bar and restaurant filled with flowers. It was a magical night. It was Harry Met Sally time. Forty-three years ago.

About ten years ago, our good friend Arlene Hurson invited us to a dinner party at her home in Boca Raton. She invited us with Bess who was an old friend. Still beautiful and elegant in her late eighties, she was happy to see us again and admitted that she had tried to be a matchmaker.

I'm grateful to her.

Eileen turned my life from black-and-white into color. She infused texture, humor, passion, and the joy of living into every aspect of my existence. She is the smartest person I have ever known. I learn from her every day. And I'm still hoping to beat her in completing *The New York Times* crossword puzzle.

Initially, we worked apart. I had politics and she had law. But, in the past twenty years, we've merged our work and do it all together. We write our books (this is the twentieth) together and often worked on foreign campaigns together, too. .

We laugh a lot, love to travel together, and enjoy time with our family and friends. We are truly each other's best friend. And she has my back. Always.

And, then there is her family. As an only child, I grew up lonely and bonded with people outside of my political relationships. But Eileen comes replete with a full Irish family—a brother and two sisters. We are all very close, see one another often, and revel in our times together. Fortunately, all her siblings have married people I love and have given us six nieces and nephews. They are each, unusually enough, beautiful, fun, brilliant, nice, successful…and sane. Quite a blessing.

17. My First Meeting with Bill Clinton

I was able to get my first meeting with Bill Clinton in November 1977, around my thirtieth birthday, by fibbing that I had to come to Little Rock to meet a commercial client and was wondering if I could drop in to see him while I was in town. By taking the onus of inviting myself, I had made it clear that Clinton need not pay my expenses. Intrigued, Clinton agreed to a fifteen minute meeting. It lasted three hours.

I was worried that Clinton might be put off by my youth—I was thirty—but I need not have worried. He was only thirty-one!

I could hardly have imagined that this meeting would be the foundation for decades of a relationship with Bill Clinton.

He was then the new Attorney General of Arkansas (elected the year before) and was contemplating his next step up the ladder.

1978 was shaping up as a watershed year in Arkansas, a state where politicians held onto office for decades. But a vacancy opened up that year when Senator John McClellan died while serving his sixth term. Mortality, at last overcame seniority and applicants lined up to fill the vacant job.

The main contenders were Governor David Pryor and Congressman Jim Guy Tucker. With Pryor leaving the governorship to run for senate, Clinton wasn't sure whether he should run for senator or for governor.

He told me he'd rather be senator than governor, but he didn't know if he could win.

I explained how polling could help him to make the decision. Of course, I said, I would do what all pollsters did and match him up against potential candidates.

But that, I said, is no sure indication of eventual success or failure. Just basing your decision about your chances on the head-to-head polling was like assessing if you could climb a mountain only by measuring its height. You had to see if there were handholds and footholds—issues—that you could use to pull yourself up.

I explained that my poll would create a hypothetical campaign for him and each of his potential opponents, run the campaigns past the voters, and measure their reactions. From these calculations, I said, we could predict the election's outcome.

I borrowed some techniques I had learned were used in Hollywood to test whether movies would be successful. The producers would take publicity blurbs that copywriters had written about the films and read them to potential viewers over the phone. Hollywood even used these surveys to determine where to shoot James Bond movies or what to put in the Jaws and Rocky films.

It was easy to apply this technique to politics. Write the ads you and your opponent would likely use and read them to the voters to determine their reactions. Take the two-dimensional head-to-head measure of voting intentions and add a third dimension, charting how the campaigns would play out as they unfolded.

Bill was fascinated. Now politics, which had previously been opaque and mysterious to him, could become rational and predictable. He was hooked.

And I was hooked on him. I called Eileen that night and told her I had just met with a guy who I thought would be president. I'd never said that before.

Clinton hired me to conduct a poll. The results indicated that he would have a hard time getting elected senator, but could easily walk into the governor's chair. So Clinton ran for governor.

Our meeting was in the Arkansas Attorney General's office, a space that resembled a 1960s suburban finished basement playroom. All that was missing was the ping pong table.

As our meeting ended, I had to use the bathroom. He showed me to his private one and I closed the door behind me. There, on the door was a floor to ceiling pinup of a shapely blonde spilling out of a wholly inadequate white bikini. s I returned to his office, I asked if he felt it was OK to have that poster decorating his bathroom. "It's the Bible Belt," I reminded him.

"Don't you know who that is?" he asked, astonished that I did not recognize the woman.

"That's Dolly Parton!" he blurted out, his tone suggesting that anybody would know that. "Who?" I asked.

"Oh man!" he shook his head. "You really are from New York."

But, it turned out, getting elected governor wasn't enough for Bill. He had another agenda, too. He wanted Pryor to win the Senate race. Not so much because of any love for the former governor, but because he wanted to block Congressman Jim Guy Tucker, Pryor's opponent. He wanted to thwart Tucker's career even as he advanced his own.

It wasn't that there was any bad blood between them, but Tucker was very much like Clinton—young, handsome, articulate, educated, modern and liberal. So like him that he threatened to usurp the space in Arkansas politics that Clinton wanted for himself. That niche was already feeling too crowded.

They were the poster boys for the new Arkansas, freed from the bad old days of segregation and ignorance.

Bill went to Yale Law School and Jim Guy attended Harvard, but there was only room for one of them in the small state of Arkansas. Each vied with the other to become its modern face.

So Bill met with Governor Pryor to offer his help in beating Tucker for the Senate seat. In effect, Clinton asked Pryor to let him run the campaign. Pryor was a very nice guy, but Bill—and Hillary—doubted his ability to win a tough campaign.

Pryor, who shared Bill's doubts, eagerly agreed. And, infatuated with my polling, Clinton brought me in on the deal. My new mission was not only to elect Clinton Governor (easy), but help defeat Tucker and elect Pryor Senator (much harder). Together, sitting side-by-side, we plotted the campaign strategy for Pryor, wrote the negative ads against Tucker, and played key roles in piloting Pryor to victory.

It was over the hours devoted to these strategy sessions that my relationship with Bill Clinton began. During the ensuing decade, we learned together how to win elections and our ideas on political strategy matured at the same time. It was as if we were a consulting firm and first Pryor and then Bill himself was our client.

Tucker's campaign theme tapped into public perceptions that David Pryor was weak. His slogan was "the difference is leadership."

But, we had a surprising new issue. Eileen had meticulously researched Tucker's voting record as a Congressman. (A cumbersome process in the pre-computer age that involved manually checking each vote in the records at the local library.) She found that Tucker had an extremely high rate of absenteeism. He just never came to work while he was running for office.

In those days, the insiders (like me) shrugged off missing votes, claiming that they didn't make much difference anyway and that voters would understand that the candidate had to spend time campaigning. But Eileen saw what a great issue it was and insisted that voters –expected elected officials to show up for the job they were paid for—particularly when their salary of $60,000 a year was almost seven times the average annual income of workers in Arkansas.[8]She also believed that the average voter would not expect to continue to get full pay while they looked for another job, as Tucker did.

The polling supported her thinking. The people of Arkansas didn't like what Tucker was doing.

So Clinton and I designed a radio ad where the clerk of the House of Representatives called the roll of Arkansas Congressmen for a vote: "Mr. Hammerschmidt votes aye. Mr. Thornton votes nay. Mr. Tucker? Mr. Tucker? How does Jim Guy Tucker vote? Can anybody find Mr. Tucker?"

The ad ended with the ultimate putdown/rebuttal to Tucker's slogan "the difference is leadership." Our ad said: "You can't lead if you're not there." It was devastating and played a key role in defeating Tucker and electing Pryor. Most important for me, it helped solidify my relationship with both Bill and Hillary (who especially relished good negative ads).

These early victories came as I was also helping Ed King beat Mike Dukakis for governor of Massachusetts after he had trailed 72-11 in the early polls.. I discovered in my polling for King that Massachusetts voters had no idea that Dukakis was a liberal. The key to beating him, I realized was to portray, scrupulously and accurately, the actual positions Dukakis took on key issues. Capital punishment? (opposed) Drinking age? (he wanted to keep it at 18). Tax limitation initiatives? (Dukakis didn't like them). Abortion? (pro-choice). When voters learned how liberal their governor was, they turned to King instead.

King won the Democratic Primary in a spectacular upset that attracted national attention.

But he wasn't out of the woods yet. King still had the general election ahead of him. The Republican candidate was the Brahmin GOP leader in the State House, Francis W. Hatch.

Hatch was a conservative who agreed with King on all the issues we had used to beat Dukakis in the primary, so we couldn't use them to differentiate the two in the general election.,

Besides, a great many of the Dukakis supporters, shell shocked at his totally unexpected defeat, couldn't bring themselves to back King as the Democratic candidate and would either vote Republican or stay home.

I racked my brain trying to find a way to use the cultural divide between the classic blue collar Ed King and the quintessential elite Frank Hatch.

There was a vast difference in their pedigrees. Hatch was a Brahmin of the sort that had dominated Bay State politics for centuries. King was a working class former pro football guard for the Baltimore Colts in 1950.

But how to capture the difference on television?

It came to me in a dream.

When I woke up, I ordered a helicopter to film our next ad. It flew over Hatch's house taking photos of the mansion from every angle. Then we routed it over King's house, an ordinary two bedroom affair on a line of identical houses in a working class area.

The text ran: (with birds chirping in the background) "Up here, in Beverly Farms, where Frank Hatch makes his home (the film showed his mansion) taxes are reasonable and crime's not too bad. So Hatch opposes the death penalty and sees no need for tax limitations. (now the sound shifts to cars honking, police sirens, garage trucks making noise) But here, in Winthrop, where Ed King lives, taxes are killing and crime is out of hand, (now the announcer is shouting to be heard over the din) that's why King is for capital punishment and a Prop thirteen tax limitation for Massachusetts."

The ad played very well. Hatch's wife helped assure our success.

Providentially named "Bambi," she told the Boston papers that she had sat up all night in fear, gun in her lap, now that her house was on television.

Ed King's hardy Irish wife, Jody, said, "We live a few blocks from a mental hospital and I don't even own a gun."

The election was all but over.

My work in the King, Clinton, and Pryor victories launched my consulting career.

In the next election cycle, 1980, my momentum continued, but this time the three Senators I helped elect were all Republicans—Warren Rudman in New Hampshire, Mark Andrews in North Dakota, and Paula Hawkins in Florida.

In 1982, I worked for two winning Senate candidates (Jeff Bingaman, Democrat from New Mexico and Pete Wilson, Republican of California. I also worked for three winning Democratic governor candidates (Mark White, Texas, Harry Hughes, Maryland, and, of course, Bill Clinton in Arkansas).

I kept thinking: What an exhilarating career choice I had made! What an adventure!

18. Welcome To Charleston…The Wrong One

"Welcome to Charleston" the banner at the airport read.

I was arriving on a plane from New York's LaGuardia Airport for a meeting with my client running for Governor of West Virginia. I had flown to Charleston to keep our lunch appointment.

But, as I proceeded through the airport, I was puzzled at the poster that said: "Don't kill the golden goose. No new taxes in South Carolina."

Why, I wondered would some stupid ad buyer have placed a billboard in a West Virginia airport about taxes in South Carolina? Some new way to bilk the state out of money?

The security guard policing the exit area appreciated my thanking him as I walked by. But it was puzzling when he replied, "Have a nice day Y'all."

Well, West Virginia is sort of a southern state.

Then I went to the curb to get in a taxi with the logo Yellow Cab, Charleston. But the driver, also with a drawl, didn't recognize my destination. After studying his map (such things existed before GPS), he turned up a blank.

So I went to the taxi dispatcher and gave him the address. Still no response.

"Is the street in any town in West Virginia?" I asked, thinking it might be in a suburb.

"West Virginia?" the dispatcher blurted out. "Son, you're in the wrong place. This here is Charleston, South Carolina!"

I knew the flight seemed longer than I had expected.

South Carolina?

Embarrassed, I called my client and was greeted with a roar of laughter. "Don't you go billing me for a trip to South Carolina, now." And, for good measure, he added, "Don't get me elected in the wrong state, now. I want to be governor of West Virginia. Got it?"

19. How and Why I Became a Republican

There wasn't a single issue or event that led me to become a Republican. It was a long journey over a period of years.

When I started out as a young Democrat, that was all I knew. In fact, that's all there was.

It didn't occur to me that there was something else to even consider.

I'd never even met a Republican! That's mainly because I focused only on that very small part of Manhattan where I lived and where Democrats reigned.

Of course, I knew there were Republican elected officials throughout New York State, but I didn't know any of them. "Rockefeller Republicans," these pro-business social liberals like Governor Nelson Rockefeller, Senator Jacob Javits, and New York City Mayor John Lindsay worked hand-in-hand with the Democrats. Their policies were indistinguishable. And none of today's bitter ideological divide between the parties existed. But that breed of Republicans is long gone. Extinct.

So, I had no historical animosity towards Republicans; they were just not a big presence or consideration.

But the Vietnam War began to change my benign view of the Democratic Party. President Lyndon Johnson's hawkish policies that escalated the war sickened me. And the Democratic Congress was no better. They never even challenged him. Mindless sheep—with a few exceptions - they let Johnson broaden his powers and increase the violence, the casualties, and the spending. Worst of all, they never demanded that he tell us the truth.

Perhaps if the Democrats had done their job and dared to question the President, we might not have lost over 58,000 young men and spent almost a trillion dollars (in today's money) for a war that made no difference whatsoever.

I watched as even the solidly Democratic West Side of New York began to turn on the President and was awash in anti-war fervor. But a lot of the local Democratic leaders, governed by steadfast party loyalty, refused to support anti-war candidates in the 1968 election, even though they agreed with them. They still flocked first to Johnson and then to Humphrey to please the national party and sustain the war.

I wondered, too, about the party's domestic and local agenda. In 1975, I watched in horror as City Hall's Democratic leaders were so fiscally irresponsible that New York was on the verge of collapse. They had rolled over its permanent deficit year after year until it could no longer be ignored and swept under the rug.

As I studied City government in my first job—at the Citizens Budget Commission—I came to realize that many of these programs, designed to help the poor, often did little for them. Instead, the biggest beneficiary was the party's core constituency—unionized middle class workers in the bureaucracy whose donations and votes re-elected the Democratic municipal leaders.

I wrote about it in a series of articles for the left-wing weekly, *The Village Voice,* that led to the publication of my first book, *Bum Rap on American Cities.(*Prentice Hall,1977)

One chapter, *Let's Get the Middle Class off Welfare,* exposed the fact that the bulk of the City's welfare budget was paid to landlords, doctors, hospitals, and social workers—not to the indigent people it was designed to help.

I was influenced by Howard Samuels

Howard's mantra was that liberal intentions made no difference if they were not matched by productivity in delivering services to the people. I saw the massive waste in New York's Democratic government and realized that little really seeped through to the poor.

In 1976, I held my nose and voted for the incompetent and clueless Jimmy Carter. But as the years passed, I grew more estranged from the political party I had inherited from my liberal Democratic parents.

When I began working outside of New York in 1977, my first two clients were both Democrats: Bill Clinton, an Arkansas liberal, and Ed King, an arch-conservative from Massachusetts. They could not have been more different. Each was bright, innovative, and exciting to work with. But there was only one thing they had in common: They were Democrats. Other than that, they seemed to be from very different political planets.

Ed King was challenging Massachusetts Governor Michael Dukakis in the Democratic primary.

Tone deaf, arrogant, condescending, and elitist, Dukakis was a leftist robot who had no common sense and showed no emotion or even concern for his constituents. He knew better than they did what was best for them.

Dukakis clung to his liberal catechism and, as Tallyrand said of the Bourbon kings of France, he "learned nothing and forgot nothing"[9] even as events changed the world around him.

He would do whatever it took to maintain the support and admiration of the Harvard liberals, in part because of his narcissistic need to please his intellectual patrons. His platform was chiseled on the sacred tablets handed down from Cambridge to the liberal left and could not be modified.

What really bothered me, though, was that Dukakis and his supporters didn't just disagree with Ed King. They looked down on him. He was way too conservative for liberal Massachusetts. That made him uncaring. He didn't go to Harvard. That made him intellectually inferior. He went to Boston College and, even worse, starred at football and later played as a pro for the Baltimore Colts as an offensive guard. He wasn't part of the club. He was very much an Irish Catholic—too much so for the Brahmins. King was just not governor material.

I came to realize that Democrats only wanted members of their own class in public office. The great unwashed—and the bulk of the country—could vote for them, but didn't know enough to govern, an insight that Donald Trump understood decades later. He, too, doesn't meet their exalted standards.

At about this time, I thought about how little George Wallace and Ted Kennedy had in common. Both were Democrats, but totally apart on ideology. So, I wondered, what did the Democratic Party really stand for?

My journey across party lines began in 1980 when I started handling campaigns for both parties. My first Republican clients were Paula Hawkins in Florida, Warren Rudman in New Hampshire, and Mark Andrews in North Dakota. All three were elected to the Senate and were refreshing, brilliant, and, well, *different.*

It turned out that the Democrats didn't have a monopoly on ideas or effectiveness. Warren Rudman, for example, was a remarkable candidate and an outstanding Senator who persistently crossed party lines and forged compromises to cut the deficit. He absolutely refused to take special interest PAC money.

Shortly after we first met, he and his wife, Shirley, invited Eileen and me to their house in Nantucket for a winter weekend. In front of the fire, we spent hours discussing his possible candidacy. I was astounded by his grasp of issues. Early on, he carved out his signature concerns: a balanced budget, reform of campaign financing, and strict oversight of Congressional ethics. He became famous for the Gramm-Rudman Act that provided for automatic budget cuts if the President did not meet certain benchmarks.

Paula Hawkins was a strong consumer advocate and had made her name battling against the Florida utilities as the Republican member of the Public Utilities Commission. She was the first woman elected to the Senate who had not been the wife or daughter of a male predecessor. She was elected on her own!

All these Republicans heavily influenced me. But perhaps the biggest pull to the right came after many early morning walks around Washington with Newt Gingrich, who tutored me in the core curriculum of conservatism. There could be no greater teacher.

It was a different time. Now the two parties are like opposing football teams, lined up against one another. Nobody—or very few—breaks party ranks and those who do rarely live to tell about it.

But my migration to the GOP was not just professional; it was personal as well. At the start of the 1980s, I voted Democrat, in part because I supported a nuclear freeze, opposed Star Wars, and supported arms control treaties. Reagan didn't see things my way. But, as the decade unfolded, I came to realize that he was right and I had been wrong.

The best way to save the world from nuclear annihilation turned out to be Reagan's way: Win the cold war and wipe out communism by forcing them to go broke. In fact, had Reagan followed my advice and curbed his defense spending, Russia would have gladly followed suit and not have exhausted itself economically. The Cold War could still be raging. The lesson sank in.

My transition from Democratic blue to bipartisan purple stemmed, in part, from my chats with my leading Democratic client, Bill Clinton, late at night in the kitchen of the Arkansas Governor's Mansion as he raided the fridge. We both thought Carter's policy of handing out grants to every manner of neighborhood group didn't really do much to help the actual poor people.

We came up with the idea that became central to his presidency—much to the discomfort of hard line Democrats—of a contractual relationship: We give you help and you take responsibility. Welfare-for-work. Student loans-for-public service. A new social contract.

From there, it was a short jump to the Republican Party. I came to see the Democrats as more interested in getting the poor to continue vote for them then in lifting them out of poverty. And all the while, adding more and more government employees who contributed to the Democrats.

My policy goals didn't change. But I saw that the direct approach most Democrats adopted didn't work as well as the more sophisticated way Republicans went about achieving them. Where Democrats pandered by handing out checks, Republicans stressed independence and self-reliance.

When I was young, I believed that people got more conservative as they got older and richer so they could keep their money. Increasingly, I came to realize that many also got more conservative because they saw that conservative means were the best way to achieve the idealistic ends they had cherished in their younger days.

So, first intellectually, then professionally, and finally emotionally, I became a Republican.

I went on to handle the winning campaigns of eleven Republicans for Senator or Governor including, in addition to Rudman, Hawkins, and Andrews, Pete Wilson of California, Tom Ridge of Pennsylvania, Don Sundquist of Tennessee, Trent Lott of Mississippi, Jesse Helms of North Carolina, Mike Huckabee of Arkansas, Dan Coats of Indiana, , and Bill Weld of Massachusetts.

And eight Democrats: David Pryor and Bill Clinton of Arkansas, Mark White of Texas, Jeff Bingaman of New Mexico, Harry Hughes of Maryland,

Ed King of Massachusetts, Buddy Roemer of Louisiana, and Bill Allain of Mississippi.

20. My Walks with Newt

During his years in Congress, future Speaker Newt Gingrich developed the habit of walking around Washington each morning taking a circuitous route that brought him to the Washington Monument, the Lincoln Memorial, and various other sites. He did it for exercise, but being Newt, he didn't listen to music on headphones like the rest of us do when we do aerobics.

Instead, he would schedule walking partners to hike around Washington, DC with him. His aim was mental as well as physical exercise. During these walks, the history professor in Newt came to the fore, eclipsing the politician. Indeed, on these jaunts, he eschewed talk of politics and loved to discuss interesting topics in world history.

I was thrilled when Newt's scheduler called me—in my pre-White House days—to say that Newt wanted to walk with me. It was great fun and it was a high honor. (Even higher when he asked me three or four more times.) I was relieved when she made a point of telling me that the walks were always leisurely, never aerobic.

The shadow of Newt Gingrich had begun to loom over Washington. He had not yet toppled the Democrats and taken the Speakership—after the Republican Party had waited forty years in the minority. But his imprint was making itself felt in the Party. More often than voters suspect, the brightest people move to the fore in politics and Newt's was clearly just such a case.

Each walk had a topic about which Newt's scheduler had told us in advance. We discussed subjects like what made Napoleon decide to invade Russia, how he would rate Eisenhower and Grant as generals, and why Churchill was defeated at the polls right as Germany was surrendering in 1945.

Some of his walk topics grew in magnitude until they became books. For example, his musings about the battle of Gettysburg matured into his book *Gettysburg: A Novel of the Civil War* that explored the hypothetical consequences of a Southern victory.

How wonderful to be passing the Jefferson Memorial while we discussed whether Jefferson was really a philosopher in politics or one of the most cunning, subtle, and astute of our founders! Or to be discussing the politics of Lincoln's Emancipation Proclamation as we passed by the great statue of the former president peering out through the columns of his memorial at the machinations of Washington DC!

Newt's knowledge of history is not only deep and profound, it is speculative. Newt the historian recalls events. Newt the politician wonders how things could have been different and critiques the moves of statesmen past with the shrewd eye of a modern political practitioner.

The walks were part of Newt's unusual fitness program. The other part was his refusal to sit down. He would conduct his work and meetings in his Congressional office while standing at a chest-high desk that looked like a lectern. When ushered into his office, you were always offered a seat, but, if you took it, Newt would be standing looking down at you the entire time.

While Newt wanted to talk history during these walks, I was determined to use them to expound on my political ideas about strategy and tactics. I would inveigh against the conventional wisdom of Republican consultants that included the dictum "don't answer negative attacks." I always felt I could score more points on rebuttal than with a purely negative offensive. I would urge more focus on early advertising rather than the then fashionable trend of saving all your ammo until the last month of the campaign.

On one walk, Newt criticized my work for both parties. I had renounced working for Democrats in 1988, but still kept Bill Clinton as a client, citing my decade-long relationship. Newt was quite blunt in telling me that, as long as I worked for Clinton, he would not support Republicans who wanted to hire me. While I ignored his advice and worked for Clinton in 1990, I did not work for any other Democrats until I rejoined Clinton in the White House at the end of 1994.

21. Mike (Huckabee) and Me

One of the most amazing people I have ever worked with is Mike Huckabee, former Baptist Minister, former Governor of Arkansas, presidential candidate, author, and TV host.

Mike is a whirlwind of ideas, creativity, and good will. He is also one of the most positive people on the planet.

I first learned about him when he ran unsuccessfully against incumbent Arkansas Democratic Senator Dale Bumpers in 1990.

When Bill Clinton became President, Lt. Governor Jim Guy Tucker became the new Governor, leaving a vacancy. So Mike decided to run for Lt. Governor.

I had become a full-time Republican by then and I was instantly drawn to Mike and believed he could be successful. He was refreshing, bright, honest, and enthusiastic—very different from the average Arkansas political hack. On top of that, he was a talented musician, had a great sense of humor, and easily connected with people.

I flew down to Texarkana, which, as the name implies, was on the border with Texas in the very south of Arkansas. Mike, his amazing wife Janet (a pilot), and their great kids, John Mark, David, and Sarah all joined in the meeting in his living room and I quickly came to realize what an active role his family played in Mike's life and career. That continued in all of his endeavors.

I immediately bonded with Mike and the entire Huckabee family.

Mike had a tough road to travel. At the time, all statewide offices and three of the four Congressional seats were then held by Democrats and no Republican was given much of a chance.

But I wasn't convinced. I realized early on that Mike had the kind of persona, charisma, and credibility to create a new political reality.

And he did.

I had long been fascinated by the Christian right and wondered how its agenda might play out. I told Mike "ok, you oppose abortion and gay marriage. So what would you do with the rest of your governorship?" I was eager to see how the agenda of the Christian right would play out in education, prisons, environment, and all the other areas of state government. We spent hours discussing issues and formulating policies.

Mike was no typical cookie-cutter evangelical Republican. He had clear and firm ideas of what he wanted to do—and what he wouldn't do. Once, I asked him if he opposed parole for violent felons, expecting him to check a box on the standard GOP agenda. But he surprised me. I was rocked back when he said, "No, of course not, forgiveness is essential to our values and heritage." His evengelicism instilled him with compassion, not anger or self-righteousness.

For his part, Mike knew that I had worked with Bill Clinton in Arkansas for years and understood the political landscape. He was amused, I think, to

61

welcome into his camp someone so prominently identified with the "dark side."

When Mike ran for Lt. Governor, the Democrats nominated Nate Colter, a card carrying member of the entrenched Democratic state establishment, to oppose him. After a fierce campaign, Mike won by a hair -- the first Republican to win statewide office in thirteen years.)

Yea, Mike!

But Mike's problems with the state Democratic establishment didn't end with his victory. As he recounts in his autobiography, *From Hope to Higher Ground*, when he tried to move into his new office as Lt. Governor, "the doors to my office were spitefully nailed shut from the inside, office furniture and equipment were removed, and the budget spent down to almost nothing prior to our arriving. After fifty-nine days of public outcry, the doors were finally opened for me to occupy the actual office I had been elected to hold two months earlier."[10]

Mike didn't stay Lt. Governor for long. In 1996, Governor Jim Guy Tucker was convicted of corruption and had to resign. Mike moved up and became the Governor!

It wasn't as easy as it sounds. Although the Arkansas constitution prohibits convicted felons from serving as Governor, Tucker insisted that it allowed him to take a leave of absence while his appeal was pending and he refused to resign. Voters were outraged. Mike firmly took the lead, announcing that he would call the Legislature into session at 10 p.m. that night to start impeachment proceedings. Finally, Tucker said good-bye. But not before he made 287 eleventh-hour appointments to State Boards and Commissions and released millions of dollars to favorite Democratic projects.

Long before Michelle Obama uttered the words "childhood obesity," Mike was a nationally recognized advocate for better food and nutritional standards for kids. Learning from his own brush with Diabetes 2 and his successful regimen to lose over 100 pounds, Mike traveled the state—and the country—to advocate a change in childhood eating habits and an increase in exercise. It was his persistence that raised this to a national issue.

I was increasingly drawn to Mike's Christianity and kindness. I remember at one of the lowest points in my life, Mike sent me a Bible with my name inscribed on the cover!

In 2008, Mike told me he wanted to run for the Republican nomination for president. While I had no paid, official, or public role in his campaign, I spoke with him often.

My core message to him was that he could not compete with the other candidate, Mitt Romney, toe-to-toe. Mitt was willing to spend whatever it took and Mike was never going to be able to raise much money. He just didn't move in those circles.

I had seen so many other presidential candidates flame out after strong starts because they ran out of money and could not support the vast overhead they had incurred. I didn't want that to happen to Mike.

I knew he would do well in the debates. Voters would immediately be attracted to him. Mike's personality, warmth, wit, intelligence and charisma would be on display. without needing millions of dollars. And the values that he spoke of – and lived – would be compelling. But, until the debates, I advised, don't try to compete. Keep down under the radar and hold your overhead to the absolute minimum lest your need for money drive you out of the race. "Don't let the sound of your own wheels drive you crazy," I said, borrowing the line from the Eagles.

Mike won Iowa in a huge upset, but did poorly in New Hampshire. Next came Michigan, the key test of whether or not he could run in a northern industrial state without much of an evangelical base.

I went on the O'Reilly Factor TV show on Fox News and told Bill that I thought Mike would get more than ten percent of the vote there. Bill bet me a dinner he wouldn't. (Mike finished a disappointing third but got 16%.)

When I told Mike of my on-air bet with Bill that he could make 10%. He was in the midst of the presidential race. But his sense of humor, modesty, and perspective shone through and he said, "Pressure!"

Since then, we've remained friends.

But our relationship has been rejuvenated by the emergence of his brilliant daughter Sarah Huckabee Sanders. I remember an eleven-year-old Sarah hanging around, listening in, as I briefed her father on my polls. And it is wonderful to see her walk the tight rope every day as Trump's press secretary. She never falls or even falters. Her Dad's daughter.

22. Right About Trump/Wrong About Romney

Eileen and I were right on target in 2016 in predicting Donald Trump's victory. In April and May, six months before the election, we wrote our best-selling book, *Armageddon: How Trump Can Beat Hillary.*

We saw the Trump phenomenon and recognized that his common sense message, clear agenda—and outsized persona—resonated with blue collar workers in a primal way that would take him to the White House.

We saw the crowds filled with hope and wild excitement.

He was a winner. I saw the coalition forming around him and spoke about its impact.

In an interview on October 28th, with San Angelo Live radio show, I said: "White men who have only a high school education backed Trump by 16 points in the Fox News poll of one week ago, now support him by an amazing 30 points, a gain of 14 in Trump's direction. Among women high school graduates who have no college, Trump's margin has swelled by 7 points in the same period."

On election day, he carried high school educated white men by 45 points! Before election day, we predicted a Trump win with 325 electoral votes. He got 309. We accurately predicted Trump upsets in Florida, North Carolina, Michigan, Pennsylvania, Ohio, Wisconsin, and Iowa. We only got Virginia and Nevada wrong .

It's very hard for me to predict the outcome of political races when I'm not directly involved in the campaign and have no access to the daily polling and field reports. I have to rely on public polls that I don't actually conduct and hope they are accurate. And I can't always account for last minute events that might swing a race. Without knowledge of, or control over, the variables, it's often a tough call .

But I missed it in the 2012 Obama win over Romney. Boy did I miss it! Here's why:

Accurate polling was impossible in the week before the election when Hurricane Sandy hit. With no phones or internet in over 8,000,000 homes in 17 states, pollsters were flailing in the dark.[11]

In their final polls, Rasmussen and Gallup both had Romney ahead. CNN, Politico, and Monmouth had it tied. The *realclearpolitics.com* polling average had Obama up by a razor thin 0.7%. No-one predicted the late Obama surge that brought him a 4.1% victory.

It happened only in the last few days, largely driven by Obama's highly publicized tour of storm damage accompanied by the outspoken Republican governor of New Jersey, Chris Christie. If the partisan Christie could compliment Obama, a lot of swing voters felt it was now OK to come over and back him.

I never saw the race as the coronation march for Obama that the mainstream media said it was. I felt, accurately, that Romney came on strong at the end, until Obama sprinted past him, at hurricane speed, in the final days.

Remember Obama and his new best friend Chris Christie hugging and helicoptering over New Jersey a few days before the election?

That made a huge difference.

23. My Meeting with the Future Pope Francis

It was one of the greatest thrills of my life to meet Cardinal Jorge Mario Bergoglio, the future Pope Francis, in 2009 in Buenos Aires, Argentina.
Of course, I had no idea at the time that he would become Pope in four years. But what I did know was that he had a wide reputation as a brilliant yet modest and unpretentious cleric, who was fearless in calling out those in power when he believed they ignored their moral duty to protect and better their citizens.

I was very curious about the personal side of this powerful man and spiritual leader who lived his life in utter simplicity. Unlike his predecessors who made their residence in the royal-like splendor of the Fernandez Anchorena Palace on the poshest street in Buenos Aires, Cardinal Bergoglio chose to live in a modest apartment with only a small gas stove for heat.

Eileen and I heard him interviewed on a TV show during a visit to Argentina. His empathy—and advocacy—for the poor was obvious and sincere, even through the translation. His calls for specific reforms were right on point.

I had worked in Argentine politics, helping reformers topple the corrupt Peronist regime in 1999. A few years later, in 2003, I collaborated with my Argentine friend Luis Rosales in running a campaign for Ricardo Lopez Murphy against the Peronist candidate Nestor Kirchner. We came within a whisker of keeping the plague of Kirchner and his wife Christina from infecting the presidency of Argentina.

The Kirchners—first husband Nestor and then, his successor as president, wife Christina—were truly the Bonnie and Clyde of Argentina, plundering hundreds of millions to benefit themselves and their cronies.

At the time, Cardinal Bergoglio fiercely opposed the Kirchners' corrupt and near dictatorial regimes, criticizing their "lack of interest in the poor, rampant corruption, distorted inflation figures, and a penchant for confrontation instead of dialogue."[12]

It was highly unusual for the leader of the Catholic Church in the most influential province in Argentina to openly challenge the Peronists, but Bergoglio was outspoken and courageous.

He denounced the Kirchners for their pervasive corruption and failure to provide social welfare services to the poor and the elderly. He also lambasted their attempts to suppress free speech and the political opposition. Their self-serving economic policies led to financial ruin for many Argentines—and unimaginable wealth for their cronies.

Cardinal Bergoglio was determined to do what he could to guard against their excesses. When he learned of their secret strategy to try to change Argentine law to extend their terms of office, he personally organized opposition to this "perpetual re-election opposition."

Luis knew of my admiration for the Cardinal and he told his aide that I was a recent convert to Catholicism. and would love to meet him. The Cardinal knew of my work against the Peronists and agreed to receive me.

Besides religion, we had a lot in common. I shared his contempt for the Kirchners and his belief that they were ransacking and destroying Argentina. I also applauded

his interest in developing policies for economic and social reform and believed that the Catholic Church in Latin America had the ability to lead the way, especially against dictators.

I was humbled when, several weeks later, the Cardinal invited me to call on him.

Under Luis' wing, I took a taxi to the Metropolitan Cathedral in Buenos Aires where the Cardinal worked from a small office.

I had been to the Cathedral many times during my work in Argentina. Eileen and I frequently stopped in on our way to and from the Casa Rosada (the Pink House) where the Argentine president worked, right across the famous Plaza de Mayo and the balcony Evita Peron used to address the nation.

Each time we visited the Cathedral, we were particularly moved by a statue of Jesus on the cross with pain graphically etched on his face and the wounds bleeding in his side. The wood on the right foot of the statue was visibly worn down after decades of visitors stroked it.

But our favorite statue was one of St. Francis of Assisi, recognizable in his brown burlap robe and posed as if he was about to stride across the church. It was not surprising that a Cardinal from that church chose the papal name of Francis.

I loved the classical architecture and beauty of the Cathedral. On the outside, it looked more like a grand court house with large columns. But inside it was filled with ornate alters and frescoes. On this visit, I walked to the back of the church stopping in front of a simple, unadorned glass office door that led to Cardinal Bergoglio's understated office. It could have been the office of the music director, it was so plain—in sharp contrast to the regal trappings of the rest of the church.

An unassuming man whose face is now known throughout the world greeted Luis and me. Taking my hand in both of his, he gently steered me into his office. There, he sat in front of a plain desk after he pulled up chairs for us. We talked for almost an hour.

The Cardinal and I spoke two different languages—he spoke love and I the language of politics. Luis easily translated English into Spanish, but the other language gap was harder to bridge. I would refer to the need to raise education standards and he would speak of the hopelessness a poor family felt when they realized that the schools their kids had to attend were bad and that their children could not count on the education available to them to move them out of poverty.

Or I would discuss the need to raise incomes and he would focus on the pain of poverty. As we connected, though, it became obvious that good politics and policies should be an extension of love.

We discussed the problems of Brazil, Chile, Colombia, Venezuela, Mexico and the other principal Latin American nations where I had worked. I told him that I felt that the current regimes largely failed in articulating and developing an alternative path out of poverty that could compete with the radical socialist movement led by Hugo Chavez, the dictator of

Venezuela. I said that I felt the Church had a major role to fill in promoting answers to social problems that did not involve dictatorship and despotism.

Bergoglio, for his part, spoke of his disappointment at the "invisibility" of the poor to the national leaders. He spoke of the agony that poverty brought, constantly referring to his own experiences in witnessing it firsthand.

We discussed the deplorable absence of social welfare and nutrition programs in much of Latin America. I said that the continental embrace of capitalism had come about without a concomitant strengthening of what we Americans call the "safety net."

He heartily agreed, and discussed not programs or funding but love and caring. I was incredibly moved. I remember feeling that this is what Jesus must have been like in person.

I told him about my own spiritual experiences that led to my religious conversion. He said he was deeply grateful for my sharing and we hugged each other. I was weeping. His warm embrace has lingered in my heart ever since. I can still feel it.

There were some signs that he might become Pope. Much later, I heard that, when the future Pope Benedict XVI was chosen to be the pontiff, Cardinal Bergoglio had finished a strong second in the College of Cardinals.

Of course, he had never mentioned anything about it and there's no way to know for sure what I had heard was even true—the College's proceedings are supposed to be secret. But that was the word in Argentina.

Several years later, when Pope Benedict announced that he was resigning, I wondered whether the relatively unknown Cardinal Bergoglio would be the first Latin American Pope.

When the white smoke came out of the chimney and the name Bergoglio was announced, I wanted to cheer.

I never thought I would see him again, but in 2015, Chris Ruddy, the CEO of NewsMax, invited Eileen and me to the Vatican ceremony to canonize simultaneously the two former popes, John Paul II and John XXIII, for the first time in history.

The ceremony, attended by millions, was upbeat and joyous. Particularly moving were the tens of thousands of Poles who had turned out in tribute to John Paul II. We were seated next to a group from Ghana, dressed in their colorful traditional robes and dresses. We chatted with them and I introduced them to Michael Reagan, who was with us. The name Reagan was magic and it was half an hour before they finished taking all their selfies with him.

A few days later, we attended the Pope's weekly blessing in the Vatican.

We were seated in the section reserved for Argentines on the platform above St. Peter's Square where Pope Francis spoke. (To mount the platform, we had to go through the Basilica itself.)

He seemed to have invited half of Argentina. Hundreds of his fellow countrymen were packed into the area directly behind the Pope.

It was a hot day and his introductions of the many visiting cardinals who had traveled for the canonization to the crowd and his recitation of the blessing took about an hour. It was a warm, sunny day and we wondered if the heat was bothering him. But it sure didn't stop him.

After he spoke, the Pope walked down from his lectern to greet, touch, and often kiss, dozens of wheelchair-bound faithful. Then, after that, he went over to personally greet the church dignitaries and ordinary people who had attended the blessing. All of that took another hour.

Finally, seemingly impervious to the heat, he rode his Popemobile back up to the platform and walked over to Argentine section. As he approached, the many young people in the group began to chant "Ar-gen-tin-a" as if at a football match. He smiled broadly and slowly made his way along the rope line, shaking each hand and pausing to let the Vatican photographers, who swarmed around him, snap pictures.

When he approached Eileen and me, our friend Luis reminded him, in Spanish, of our meeting years before. He said he remembered it well and gave us a warm greeting.

I will always remember his warm hands on my forearms as we spoke. The photo of our moment together, the warmth, and the love are still with me. Then, as he started to move on, he took Eileen's hand and looked into her eyes and said, "Please pray for me."

NOTE: In September 2018, Argentina's former president Cristina Kirchner was indicted on charges of directing a corrupt criminal enterprise by accepting an estimated $160 million in bags of cash bribes from construction companies in exchange for public works contracts from 2003-2015. The eighty-seven payments were documented in a chauffer's notebook.

24. The Strange Case of the Vince Foster Phone Call

One summer morning in July 1993, I was surprised to get a call from Clinton's Chief of Staff, Mac McLarty, at about 11:00 in the morning at my home in Connecticut. It was a beautiful sunny day and I was still sleeping when Eileen handed me the phone.

I didn't know Mac at all—I'd never met him or spoken with him by phone.

What was he calling me about? I wondered.

He immediately began asking my advice on how Clinton should handle a fairly simple procedural matter in Congress. I was puzzled. Why would he call me to discuss something that was not in any way my specialty? I didn't work with Congress. There had to be ten people in the White House who could answer his question. Furthermore, I was not in touch with the Clintons very much at that time. So why call me?

The issue was so simple and so completely irrelevant to anything I did, I began to think it must be a pretext for the call. It had to be.

I waited for the real reason to become apparent as he continued chatting.

Then he asked if I'd heard the news about Vince Foster. I'd just woken up and, back in those pre-Internet, pre-cable news days, my newspaper was at the end of the driveway, almost a half mile away, so I hadn't. McLarty told me about the Foster suicide on the previous night, July 20th.

I knew Vince Foster only in passing. Occasionally, he would be leaving the Governor's Mansion as I was arriving. So I literally knew him only in passing.

McLarty kept me on the phone for a few more minutes, casually asking questions about Foster. When had we last spoken? Had I ever discussed Whitewater with him? On and on.

To this day, I don't know for sure why McLarty was calling me. What I believe, in retrospect, is that the Clinton folks must have thought that I knew something. Something that related to Foster. Something that they wanted to keep quiet. I have no idea what it was.

But one thing is clear: there is no way that McLarty was focusing on Congress on that sad morning. Congress would be the very last of his concerns.

As the story and the investigation of Foster's death unfolded, McLarty's call became even more baffling.

By all descriptions, on the morning after Foster's suicide, the White House was in complete chaos. As Chief of Staff, the tragic and high profile suicide of a White House Counsel put McLarty under tremendous pressure. And it had to be personally difficult for him; Foster was not just another senior White House staff person, he was a childhood friend.

McLarty would naturally have been distraught and overwhelmed by what had happened. In addition to his own obvious feelings of loss, he had to lead the grief stricken staff, monitor the investigation into the death/suicide, respond to rampant press inquiries, and address law enforcement concerns. It was a lot.

But there was one more thing to worry about. Hillary Clinton, in yet another one of her paranoid coverups, was directing her own black ops through numerous phone calls, creating yet another signature scandal.

Within minutes of learning of Foster's death at her mother's home in Little Rock, Hillary dispatched her closest aides to go to Foster's office—ostensibly to look for a suicide note. (They claim to have missed the torn up one ostensibly found thirty hours later.) Although Hillary and her aides deny it, credible witnesses claim to have seen aides removing boxes from Foster's office. Were they taking out anything that would be embarrassing or compromising to the Clintons? That would be vintage Hillary.

Foster's office was unlocked after three longtime Hillary aides—Maggie Williams, Susan Thomases, and Patsy Thomassen—arrived after 11:00 p.m., at the First Lady's request.

It wasn't until 10:30 a.m. the next morning that Foster's office was locked and secured.

And the call to me was right after that.

Why was he calling me? Had they seen something related to me?

There was a strange sequel to all of this. Two years later, as Congressional committees were investigating what happened in the White House on the night of Foster's death, I received a call from someone in the White House who said he was involved in preparing responses to a Congressional Committee. By that time, I was working in the White House. I don't remember who called; I didn't recognize his name. He read me two phone numbers and asked if either had ever been my phone number in July 1993. It seems they were tracking calls that were made either to or from the

White House immediately following Foster's death. The numbers had never been mine. I wondered why they would think they belonged to me.

The White House ultimately provided Hillary's mothers phone bill to Congress. It confirmed that a ten minute call had been made from her house at 10:41 p.m. to the number (202) 628-7087. The White House ultimately told the Committee that phone telephone number was "an unlisted trunk line that rang on the White House switchboard. The number was installed as a bypass to the main White House switchboard, so that calls could be made from the White House in the event the main switchboard failed. The number was also used as a means to get through to the White House when the switchboard was overloaded, and were provided to certain individuals for that purpose."[13]So someone like Hillary could call in without the switchboard knowing about it and without any record of the call – as happened that night.

Why would she do that? (Despite the evidence of the call, Hillary later said she did not recall making it. That's her standard way of circumventing perjury charges. Don't answer, just say you can't recall.)

Apparently the call was received by Bill Buton, an aide to Mac McLarty and former Rose Law associate, who was working in McLarty's office that night. So was Hillary calling Burton or McLarty?

And why did McLarty take time out of a difficult and frantic day to call me?

Had Hillary suggested something.?

My only interaction with Foster had been almost ten years earlier.

Foster was Bill's and Hillary's White House point man (more her's than his) on the burgeoning Whitewater scandal. As the Clintons' attorney, he knew all their secrets about the land deal gone bad. He was also Hillary's best friend in the Rose Law Firm.

One clue might be my work with Hillary over the Grand Gulf nuclear power plant in Mississippi.

Bill had come back to office after his 1980 defeat partly by attacking the utility rate increases his predecessor had approved. But as he was preparing to take office in 1982, the Federal Energy Regulatory Commission (FERC) approved a big hike in utility rates in Arkansas to fund the Grand Gulf Nuclear Power Plant. Located in Port Gibson, Mississippi, Grand Gulf was to serve the tri-state area of Arkansas, Mississippi, and Louisiana. Clinton opposed Grand Gulf, but he had no veto over the multi-state plant. So, when the FERC ordered a rate increase, he sued on behalf of the ratepayers of Arkansas.

Good move. But he chose Hillary's firm (the Rose Firm) to handle the suit. He claimed he didn't trust anyone else.

I was telling Eileen about it and she spotted the blatant conflict of interest. "How can Hillary represent the state on this matter and get a fee when she is the governor's wife?"

On my next trip to Little Rock, I repeated the concern, suggesting that the State break all ties with the Rose Law Firm. Hillary was livid, maintaining that only she was competent to bring the case and pointing out that all previous governors had used the Rose Firm for bond issues. She was not going to give up the fees she would get for that work.

Eventually, I persuaded her to redo the partnership agreement at the Firm so that she would not share in fees generated by state business.

Actually, she engineered it so she would get a larger share from the non-state business pool and forego the share of the State business.

Vince Foster, a partner at Rose, sent me a comprehensive memo in 1984 explaining the new fee arrangement and addressing my concerns. He outlined why certain other Arkansas firms were inadequate and why Rose had to handle the case. I came across the memo in the late nineties.

In fact, the issue did come up. In the campaign of 1984, as Bill sought re-election, his opponent, Frank White (the man who had defeated him in 1980) attacked the Grand Gulf fee arrangement.

Bill ridiculed him and said, "Frank, its ok to attack me, but not my wife. After all, you're running for governor, not for first lady."

The campaign published literature and billboards saying "Frank White for First Lady," and drowned the issue in laughter.

But White had a point and Foster's memo to me proved it. The fee arrangement was a conflict of interest and showed that Hillary was profiting from state business despite her denials. Could that have had something to do with Mac's phone call? All those years later?

We'll never know.

NOTE: While Hillary frantically called her aides after Foster's death, her phone records show that she placed no call to his widow.

25. Bill Clinton Takes an Intern to Dinner with Eileen and Me

Eileen and I first became aware of Bill's womanizing ways right before Christmas 1981. We had invited Bill and Hillary to dinner at Manhattan's posh Four Seasons Restaurant. I had spent most of the day in New York with Bill filming ads for his upcoming effort to regain the governorship he had lost the year before.

While we were filming, Bill told me that Hillary was tied up in Washington and couldn't join us, so I switched the reservation to three. Then, a few hours later, he called and asked, "Is it OK if I bring a reporter to dinner… if I pay?" I immediately told him that paying wasn't the issue and told him that we shouldn't be talking about the campaign in front of any press. He quickly assured me that it wouldn't be a problem. "I promised this reporter an interview, but don't worry about it."

The gender or name of the "reporter" was never mentioned.

Eileen taught me long ago that when a man speaks repeatedly of someone without revealing their gender, it's usually a member of the opposite sex.

When we arrived at the restaurant, Bill was already at our table with the "reporter." Sure enough, she was female—a nineteen-year-old beauty with hair so long, she could literally sit on it. Not exactly a reporter, she had been an intern at the Today Show when Bill had been a guest the previous summer.

Bill's other intern.

Throughout the meal, they were holding hands under the table and their knees were always touching. It was inconceivable that Bill could think we didn't notice. And, anyone else looking at them would presume that they were on a hot date.

Eileen couldn't believe how reckless Bill was. For one thing, he was trying to get reelected and could easily have been recognized by someone. It's really a small world and, it definitely would not be good press if that story leaked.

But it was even worse. At the time, Eileen worked as a lobbyist for the New York City Legal Services project—the federally funded program that represents the interest of the poor in civil actions. Hillary Clinton happened to be the Chairman of the Corporation Board. Although she certainly wasn't

Eileen's direct boss, the Legal Services community was small and well connected—especially at that time, when the programs were fighting the Reagan proposals to defund them.

Bill had only met Eileen once before and should have been concerned about flaunting a date in front of her. She was discrete, but he had no way of knowing—or assuring—that.

But he didn't show the slightest concern.

The teenager was very clever. She knew her stuff. It turns out that she was working on a book—apparently never published—about thirty men who "made it" by the age of thirty and she was "interviewing" Bill.

After dinner, we went outside on fifty-second street to hail a taxi. Bill turned to his babe and asked solicitously, "Have you ever seen the Christmas tree at Rockefeller Center?" (It had gone up that week.)

"Why no," she answered.

Bill was the height of courtesy and generosity. "No need for a taxi for us. I'll take her over to see the tree and then drop her off at her hotel. Y'all go home and don't worry about us."

We didn't. But we did wonder just how stupid he thought we were.

26. How I Wore a Borrowed Waiter's Tuxedo (way too small) to My First State Dinner

When my work with President Clinton became public knowledge in April 1995 (I had been working for him secretly for six months before that), the media had no photos of me on file. No B roll footage because I had assiduously avoided any press coverage for my previous sixteen years of political consulting. So when the White House announced that Eileen and I would be attending a black tie state dinner for the president of Mexico, the media photogs were all determined to add me to their file footage.

That morning, I left our home in Connecticut before Eileen. I always pack very lightly. Underwear, shirts, ties and that's about it. But today, I'd have to bring a garment bag with my tuxedo and schlep it around a full day of meetings.

Hey, I thought, Eileen needs a garment bag for her formal dress and why bring two bags? So I hung up my tux carefully in her garment bag that was hanging on the bedroom door, but I forgot to tell her.

"Did you pack your tux?" she asked me dutifully as I left that morning. I blithely assured her that I had "taken care of it" without bothering to tell her that I had done so by putting it in her bag.

Ooops. That wasn't the garment bag she was going to bring. So my tuxedo was still decorating our closet in Connecticut.

"Where's your tux?" she asked as we changed early that evening. "In your bag," I answered. "No, it's not." Oh shit!

Everybody takes state dinners really seriously in Washington and it was a huge faux pas not to wear a tuxedo. And I had half the DC press corps waiting with cameras ready to photograph Clinton's new advisor.

I was stuck. I didn't realize that I had no tux until 6 p.m. The dinner was at 7. No tuxedo rental place was open. Ever resourceful, Eileen suggested I ask the hotel if I could borrow a tuxedo from one of the waiters who was off duty that night. They sent one up.

But it was worn, shiny, and too small. The sleeves only came up to my wrists. The pants down only to my ankles – floods. But it was that or nothing, so I put it on and we ran out of the hotel

When Eileen, elegantly dressed, and I in my borrowed tuxedo, entered the ballroom late—almost the last to arrive. We were announced by the usher in his usual loud voice: "Mr. Dick Morris and Ms. Eileen McGann." The paparazzi perked up and the flashbulbs started popping.

My hopes of slipping by without notice or comment evaporated when Eileen entered the receiving line to greet Hillary and promptly spilled the beans, telling her my tuxedo saga. Hillary laughed and said, "I know someone who had that problem, too, but he was a lot taller and it was a lot harder to find a tuxedo to fit."

Next was the president who just smiled at my tale. But, in the meantime, Eileen had proceeded to Al Gore, next on the line, who collapsed in a fit of laughter.

The next day, the *Washington Post* ran the story with photos of my ill-fitting tux.

At the White House the next morning, Vice President Gore was scheduled to join the president and a group of us in a meeting in the residence. As he walked in the door and came up behind me, he paused to rub the label of my suit jacket between his fingers as if to feel the fabric. "Yours?" he asked.

27. Saving Justice Kavanaugh

On September 24, 2018, just as Christine Blasey Ford was bringing forth her allegations against Judge Brett Kavanaugh during his confirmation process, I got an e-mail from an acquaintance:

"I have a close friend in California," he wrote, "who has very pertinent information about Dr. Ford who has made accusations against Kavanaugh, based on a long-term relationship with Dr. Ford." He noted that his friend had tried to give "his information to the *Wall Street Journal* but they buried it." He said that his friend "is very upset about that and is looking for someone with the courage to help him get it to the public."

He concluded his e-mail saying, "If you have an interest in pursuing this story, I will put you in touch with my friend and you two can take it from there. Just let me know."

This e-mail began a fascinating week-long stretch of phone calls back and forth from California and intense discussions with contacts on the Senate Judiciary Committee.

(At the request of those involved, I have not used names in recounting this tale.)

I called my friend's California friend who told me that he was in touch with a man who had been Dr. Ford's boyfriend/live-in-lover for much of the 1990s. When I got Dr. Ford's ex on the phone, he had quite a story to tell.

For about eight years, he and Ford were together, sometimes off and sometimes on.

He began by telling me that she was a "liar" and "quite a handful" whose word could not be trusted. He had never heard of any sexual abuse in her past and she "showed no scars from any prior incident."

As evidence of her tendency to lie, he said that he had read that she now professed to have a fear of flying, but noted that she frequently flew back and forth from Hawaii during their relationship, apparently without trepidation.

I listened, somewhat bored, concluding that this was all just post-breakup sour grapes when I found myself jolted to attention by his discussion of Dr. Ford's ability to manipulate lie detector tests. Dr. Ford, of course, had taken and passed a lie detector test in the days before she went public with her charges, a test she loudly proclaimed as attesting to her veracity and credibility.

Her ex told the story of Dr. Ford's encounter with a woman who was subsequently identified as Monica McLuhan. (He remembered the name "Monica" but couldn't remember if her last name was "McLuhan" or "McCann.")

Monica, he told me, was applying for a job with the FBI and was worried about having to take a lie detector test. He was not clear about what particular questions might cause her concern, but remembered that she knew that Dr. Ford had conducted professional research on self-hypnosis and other stress minimization techniques.

He recalled that Christine regaled him and her other friends one evening with the story of how she had successfully coached Monica to pass her FBI test and was pleased that she was now an agent.

Promising to keep his name out of it, I asked for his permission to tell his story to contacts that I who were close to the staff of the Senate Judiciary Committee. He said he hoped I would.

I relayed the details of my conversation, but there a concern that Dr. Ford's testimony before the Committee would not really focus on the issue of her lie detector test. So I left the matter in his hands.

I was pleasantly surprised to hear Arizona prosecutor Rachel Mitchell—who had been retained by the Republicans on the Committee—ask Ford if she had ever coached someone to help them pass a lie detector test. The fact that she denied ever doing so underscored the obvious point that she was not telling the truth.

Then, on October 2, Judiciary Committee Chairman Chuck Grassley (R-Iowa) wrote telling the FBI that "The Senate Judiciary Committee has received a sworn statement from a long-time boyfriend of Dr. Ford's, stating that he personally witnessed Dr. Ford coaching a friend on polygraph examinations."

The story spread across the country like wildfire and did much to damage Dr. Ford's credibility and help assure Judge Kavanaugh's confirmation.

Justice Kavanaugh will make a fine addition to the Supreme Court. And his confirmation—and the lengths to which Democrats went to block it—unmasked the extreme left wing of the party and showed how irresponsible it really is.

I was delighted that the chance to help make a difference dropped into my lap and thank those who helped bring her lack of credibility to light.

28. Bill Brings Me Home to Meet Mama

Bill Clinton was always a bit "eastern" or "northern" for Arkansas. College at Georgetown in Washington, law school at Yale, a year at Oxford—not your typical Arkansas resume. After a century and a half of being left behind, Arkansas was eager to shed its past and build a new future. But it didn't want to elect a governor who didn't understand who they were and where they came from.

So they embraced Bill Clinton and followed him, but always warily, always alert for signs that he had strayed too far from his roots.

When Bill first ran for governor, we needed to establish his connection with the razorbacks (the state's football mascot) and emphasize his Arkansas roots. What better way to do it than to bring a camera crew to his mother's home and film his down home origins.

But when I suggested it, I didn't know Virginia Kelley, Bill's mom. She was no stay-at-home wallflower or down home hillbilly.

When we showed up at her house to film the commercial, she emerged dressed to kill, accompanied by Bill's first grade teacher. Although it was a hot afternoon, she was wearing a mink stole. And she wore heavy makeup, fake eyelashes, high heels, a tight skirt, flashy jewelry, too much rouge. You get the picture. She was dressed for an Academy Award ceremony, not for an ad about rural Arkansas roots.

But how do you tell a candidate that his mother needed a bit of a makeover for the ad?

Eileen and I were sitting on the curb across the street from the house, perched to watch the filming on the lawn. Despite the crazy outfit, there was a palpable presence to Virginia Kelley. She had her own charisma. But the look was wrong for the ad.

I had to say something to Bill.

I walked over and gently told him that perhaps she was a bit "overdressed" for the ad. He got it right away and beckoned her back inside the house, entering right behind her. They were inside for about half an hour and, when they emerged, she looked a bit more like Arkansas.

To her credit, she didn't object and understood the concern. Willingly, she read the script about Bill's upbringing and Arkansas roots—and even dressed the part.

The ad, the first of our campaign, served to introduce Bill to the voters and get the campaign off to a good start.

When Virginia passed away in January 1994, during Bill's presidency, I wrote him a note of condolence mentioning our filming session. He wrote back a handwritten reply recalling the anecdote and adding "after that, she dressed as she pleased."

29. Bill Clinton Tackles Me; Hillary says, "He only does that to people he loves."

It's easy to recall the exact moment when my relationship with Bill Clinton cooled. It was when the sitting Governor of Arkansas tackled me, threw me to the ground, and drew his fist back to punch me in May 1990.

I'll never forget *that*.

It was only Hillary's swift intervention that stopped his swing.

We were at a midnight meeting in the Arkansas Governor's Mansion, working on Bill's last campaign for governor.

For a long time, he had been undecided about whether he should run for a final term in 1990. Since he was definitely planning to run for president in 1992, he would have to start working on the presidential race almost immediately after starting his new term.

He pondered: Should he emulate Jimmy Carter who gave up the Georgia governorship in 1976 to run for president or should he follow the example of recent Democratic nominee, Mike Dukakis, who stayed on as governor of Massachusetts in 1988 as he sought the highest office?

There was one other complication: Running for Governor again would inevitably lead the Arkansas voters to pressure him to make a commitment to fill out his term and not run for president in 1992. Eventually, although he knew perfectly well that he was going to run for the White House, he made the commitment.. After he was elected, he simply broke his promise.

For months, I had argued that there were good reasons for him to run again for governor. First, he couldn't trust the man who would take his place as governor if he left office to run for president—the Lt. Governor Jim Guy Tucker.

Tucker could easily run the state into the ground—or raise taxes sharply—and blame it on Bill. Tucker and Clinton were not friends, not by a long shot. Clinton had worked to defeat Tucker in his 1978 race against David Pryor. Then, in 1982, Tucker ran for Governor in the Democratic primary against Clinton. He didn't even make the runoff. There was definitely a history.

I also feared that Tucker might use his access to confidential information and the state police to discredit Clinton. As we later found out, there was plenty there to work with.

There was another important reason for him to stay on as Governor that I felt strongly about. If he was still in office, Bill could announce new programs and initiatives and easily shape a positive image. It wasn't that easy or effective to do that from the outside.

Bill thought carefully about whether to run. At one point, he floated the idea of Hillary running for Governor in the event that he sat out the race. Would the people of Arkansas accept that?

I fielded two polls to figure out if she could run in his stead, but they both came out badly.

Oddly, back then, Arkansas voters did not see Hillary as an independent political figure. They felt that she would be merely assuming the governorship as a "place holder" in case her husband lost the presidential race and wanted to come back to Arkansas politics. (exactly what Bill had in mind)

When I reported the results, I tried to explain it in the context of events that had occurred in neighboring states. Hillary was infuriated when I drew a comparison with Alabama Governor George Wallace who got his wife, Lurleen, elected in his state when he was term-limited and had to leave office. "I am no Lurleen Wallace," she screamed as she and Bill stumbled all over themselves to spell out her achievements.

I think that may have been the first time that Hillary realized that she might not have the image she thought she had and would have to carve out her own credentials on the national stage in order to have a future political career after Bill left office. It wouldn't happen automatically.

So, for lots of reasons, Bill ran again, but this time voters weren't so enthusiastic about re-electing him after he had already served ten years as governor.

Clinton faced unexpectedly strong opposition in the Democratic Primary from Tom McRae, a total unknown. Even though he was a novice, McRae ran a great campaign. He emphasized Bill's many years as Governor and made the case that he was more interested in a presidential campaign than what was going on in Arkansas.

One of his TV ads featured clocks stretched into all shapes and sizes as in Salvador Dali's famous painting, *The Persistence of Memory*, all to remind voters how long Bill had been in office. Another showed crowds of Arkansas voters at the airport waving good-bye to Bill's plane as he took off, yet again, for Iowa to run for president.

In the last month of the campaign, my polls showed that McRae was beginning to close the gap with Clinton, pushing the incumbent governor below the 50% threshold. This was alarming and showed Clinton was in serious jeopardy.

Bill, who was expecting a cakewalk, was totally freaked. His presumed presidential bid—in fact, his entire political career—was hanging in the balance.

I flew to Little Rock to meet him and map out our strategy. I was feeling a little rocky that day because I had been in bed for the previous five days, recovering from painful oral surgery. In fact, I actually needed to stop at my oral surgeon's office for follow-up treatment on the way to the airport. I was really uncomfortable, but didn't want to take pain killers because I needed to be sharp for the meeting with Bill scheduled for 8 p.m..

But when I got to the Governor's Mansion, I learned that Clinton would be late—very late. He was taping a Nightline episode. So, the meeting was postponed several times and didn't get started until almost midnight. I waited, exhausted, while my tooth throbbed in agony.

When Bill finally arrived, he was in a fowl, angry, and self-pitying mood. I'd seen that before and it was not a pretty sight. I wondered if he had been drinking. Although he was generally a teetotaler, he occasionally had a drink. I had once seen an abrupt change in demeanor when he drank a Tom Collins at my home in New York and I wondered if he had imbibed.

There was Bill Clinton at his worst. He immediately launched into a vitriolic, obscenity-laced diatribe such as I'd never heard from him before. He accused me of luring him into the reelection race so I could make more money from polling and said I was spending all my time working for other candidates and neglecting him.

Two years before, in 1988, I had switched parties and become a Republican. Many prominent members of the GOP—like Newt Gingrich—

insisted that I drop Clinton as a client and represent only Republicans. I wouldn't do it because of my long relationship with him. I "grandfathered" Clinton in and kept working for him.

So when Bill went so far as to imply that I was "throwing" the race—deliberately letting him lose—I was outraged. He shouted and cursed at me and I yelled back. Things got very heated and I got up and stormed out of the Mansion saying over my shoulder as I left "OK. OK. You've got it. I'm going to be a fifty state Republican now and you can lose this damn election on your own!"

That did it. Bill charged up behind me and, as I reached for the kitchen door to go out, he tackled me. While I lay on the floor, he got up on his knees and drew his fist back to hit me. At that point, Hillary came to my rescue, throwing her arms around Bill's cocked fist and pulling him back. She screamed at him: "Bill! Bill! Stop! Think of what you are doing! Bill!"

Only then did Clinton snap out of his vicious mood and, realizing what he had done, backed off.

I got up ran out the door. Bill was yelling to me to stay as I left the Mansion.

Hillary quickly caught up with me outside. She put her arm around me and walked me around the grounds of the governor's mansion. "He didn't mean it," she said, trying to soothe me. "Dick, he values you and he needs you and he's got faith in you. He's just very tired and tense and don't let this get to you."

Then she said something I will always remember: "He only does this to people he loves."

Hmmmmm. I wonder who those other lucky folks were.

My relationship with Bill was never the same after that. We continued to work together, but I would never describe him as a friend, just a client.

30. The Coverup: The Media Tries to Report the Story During the 1992 Campaign

The sequel to this lamentable tale was Hillary's subsequent effort to cover it up. Word leaked out via a political consultant friend in whom I had confided when I saw him at the hotel bar immediately after the incident. Several years later, he was working for a candidate opposing Clinton for the Democratic party nomination for president. The story I had told him two years earlier was too juicy to ignore and he relayed the saga to a reporter in an effort to besmirch (or accurately portray?) his opponent Bill Clinton.

I didn't know about his leak until early May 1992, in the middle of the presidential race. Eileen and I came home to our house in Connecticut from a relaxing Friday night dinner and listened to a message on our answering machine from someone who identified himself as a reporter for the *Los Angeles Times*. He said he wanted my reaction to the Rodney King beating by L.A. cops that was dominating the news back then.

I didn't think much of it and figured that I'd call him back on Monday. But he was apparently not going to wait. On Monday morning, I was awakened to some yelling downstairs. It was early—about 7:15—and Eileen was loudly telling someone to get out of the house.

Apparently, she had just gotten out of the shower when she heard some banging on the front door. She came downstairs and saw a man and woman getting out of an SUV in the driveway. The pair was unloading video camera equipment.

The man introduced himself as a reporter from the *L.A. Times* and asked if I was "ready" for his interview. Eileen asked if I was expecting him and he said yes. She thought that was odd because I hadn't mentioned it and never ever make appointments at 7:15 in the morning if I can help it. I'm rarely up at that time.

He asked if he could set up the equipment inside, while the woman began setting up additional equipment outside the front door.

Eileen began quizzing him about why he was there so early. She asked if it was about the L.A riots and he seemed uninterested in talking about them. When he asked if there were any photos of Dick with Bill Clinton, she knew something else was up. What would those photos have to do with the L.A. riots?

Her suspicions grew as he began asking about my relationship with the Clintons. Amazingly, the "reporter" wasn't budging and it was beginning to sound like a brawl.

I ran downstairs in my robe, annoyed at the intrusion. But, when I found out that the L.A riots were only his pretext for coming and that what he really wanted was the low down on my fight with Clinton, exasperation turned to rage. I shouted at him to leave my house and picked up the phone to call the police. He started to leave, but all the way out, he was asking about Clinton attacking me.

I would have run after him in my bathrobe to his car, if Eileen hadn't reminded me that the photographer was outside. I was quite a sight—hair sticking up and no shoes!

As soon as he left, I called Hillary to ask how to handle it. She had Betsy Wright, Bill's chief of staff, call me back with her suggested response: "Just say it never happened." That's what Hillary always says.

There was no way that I could say that, since there was definitely one person to whom I had told the story—a well-connected, reputable consultant.

I steeled myself and waited for the story to come out.

But, it's a small world. At the time, Eileen was the General Counsel for the Connecticut Daily Newspaper Association that included the *Hartford Courant*, which had the same owner as the *L.A. Times*. Coincidentally, she was headed to a meeting in New York City that morning with representatives of the *Courant* and the *L.A. Times*.

After they finished their business meeting, she complained to the people from the *L.A. Times* about our uninvited, aggressive, untruthful, and obnoxious early morning visitor. They made a few calls and then apologized, claiming that the "reporter" was not an employee of their paper, but an independent investigative journalist who was chasing a story. Although his stories were sometimes published by the *Times*, they insisted that he was not on assignment for them. Whatever he was, the story never appeared in print during the campaign.

Later, I learned that Clinton flunky Gloria Cabe, who was the only person, apart from Bill, Hillary, and me, who witnessed the incident, had confirmed the story to Clinton biographer David Maraniss.

But, my relationship with Bill was never the same again.

31. Family Hold Back (FHB) in Paris...and a Call from the FBI

In the spring of 1996—right in the middle of the Clinton campaign—Eileen and I planned a week-long vacation in Paris. We chose Easter Week because we knew it would be a quiet time in the campaign before the busy summer that would culminate with the August convention.

Eileen rented a large and wonderful apartment near the Eiffel Tower and we invited her brother Paul and his wife Jean, as well as our niece Katie, who was only fourteen, but already a seasoned traveler. At the last minute, we invited my Chief of Staff, Tom Freedman, and his girlfriend at the time. Tom had worked closely and intimately with me every day from early 1995 until I left the campaign over Labor Day weekend in 1996. He was extremely bright, watched my back like a hawk, and was great fun.

A good friend of Eileen's lived in Paris and we had made plans to see her and her husband while we were there. About a month before we were leaving, she called and told us that a friend of hers, who was active in *Democrats Abroad,* wanted to invite me to speak to the group one afternoon and then come to dinner at her house afterward.

We had met the woman and her husband before at a Thanksgiving dinner party in Paris. She was an American who had lived in Paris for at least thirty years and was a respected writer and university professor. We immediately accepted and looked forward to it.

A few weeks later, we had our first clue that the dinner might get a little complicated. The woman sent a fax and asked who we would like to include in the dinner. We listed our two Paris friends and asked if our family members could also join us. She wrote back asking how old our niece was. When she found out that Katie was only fourteen, she suggested that "it would be best for the teenagers to stay home." She had also mistakenly concluded that my thirtysomething brother-in-law was another teenager and suggested that he stay home, too.

That didn't sit right with us, but we didn't object at first because we thought it was going to be a small dinner party and didn't want to impose on her.

When we got to Paris, though, she sent another fax and indicated that more than fifty people would be coming. Once again, she asked if there were people we wanted to invite. At that point, we repeated our wish that we would like our family members and Tom Freedman to come. Amazingly, she objected to our niece again. At that point, Eileen insisted that I tell her that if Katie couldn't come, then I wouldn't be coming. No more negotiations.

That settled it. Katie was permitted to join us.

When we arrived at the reception before the late afternoon speech, I saw the woman pull Eileen aside and whisper something to her. I couldn't tell what she was saying, but I did see that Eileen had her "Are you kidding me?" look on her face! I'd seen that before.

A few minutes later Eileen joined me. "What's up?" I asked her. With a deadpan expression, she told me that the woman asked that Eileen's brother and Tom wait until the very end to take their food from the buffet table and, even then, take very small portions, as she wanted to be sure to have enough food for everyone. I looked at her quizzically. Suddenly she burst out laughing and said, "Good luck with that one."

She reminded me of stories that her mother used to tell me about a code in her family when she was growing up. The initials FHB would be whispered and everyone knew what it meant. It stood for "family hold back." If there was a concern that there wouldn't be enough food for all of the guests, FHB was invoked and the family members knew to take small portions and hold back on seconds.

Although we were not her family, the woman was clearly demanding that our family skimp on their portions and hold back.

There was no question that they were not welcome. She made that quite obvious.

On the way from the speech to the dinner party, we wondered if we had made a mistake in insisting on the family joining us. After all, she was inviting us to her home and she was providing the food.

Imagine our surprise when we entered the apartment and saw lines of people waiting to PAY for dinner.

Unbeknownst to us, the dinner party was not private at all, but a fundraiser for *Democrats Abroad*. The guests were paying $25–$50 to meet me and hear me speak. Anyone could come. (except our family!) The hostess had never mentioned that she was charging guests or that she advertised the chance to spend the evening with me. Copies of her flyer advertising the event—with a big photo of me—were spread on the table.

We were amazed.

I immediately wrote a check for all of us. I had no problem giving an unexpected second speech, but she had been so gratuitously rude and ungracious, I insisted on paying for everyone's dinner. We didn't want free food from her.

When she found out that we had left a check, she came over and told us that we didn't have to pay for ourselves, but we insisted. (no mention of the others)

As soon as Eileen saw Tom Freedman and her brother arrive, she went over to them and said, "I hope you guys are really hungry tonight and have a big appetite. Dig in. No need to wait." She knew her brother's appetite and after dozens of lunches and dinners with Tom, knew his, too.

No FHB!

In fact, there was enough food. But it wasn't much good. On the buffet table, there was a huge glass bowl filled with an uninviting veal stew with a white sauce and another glass bowl filled with white rice. A green salad was on the side.

So, after the dinner, we went around the corner to Deux Magots and ordered delicious club sandwiches.

We actually enjoyed meeting the people who had come to the secret "fundraiser." The late Flora Lewis, the longtime foreign affairs columnist for *The New York Times* was there as were other well-known journalists.

The rest of the trip was wonderful. We went to great restaurants every night—a moveable feast—as well as great museums and shops every day. On Easter Sunday, we cooked a big leg of lamb for dinner and enjoyed it in the apartment's large dining room.

Throughout that week, I spoke to the President every day about the polling and the ad scripts I was suggesting. The time difference meant that I had to stay up until two a.m. every night in order to speak to him early in the morning, his time.

Almost two years later, I got a call from the FBI indicating that they wanted to talk to me. They came to my apartment and asked me if I recalled a phone conversation with the President on a specific day in April 1996. Eileen checked our calendar and saw that it was Easter Sunday.

I told the agents that I had spoken to the President every day—sometimes several times a day and didn't remember anything special about the call.

I asked if they were looking for something specific. They declined to elaborate. But when the Starr Report was released, I learned that Monica Lewinsky had told the FBI that she was having oral sex with the president while he was speaking to me. They were trying to confirm her statement.

He never let on!

32. The Challenge of Working in Foreign Countries

After I left Clinton in 1996, I was surprised to be invited to work for candidates in several foreign countries. It was a new challenge and I embraced it wholeheartedly. I wondered if I could use my skills to help elect candidates committed to democratic ideals, and, at the same time, explore culture and politics outside the U.S. with Eileen. We did and it was a great adventure.

Since then, I've worked in more than forty countries and helped to elect twelve foreign presidents or prime ministers in Mexico (twice), Argentina, Uruguay, Russia, Poland, Hungary, Spain, Taiwan, Ukraine, Japan, and Kenya. Eileen and I also worked for the United Kingdom Independence Party (UKIP) that laid the foundation for Brexit, the initiative that took Britain out of the European Union.

I loved the challenge of working abroad and learning everything possible about new cultures and politics from scratch. At the start of each foreign campaign, I would completely immerse myself in the history and politics of the country reading everything I could get my hands on. Then I would meet with experts and learn about the current political issues and parties and ask a million questions about what could be done to solve some of the country's massive problems. Then I would spend hours with the candidate and his/her staff discussing everything I had learned and getting an understanding of the candidate's passions and ideas for the campaign.

From all that, I would develop a questionnaire to test support for the candidate, the issues, the themes, and the possible message. We also needed to understand the feelings of the voters about all the opponents and ask them to describe in their own words what they felt about the candidates and the problems facing the country.

Unlike the U.S., where a poll can be completed overnight, it often took over a week to get the results. The interviews usually had to be done in person since many voters either had no phones and those that existed were usually unreliable.

As I worked in many different countries and cultures, I came to believe that each nation had a single word that aptly described its goals and political focus. It didn't always reach its objectives, but it always aimed at them. The key to understanding the country is to find out what the word is and use it as a lodestar in guiding the campaign.

For the United States, I think it is liberty. For Britain, tradition, France, joie de vivre (joy of living), Russia, power, Japan, co-operation, Germany, efficiency, Italy, romance, Brazil, festivals and joy, China, money, and Canada—they call it "distinction"—being different from the U.S.

The candidates and campaigns I backed had a theme and a consistency – I wanted to help to rid the world of regimes that, while ostensibly democracies, were actually corrupt autocracies that had ruled their countries for decades, keeping them down and poor.

For example, Eileen and I have worked especially hard in Eastern Europe fighting against the "post-communist" political parties that are usually only cosmetically different from the people's republic regimes that preceded them.

In Japan, I worked to oust the LDP—the Liberal Democratic Party—that had ruled, with increasing corruption and autocracy, since World War II.

In Taiwan, my adversary was the Kuomintang, the party founded by Chiang Kai-Shek as he fled mainland China in the wake of the communist takeover. The Kuomintang created a one-party state, based on the same rampant corruption that had so handicapped it in fighting Mao in the fifties.

In the UK, we worked to help the British people throw off the yoke of the EU bureaucracy, regulation, and restrictions on its freedom.

The highlight for me was in 2000 in Mexico where I helped to dethrone the PRI, the "Institutional Revolutionary Party" that had ruled for seventy-one years.

The presidential candidate was the charismatic Vicente Fox from the conservative, pro-democratic party—the PAN—whose election really created a viable democracy in Mexico for the first time in its history.

Handsome, brilliant, and a courageous visionary, Fox understood the challenge ahead of him and was able to excite and energize the millions of forgotten Mexicans who had long ago given up on ever being protected by their government.

I remember the first time that Eileen and I met Vicente Fox. Our good friend, Juan Hernandez, who became his campaign manager and a leading activist for Mexican-Americans, invited us to dinner at his home in Dallas. At the time, Fox was the Governor of the Mexican state of Guanajuato in the center of Mexico.

We were immediately blown away. It's not often that one meets someone like Vicente Fox. His unique presence dominates any space he occupies. And it's not just his physical size—or his trademark cowboy boots. He is tall, attractive, and lithe, but there's much more to him that causes one to pause and pay attention. His dignity and elegance combine with his warmth, intelligence and demeanor to make him a compelling and magnetic personality.

His experiences and background had fully prepared him for the job of President of a new Mexico.

It was his moment.

Fox grew up on a prosperous twelve-hundred-acre ranch and vegetable farm in the picturesque town of Guanajuato, a charming town that Eileen and I visited. It is low mountains and marked by curvy pedestrian streets. We were amazed to see that the central market, a large pinkish stone building with a rounded glass ceiling, had been designed by Gustave Eiffel. It didn't resemble his iconic Tower in Paris, but it was still beautiful. Inside the bustling market were endless stalls piled with colorful fruits and vegetables, lots of other food, clothing, and traditional crafts.

The artist Diego Rivera was born there and his former home was a museum. We loved the town and then spent the weekend in the neighboring beautiful city of San Miguel d'Allende, where we've returned many times.

Fox would move a long way from Guanajuato. It started in 1964, when Fox was hired by the Coca-Cola company of Mexico. He spent some time driving one of their delivery trucks and learned first-hand what was going on in the field. But Vicente was no ordinary driver. In fact, he has never been an ordinary anything.

He tackled the job with the passion and enthusiasm of the sole owner of a small company. At the time, Pepsi controlled most of the cola market in Mexico. The goal of Coca-Cola was to change that and Vicente Fox was a general in that commercial war. He's a natural marketer and used his impressive talent to help increase the market share of Coke, day by day, town by town, person by person. Working with other drivers, he convinced establishments all over Mexico that were selling Pepsi to switch to Coke. It worked. By 1971, he was invited to join the Coke marketing team at their headquarters. There he developed an unorthodox and highly successful advertising campaign. And, not surprisingly, Coke surpassed Pepsi in sales by 2-1.[14]In 1975, his hard work paid off. He was named CEO of Coca-Cola Mexico.

I never had the nerve to tell him of my Diet Pepsi habit!

Fox was a graduate of the Harvard Business School and an accomplished businessman before he entered politics. He understood the problems that big and small businesses faced with the corruption and bureaucracy that flourished under the PAN. He also understood the difficult plight of Mexican farmers and ranchers like his family. And he had the innate skills and practical experience to convince the Mexican voters that change was truly possible and vitally necessary.

Shortly after that first meeting, I began traveling to Mexico several times a month to help develop the strategy for Vicente Fox's presidential campaign. A year and a half later, he was elected President.

A new Mexico had arrived.

During the long campaign, I used to stay at the Four Seasons Hotel in Mexico City. For security reasons, the reservations would be made in a variety of assumed names. When I arrived, a young driver would pick me up at the airport and take me to the hotel. That driver, Fredo Arias King, is still a very dear friend and a learned source of information about Mexico. The hotel was not just chosen for its well-known luxury and comfort. In addition, it offered a special layer of safety and security. At the time, there were serious concerns about violence and kidnapping directed at those working in the campaign.

While I was there, I would generally stay inside the hotel and sometimes hold meetings there. I was strictly instructed to never walk in the streets or take a taxi. Often, Fredo would come pick me up at the hotel and take me out to dinner at a discrete restaurant. He would also take me to meet the candidate. I didn't see much else in Mexico City.

But even with the extra layer of protection, anyone could simply rent a room and be able to access the hotel. And at least once, someone we viewed as somewhat questionable had somehow ended up in the room right next door to me.

That happened once in early June 2006, when I was already working on the campaign of Fox's successor, Felipe Calderon.

When another peculiar incident happened a few weeks later, my friend found a "safe house" for me. It even came with a friendly dog. We referred to it as "Grandma's house" and I stayed there for the next several years whenever I was in Mexico City.

Fox was quite a contrast with the opposition PRI. Nominally populist, the PRI exploited class warfare and animosity toward the U.S. to hold its people down and keep power while robbing the country blind. They won their elections by bribery.

The New York Times featured a photo of a PRI Governor posing beside hundreds of washing machines stacked three-high in a warehouse, awaiting distribution as bribes to voters. That is what we were up against.

After Fox won, I helped the PAN elect Felipe Calderon as his successor. Calderon took the war against drug kingpins to new heights.

33. Bringing Democracy to Mexico

There had never been a free and competitive election in Mexico. Vicente Fox changed all that in 2000 when he defeated the PRI (the Institutional Revolutionary Party). Fox had reformed his own party—the PAN—to make it less representative of large landholders allied with the Catholic Church and closer to the model of a free market-oriented party primarily backed by entrepreneurs and small businesspeople.

But, defeating the PRI was a tall order. They had, literally, twenty times more money than we did and political machines in each town, province, and city. The PRI won its elections largely through bribing the voters.

A joke circulated at the time about a Mexican who died and went to heaven where he found everybody lived the life of ease, with no work to do and plenty of food, rest, recreation, and vacation. He came back to Earth for a visit and then returned to heaven a few weeks later to find everything had changed. Now, everyone had to work twelve hours a day, no vacations, no time off. "What happened?" he asked. "When I was here three weeks ago, it was so much easier and better." "Oh," they answered, "that was during the election campaign."

Clearly voters wanted to topple the PRI and its candidate Francisco Labastida. But everyone warned us that our votes would melt away when the PRI started passing out its bribes right before the election. They always had before.

We couldn't stop the PRI from passing out bribes or the poor people from taking them. Our message—take the gift, say "thank you," but vote for Fox—was embodied in a TV ad that featured an indigenous couple sitting in their small home with a dirt floor. A knock at the door. The wife gets up to open it and asks, "Who is it?"

"Oh, Senora, I am from the PRI," comes the answer.

She opens the door, steps out, and closes it right behind her so the man from the PRI can't see in. "Who are you going to vote for?" he asks.

"Oh, like always, Labastida and the PRI."

"Bueno," he smiles and reaches into his truck to give her a big basket of food.

She smiles and waves as he drives away. When he's gone, she slips back into the house with her overflowing basket, quickly shutting the door behind her.

"Why did you say we are voting for Labastida and the PRI?" her husband asks. "We are voting for Fox and the PAN."

Meanwhile, the camera pans out to show that their room is covered with Fox and PAN posters denouncing the PRI and Labastida. Señora is sitting at the table eating her food. She gestures with her fork "For 71 years, they cheated me. Now I'm cheating them!" she explains to her husband.

The ad was a huge success.

Meanwhile, I began to notice a curious trend in the polls. The newspaper polls showed us losing by huge margins. But they were universally acknowledged to be biased and corrupted Our own polls, however, showed the race tied with about 14% undecided. Week after week we had the same result.

It's very unusual that the number of undecided voters doesn't drop as the election approaches and they make up their minds. My Mexican friends kept telling me that people lied to pollsters, fearful of retaliation or losing their jobs if they admitted that they were abandoning the PRI.

So I dug down to study the undecided vote. As I checked out their answers to other questions I realized that half were really hidden Fox voters. They said they liked the PAN, disliked the PRI, wanted change, liked Fox, but then said they were undecided when the key question came. So I told Vicente that he would get half the undecideds and win by seven points.

That's exactly what happened. Voters got the message and Vicente won by seven points.

34. Another Ad in Mexico Saves Democracy...Again

With Fox's election, a real multi-party democracy came to Mexico.
But, when his term expired in 2006—and the constitution barred him from seeking a second term—I enlisted to help keep the PAN in power by electing as Fox's successor, Felipe Calderon.

But the demagogic appeal of Andres Manuel Lopez Obrador (AMLO) loomed large in our path. In 2006, AMLO led in all the polls by a significant margin and looked unstoppable.

Back then, he was the Mayor of Mexico City and the candidate of the leftist PRD party. (After his defeat, he came back and tried again 2012 and, finally, won in 2018. He will take office on December 1, 2018. God help us!)

AMLO's appeal was based on his formidable record as mayor. He raised pensions, improved the parks, repaired and expanded the highways, and upgraded the university. A real success.

Unfortunately, his achievements were all financed by massive government borrowing akin to that which had led to the Tequila Crisis in 1994 when Mexico was saved from default only by a huge package of Clinton-ordered U.S. aid.

The average Mexican suffered mightily in that crisis. Unemployment soared, home foreclosures rose, and jobs were scarce. People dreaded a return to those bad old days.

So in the Calderon campaign , we decided to use jiu-jitsu to beat AMLO by tying his accomplishments to memories of the Crisis. The more he bragged about his achievements and his plans for the future, the more he would be raising fears of another debt crisis.

In our first ad, we showed a brick wall being built, higher and higher, while the announcer said "AMLO says he raised pensions, built roads, and improved the parks in Mexico City. But he is not telling you that he financed it all by borrowing money. And, if he is elected president, he will borrow more and more and more. And then it will all come tumbling down (here the wall collapses) just like it did 1994."

The ad worked and we began chipping away at AMLO's vote share.

But it was not until our final ad that we went over the top (literally and figuratively). AMLO had run ads showing people smiling and patting their pants pockets and their pocketbooks while the announcer spoke of the 20%

95

wage increases he would enact if he were elected. Knowing that his voters were, perhaps, not proficient in math, his ad said "If you make 2,000 pesos, you'll make 2,400. If you make 4,000, you'll make 4,800..." and all the while people were smiling and patting their wallets and purses.

So we showed a man smiling and patting his pocket as we re-played AMLO's ad. But then, the man interrupts the ad and begins to frown as he turns his pocket inside out. "But I have nothing in my pocket!" Then his pants drop to his ankles and he says, "and I'm losing my pants." That made our point well. Calderon ended up winning by a micro-hair and became president.

He was determined to get to the root of the power of the old corrupt party Fox had ousted, the PRI. The drug kingpins financed the PRI and got protection in return. Calderon really cracked down on the narcos launching a virtual civil war that led to 50,000 Mexican deaths.

Exhausted by the war and depressed by the casualties, the voters unwisely turned down the PAN in 2012 and put the PRI back in power. The PRI picked up where it had left off, renewing its protection for drugs and crime. Now Mexico has turned to radical revolutionary Andres Mario Lopez Obrador (AMLO), a Marxist Castro-like figure. A total disaster. Hard times ahead. It's time to weep for Mexico.

35. Brexit: Helping to Free Britain from the EU

In the fall of 2002, Eileen and I were enjoying a Mediterranean cruise, guests of Celebrity cruise line. In return for free passage, I was required to sing for my supper and give three speeches during the week.

There were several hundred people at the first speech and one of them was Carolyn Knapman, whose husband Roger had just been elected to lead the little-known United Kingdom Independence Party (UKIP). The Party advocated withdrawal from the European Union and rejection of the Euro—a truly radical proposition at the time. UKIP had just been trounced in the European parliamentary elections in the U.K., winning only 1.6% of the vote.

Roger Knapman, a former Tory Party MP who had served as Conservative Party Whip from 1995–1997, had taken over the nascent party with a mandate to change direction. At his side was the amazing Nigel

Farage, a charismatic young man whose zest and zeal were the perfect complement to Roger's political seasoning. Knapman had served in Margaret Thatcher's Conservative Party government but was so appalled by the power being usurped by the EU that he left the party to help found UKIP.

Carolyn approached Eileen to tell her about UKIP and ask if I would consider helping the party. I had always been a strong euro-skeptic and had just written a column for *The Telegraph* in London, Britain's Tory newspaper. In my article, I asked readers if they had noticed, particularly during the Iraq War, that "the English Channel is now wider than the Atlantic Ocean?" I felt that Britain was moving closer to the U.S. and away from continental Europe and the EU.

The column had caught Roger's eye and when Carolyn told him I was on board, he asked her to approach me.

That afternoon we met and talked for hours. He asked us to come to London and meet other members of the party.

So, on a bit of a lark, we got off the ship in France and flew to London. Roger arranged for us to meet with many of the UKIP members in order to understand the problems that EU regulations were causing. It was astounding. One after the other, they described the crippling of their businesses and local life.

I remember two brothers who were fisherman, in particular. Their family had been in the fishing business for centuries. A few months earlier, they had invested in a larger, more efficient, and, of course, more expensive fishing boat. They had taken out a mortgage to pay for it.

Historically, the procedure for substituting a new boat was simple. All that was required was to send an application to the EU to transfer the registration from the old ship to the new one.

After sending in the necessary forms and fees to the EU Fisheries Commission (the chairman was from landlocked Austria), the brothers received a devastating reply. Apparently the Fisheries Commission was performing a comprehensive review of all fishing issues. It was expected to take two years. Until then, no new registrations would be approved. It was entirely up to the EU; the U.K. government in London could do absolutely nothing about it.

Imagine the frustration: The brother's brand new boat—that would streamline their work—was stuck in dry-dock. But their hefty mortgage did not go away.

Meanwhile, the EU made sure to grant fishing rights off the European coast to landlocked member nations. So, for example, Austrians could fish in designated areas off the British coast.

In fact, the bureaucrats who ran the EU governed every aspect of life in the U.K. and the other member nations. National sovereignty, along with the historic idea of home rule, became an anachronistic joke.

Immigration policy was made in Brussels—open borders was the decree. So anyone could arrive illegally in any member country and travel and live lawfully in any other nation. Millions flocked from Turkey over the EU border to Greece or from North Africa to Spain or Italy. Then they would end up in Germany, France, or the U.K.. And nobody could touch them.

Every aspect of economic life was subject to EU regulation. At each meeting of UKIP, we listened to horror stories of over-bureaucratization.

Agriculture also was strictly regulated. But, sometimes the bureaucrats could be gamed. We learned about an Irish shepherd who deceived the EU auditor who had come to measure his herd to determine the amount of subsidy to which he was entitled. As the man from Brussels counted sheep in one pasture and moved onto the next one—presumably having stayed awake while he counted—the farmer would quickly move his herd to a third pasture and so on. So he got several times the subsidy he should have.

With all this EU regulation, the British felt that they were losing their own country. But their core demand—leaving the EU—seemed so drastic that UKIP had remained a tiny fringe party.

Their first real breakthrough was in the European Parliamentary elections of 2004. I worked with the party leaders to develop a strategy. It was a tough task. There were so many crucial issues that the EU was influencing and controlling. Would we concentrate on farming, fishing, immigration, trade, or any of a dozen impacted areas? Each group wanted a piece of the platform and the campaign slogan. Everything from food, roads, the environment, appliances, condoms, cars, and mineral ore is regulated by the EU.

Some of the more absurd regulations include:

A ban on the sale of overly curved bananas

A ban on driving by Type 1 diabetics

A ban on the sale of curved cucumbers

You get the picture.

So how to communicate the anti-Europe message of UKIP in a succinct way that captured the feelings of the British?

It was so complicated and there were so many valid issues. My head was spinning. Finally, I understood that we could succeed by simplification. My chief contribution was to suggest a one word slogan: "NO!" The O was formed by the gold stars of the EU flag on a blue background. And a ghostbusters line went through the word.

"NO!" immediately became the rallying cry, preferably pronounced the way a two-year-old would—**NO!!!** It was featured on all the UKIP billboards and caught on throughout the U.K.

UKIP, which had won less than two percent of the vote for European Parliament in the previous election, now soared to 16.1% in 2004, outdistancing the Liberal/Social Democrats to finish third among the four parties. It almost passed the Labor Party in total vote.

Before the election, UKIP was seen as an offshoot of the Tory Party. But now it was clear that it drew as many votes from Labor and the left as from the Conservatives and right.

These days, the US and Europe are awash in anti-globalist sentiment. The Trump election in the US and similar outcomes in Denmark, Sweden, Italy, Poland, Hungary, Slovenia, and parts of Germany provide evidence of deep anti-E.U discontent, particularly among workers. But the UKIP victory of 2004 was the first.

That year, UKIP broke through, winning sixteen seats in the European Parliament (out of seventy-three allotted to Britain), an over-the-top performance.

They've been unstoppable since, even winning the Brexit referendum in 2016 to pull out of the EU entirely.

36. UKIP: "We Do Well with the Dukes"

From late 2002 until after the 2004 election, Eileen and I visited the UKIP folks almost monthly. They were uniformly nice, smart, and fun to be with and deeply committed to their cause.

After Knapman's retirement, the new UKIP leader Nigel Farage led the party to success after success. His unrivaled ability to advocate the case for leaving Europe almost singlehandedly turned a fringe movement into a force that eventually succeeded in passing the Brexit referendum that favored leaving Europe. This was a colossal achievement that was beyond imagination ten years ago.

Occasionally, UKIP would ask me to help with fundraising or to give a poll briefing to individuals or groups in lots of different places in Britain. We went all over England, visiting castles and mansions, a working family vacation resort, an old RAF base, lots of different cities outside of London—Dorset, Exeter, Bristol, Manchester, and Cardiff in Wales. Each one was an adventure.

We soon got used to the ritual. At UKIP dinners—formal or not—all the diners would stand for a toast at the start of the meal. They would raise their glasses and say, in unison: "To the Queen!"

UKIP arranged for us to visit several various dukes—and an Earl. Roger Knapman liked to say that there was one constituency where he was confident of a majority: "We do really well among the dukes." There were only 31 of them, but they had a lot of influence and money.

Once, we tried to convince one of the most prestigious of them all, the Duke of Devonshire, to provide financial support to UKIP.

Eileen and I joined Roger and Caroline Knapman and a few other UKIP members and traveled north to Derbyshire for a meeting with the Duke at his iconic home, Chatsworth House, on a Sunday morning. Because it was an early morning meeting and a long trip, we went up there the night before.

I think that we stayed in Derby, but I'm not really sure. What I am definitely sure of is the unbelievable noise level in the hotel that night. A wedding was in progress and the ballroom was, unfortunately, directly underneath our room—with the blasting of the DJ continuing until four in the morning. I can still hear the booming in my head as I think about it. But we got through the night.

We left early for Chatsworth House on a beautiful sunny Sunday morning in October. The estate is breathtaking on both the inside and the outside and has been the seat of the Cavendish family since the 16[th]century. Sheep polk-dot the green grass surrounding the mansion, considered one of the most beautiful in all of England. Gardens, waterworks, fountains, and sculpture add to the beauty.

We were escorted to the Duke's private library, a stunning double height room with floor to ceiling windows overlooking the parkland and fountains. Bookcases lined the room and a fire burned in the fireplace, cutting the morning chill. The ceiling and numerous columns were painted with classical themes. Piles of magazines and books covered every table and the Duke's desk—some of them more than three feet high. A large blackboard listed the Duke's schedule for the day. He had allocated about a half hour for us.

Although the Duke was eighty-three at the time and obviously suffering from poor eyesight, he was alert and on top of the political issues of the day. He was very tall and while stretched out in a chair, his legs seemed to go on forever, extending across the room.

I started the session by briefing him on a poll showing the growing support for leaving Europe and for UKIP candidates. He was starting to stare blankly and Eileen signaled me to slow down. I was talking way too fast. The Duke asked a few questions and, too soon, our time was over. He was an early and strong UKIP supporter. He, unfortunately, died about six months after our meeting.

As we were leaving, the Duchess of Devonshire, formerly Deborah Mitford (one of the famous Mitford sisters) came down the steps and invited us on a private tour of the splendid mansion. It was breathtaking.

On another trip, we visited the beautiful Bellevue Castle, the home of the Duke of Rutland, another UKIP supporter.

One UKIP fundraiser was held in a hangar at an old RAF airfield near Manchester. A big band played as UKIPers danced and partied, dressed in 1940s clothing. Many of the men wore their World War II RAF uniforms. During one of our trips, we were the guest of the Earl of Bradford for several days. The Earl, Richard Bridgeman, had been a UKIP candidate several years before and was a big supporter of the party. We had a wonderful time with him and his family in their beautiful West Midlands home. We nicknamed him the "Duke of Earl."

37. My Debate with Germane Greer over UKIP

Shortly after UKIP fared so well in 2004, the party leaders asked me to appear on a BBC program to discuss the stunning election results. Eileen and I were in Romania and planned to get to London just in time for the TV show.

But as we were boarding our plane, I got a call and learned that the location of the nation-wide show had been changed from London to Cardiff, the capital of Wales. UKIP would have a helicopter waiting at Heathrow. We arrived in London and quickly boarded the chopper.

The ride to Cardiff was amazing—the whole way, we could look down and see the absolutely straight Roman roads built two millennia ago. (The Romans built the roads so chariots and horses could pick up speed on straight-aways. No need to deviate around someone else's property. It was eminent domain, Roman style.)

Along the way, I learned that Germaine Greer, the radical feminist would be on the show. "Yikes!" I thought, "what was that about?" Matt Taylor, a former adviser to Tony Blair would also be joining us. I expected a brawl, got one, and held my own.

I said that the U.K.'s five hundred years of democracy were now imperiled by the rise of what I called "bureaucratism" in the EU. I warned that their continental colleagues lacked the British respect for the will of the people and warned that revolt against the rule of "Brussels bureaucrats" would spark rebellions all over the continent (as they have all over.

As we were departing the helicopter, I asked the pilot if he would be taking us back to London. He wasn't. I was a little worried about how we would get out of Cardiff, but a UKIP staffer was there and took us back to the city. The three-hour drive wasn't nearly as much fun as the helicopter, but a minority fringe party can't hope to travel in style all the time.

I particularly recall the young man who drove us back from Wales. His car was a ramshackle affair that raised doubts about its ability to complete the journey. Our trepidation was not alleviated when he explained his theory of automotive purchasing.

He said that he only bought a car when he was sure to be the last owner, often after quite a few others. That way, he'd get a car for a few thousand pounds and it would last twenty or thirty thousand miles. When it died, he'd just buy another one, also on its last legs.

Somehow we got home. Apparently this was not fated to be the car's terminal voyage.

We loved working with the UKIP people and continue to support them and their truly awesome leader, Nigel Farage.

38. How to Ward Off Mosquitoes in Brazil

During the past twenty years, I've worked in more than forty countries. And had a lot of fun.

My Argentine friend and partner Luis Rosales always cracked me up. We've worked together throughout Latin America and now, in 2005, we were in Bolivia.

(Remember when Butch Cassidy tells Sundance that the deserted, overgrown, decrepit railway station there might be the "garden spot of the whole country?")

In LaPaz, we met with the candidate for president—former president Gonzalo Sánchez de Lozada y Sánchez de Bustamante (Goni for short). He was articulate and bright, but there was one problem: Luis told me that his English was better than his Spanish! He had spent so much time in school in the U.S. that he had forgotten his native language!

Bolivians felt that this was reason enough not to give him another term as their president.

Now, Luis and I had come to the best part of the trip. We were going home. Well, not home, but to San Paulo, Brazil, for our next meeting. But Luis almost didn't get to go.

When he arrived at the La Paz airport—14,000 feet up—the counter agent told him that he needed a yellow fever shot to enter Brazil from Bolivia. I had gotten my shot before I left the US, but Luis hadn't.

"We have a problem," he gravely told the ticket agent. "What do you think we can do about the problem?"

His comment seemed to be a kind of Latin American code. The woman excused herself and went behind the counter to discuss this "problem" with her supervisor who came out to attend—personally—to this new "problem."

Being a Yanqui, I expected he would just tell my friend to go back to town and get his shot. Another night in paradise!

But, no, there was another solution. Had medical science made a breakthrough when I wasn't looking, I wondered?

Apparently not.

The airline supervisor, in a gaudy uniform, his chest filled with medals, came out and repeated what a major problem it was. "For this problem, we have stopped here even Germans," he said as if to emphasize how seriously they took the requirement.

Then, as if light dawned, he remembered that there was someone in Santa Cruz (the plane's next and last stop before it entered Brazil) who could "solve" the problem.

Money was never mentioned, but Luis knew the libretto. He'd been to this particular opera before.

Pesos changed hands.

When we landed in Santa Cruz, the problem-solver materialized as we came off the plane. The layover was only 40 minutes, so I asked Luis if there was enough time to solve the problem. A trip to town, a doctor's appointment, and the trip back could take two hours.

No time to get a shot, but plenty to pick up a certificate that he had one.

Luis and his savior disappeared to a remote corner of the airport and my friend returned brandishing a certificate attesting to the "fact" that he had had a yellow fever shot. It was the least painful injection he'd ever gotten.

More pesos. But no problem entering Brazil.

That night, Luis and I relaxed by the pool at the Sheraton hotel in San Paulo sipping cognac and smoking cigars. (I don't smoke, but I allowed myself a cigar once in a while when I was in Latin America.)

Suddenly a mosquito appeared. A mortal threat. I sprang into action.

"Quick, Luis, show him your certificate."

39. My Motorcade in Colombia

In 2004, at the height of the civil war in Colombia, I was invited to meet the president and his cabinet. President Alvaro Uribe was locked in a deadly struggle to eliminate the narco-terrorist, Marxist FARC. Soon to face re-election, he had read my book, *The New Prince: Machiavelli Updated for the 21st Century,* and wanted a personal briefing.

Excerpt from handwritten letter from my mother, Terry Morris, on the morning after my premature birth day, November 29, 1947 (Morris family photo)

My mother ,Terry Morris holding me at about 4 months old. (Morris family photo)

Bon Voyage Party for my parents as they leave on a cruise to their 25th wedding anniversary, 1959 (Morris family photo)

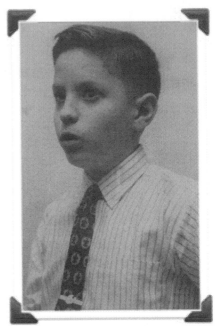

My Aunt Florence and Eileen and I at my parent's 50th Wedding Anniversary 1984 (Morris family photo)

Dick Morris, candidate for Student Government (Morris Family photo taken by Simon Rifkin)

My parents and me at the 1965 Celebration of my fathers. Eugene Morris' 30th Anniversary of Admission to the N.Y.Bar (Morris Family photo)

My niece Katie Maxwell and President Bill
Clinton with me at the White House, 1994
(Photo gift from President Bill Clinton)

Speaking to Democrats Abroad, Paris,
April 1996
(Morris family photo)

Simon Barsky and I after my speech at
the Nixon Library
   (photo gift from Simon Barsky)

Dick
Morris ,
Luis
Rosales,
and Eileen
McGann
with Pope
Francis at
the Vatican,
2015
(photo gift
of Luis
Rosales)

Bogota, the capital, in those days was not a place for tourists. (It is now after Uribe won both the war and the election.)

The FARC rebels had made the city so dangerous that Uribe sent an armored car (bomb proof and bullet proof) to fetch me at the airport. Not only that. Two motorcycle outriders on each flank. A leading car and a following car, both bomb and bulletproof, and six soldiers in uniform with machine guns. I never felt safer.

When you tap on the window in a car like that, you realize you are not touching glass, but a kind of transparent metal. The door weighs so much you need two hands to close it. If an atomic bomb went off outside, you'd probably ask the driver to "turn up the air. It's getting a bit stuffy back here."

I arrived without incident and the meeting went well. I was very flattered when I saw they all had copies of my book and that Uribe had marked and underlined almost every page. (He still calls me "professor.")

After the presentation, it came time to return to the airport in my limo and motorcade. So far, no problemo. But then, after I left the motorcade and entered airport security, things got a bit tougher.

I went through the metal detector and had my bag X-rayed. Then, the airport security people examined my passport. They saw stamps from the fifty or sixty countries that littered its pages and sent me into a side room. They must have thought me to be a well-travelled drug mule.

There, a technician made me drop my pants and raise my shirt so he could take an X-ray of my stomach to see if I had any condoms in my digestive system filled with cocaine or something. Naturally, I resented the intrusion and the suspicion. As I walked away to board my plane, I asked—over my shoulder—"by the way, do I have cancer?" I didn't want it to have been a total loss.

That was then. Now, you can stroll the streets of Bogota in perfect safety, take a regular taxi from the airport, and have lunch or a drink in one of the many and charming sidewalk restaurants that dot the city. No danger.

The difference was president Uribe. I don't think any other president or living ex-president anywhere in the world has had as much success as Uribe.

Several billion dollars of U.S. military aid and equipment (sent by President Clinton) had certainly helped the government to defeat the FARC. But the key was a unique strategy.

Uribe realized that the FARC was essentially an army of drug dealers. The days of Marxist ideology were long faded. Once it had been a genuinely revolutionary guerrilla army modeled after Castro's in Cuba. But after the fall of the Soviet Union and the end of its subsidies, it stayed maintained itself by selling drugs and forgot about communism.

To stay alive in that dangerous world—hunted by the government on the one hand and rival drug dealers on the other—its leaders needed to be protected by a small army of well-trained and well-armed bodyguards. But maybe not so well paid.

President Uribe saw their vulnerability and offered the bodyguards huge cash rewards for the hides of their employers, dead or alive.

When you offer a bodyguard a million dollar reward for killing his boss, it can be a great motivation. And so, the guards began to turn on their employers, killing them, claiming their reward, and going into the Colombian equivalent of the witness protection program. (They are probably all living happily in Miami now). Soon the leaders of the FARC were dying like flies and the rebellion collapsed. Brilliant!

The U.S. sent helicopters, smart bombs, and all kinds of surveillance equipment, but it was the cold hard cash rewards that turned out to do the trick.

40. Spy Pen in Colombia

You never really know for sure if the CIA is watching you when you work in a foreign country, but sometimes you get a strong—and creepy—feeling that they definitely are. That's how we felt one night during a visit to Medellin, Colombia.

We were in Medellin at the invitation of our good friends Jorge and Nancy Estrada. Jorge (to whom this book is dedicated) was born there and had often told us about its amazing climate (72 degrees year round) and its beautiful mountains and flowers.

But in the 1970s and 1980s, the extreme violence of the Medellin drug cartel, led by the brutal Pablo Escobar, had transformed the peaceful city into a dangerous, war-zone. In 1993, TIME magazine had singled it out as the "murder capital of the world."[15]

According to the Telegraph of London, "Drug lords lived like princes. Judges and policeman were regularly assassinated, paramilitaries invaded neighborhoods and ordinary people disappeared overnight without trace."[16]

But once Escobar was killed, Medellin was gradually rehabilitated into a safe, beautiful, and prosperous city that now attracts tourists and ex-pats. The scenery is beautiful, people are friendly, and the food is great!

We enjoyed traveling with the Estradas, who took us all over the city. It had been a long day for us when they dropped us off at our hotel at about 10 p.m. It had begun with an early morning breakfast speech to business leaders at our hotel, followed by a trip to the fantastic Botero Museum in the center of the city, and then another speech at the office of the Governor of the province of Antiochia. After that, we had dinner with Governor Luis Alfredo Ramos and his wife Maria, who had become friends.

When Jorge dropped us off that night, we made a beeline for the hotel bar and gratefully ordered drinks. There was only one other person there—a man who had his back to us and was talking on his cell phone.

Within a few minutes, the man turned around and waved at us and walked over to our table. He introduced himself as an American and said that he enjoyed watching me when I was on FoxNews.

We invited him to join us for a drink. He immediately told us that he worked for the DEA. Then he asked what we were doing in Colombia? Who was my client? How long were we staying? After we ducked the questions, he talked about the other countries where he had been stationed.

I noticed that Eileen was staring at him intently. He did, too. "Didn't I see you in the hotel lobby early this morning?" she asked.

"I don't think so," he replied, a touch defensively.

But she didn't let it go. "You were sitting right over there and reading a newspaper," she persisted, pointing to a bench in front of a separate elevator that went only from the lobby to the restaurant where I had given my speech that morning. He insisted that she must be confusing him with someone else, but I knew right away that he was lying.

Eileen is NEVER confused about stuff like that. She has a photographic memory for scenes and events. (She can easily recount the exact furnishings of her grandmother's apartment she last entered when she was eight years old.) She had also recognized his watch band, which was a madras plaid.

"How many of those are there in Medellin?" she asked me later.

Eileen kicked me; she knew she was right and wanted to get away from the man who we believed had been watching—at the very least—to see who came to my speech. Was he waiting alone on the bar to see when we returned, we wondered? It was too weird. Did the DEA have nothing better to do?

I asked for the check. We said good night and started to leave. Then, surprisingly, the DEA agent asked for my autograph.

Seriously? I thought.

I groped for a pen, but he quickly handed one to me. But the pen felt odd, way too heavy. Amazingly, it bore the logo "*Drug Enforcement Administration*." Eileen and I had the same reaction: Since when did the DEA invest in pens to give out like calling cards and advertise its existence—especially in Medellin? Did they give out pens to drug kingpins too? Did Pablo get one right before they killed him?

After I signed his paper, I moved to give him back his pen. "Keep it," he said. I didn't want it, but he insisted and I deposited it into my jacket pocket.

We ditched our interloper and walked to the elevator to go to our room. On the way up, I made a motion to Eileen to say nothing and pointed to the pen, weighing it in my palm to show her how heavy it was. She nodded.

Our room was an apartment that took up about a quarter of the floor. A guard was stationed at the double-doored entrance as we exited the elevator.

We entered silently. There was a large living room and a full kitchen. Eileen motioned for me to give her the pen and she went into the kitchen and put it in the freezer. We were laughing hysterically. To avoid speaking for fear that someone was listening, we wrote to each other on our laptops.

We'd done that before!

"INSPECTOR CLOUSEAU," Eileen wrote.

After looking up "spy pens" online, we were convinced the pen was either a camera, microphone, or some kind of a tracker. Nothing good, that's for sure. It was larger than an average pen and impossible to open.

We weren't sure how well the freezer would obstruct its purpose—whatever it was. So we removed it and went out on the huge balcony attached to our suite and threw it way out into the woods.

I called Jorge the next morning and he checked with the U.S. consulate. They confirmed that our friend, indeed, worked for the DEA, but knew nothing about his pen and seemed surprised that he was handing them out.

In our experience, the DEA—and other U.S. agencies in foreign countries—often provide cover for CIA agents.

No one could convince us that our meeting with the pen man was a coincidence.

41. Karl Rove as a Waiter in Venice

Venice is a magical place and it is very easy to become so engrossed in the breathtaking environment that you don't notice something very obvious right in front of you.

That's what happened to us!

Eileen and I were having dinner on the terrace of the Gritti Palace Hotel on the Grand Canal with our niece Marie. In the Latin Quarter It was a perfect June night and we were marveling at the light and the sky color as the sunset began at nearly ten o'clock. Gondolas, water buses, water taxis, and yachts cruised up and down the canal and there was a very festive atmosphere in the restaurant.

We were staying at the beautiful and elegant Excelsior Hotel at Lido Beach, where the beach and the pool offered relief from the hot sun. Every night, we took the hotel's water taxi to the dock of a restaurant on one of the canals. Just going back and forth to the hotel was fun—it was a bracing fifteen minute ride, bouncing on the water and zipping along.

That evening, we took the water taxi to the Gritti and stepped off the boat onto the steps to the hotel's outdoor restaurant. The dock worker who helped us off the boat as it rolled in the water, turned us over to the maître d' who escorted us to our waterside table.

A full moon made the night even more beautiful. We loved looking across at the huge illuminated dome of the church of Santa Maria della Salute and a new hotel that was reflecting its red lights onto the canal.

The food was magnificent and the service excellent...and memorable.

Memorable because, midway through our meal, a new waiter appeared with a towel draped over his arm. He bowed graciously and asked, with heavily accented English, "Meester Morris, how do you enjoy your dinner?"

I graciously replied that it was wonderful and asked his name, not looking directly at him.

"Carlos Rovera," he replied. Then I got it. The waiter in disguise was, in fact, Karl Rove, one of the top consultants in politics.

He was so out-of-context that he had almost pulled the deception off completely. We still joke about it.

(Karl was staying at the Gritti and was having dinner with some friends in the restaurant.)

42. My Fur Lined Hiking Boots in South Florida

My sartorial lapses are the stuff of legend in our family.

In 1986, I worked for Senator Paula Hawkins' re-election campaign in Florida (I had handled her first race in 1980).

Paula wanted me to come to a press conference in Ft. Lauderdale where she planned to attack a proposed gas pipeline. I was to present polling data that showed people didn't want the pipe and its attendant risks of leakage and pollution.

It was my first media appearance in the Florida campaign, a race in which both sides jumped through hoops to disguise the fact that they were using out-of-state consultants.

Hence my problem. I flew down to Florida from my home in Connecticut in mid-February, still wearing the fur-lined boots I had used to hike through the ten-inch snow that morning. I had forgotten to change shoes. I had no other shoes with me! What if the reporters noticed? What if they panned in on my boots? In 90 degree Florida? How out-of-state could we get?

When Eileen and I bought our home in Connecticut, we fell in love with the nature preserve that abutted it—hundreds of acres of woods with paths delineated by paint slashes on trees. On this winter day, we waded through the snow to marvel at the bucolic winter scene that unfolded at our doorstep.

Then, it was time to jump into the waiting car. I had to rush to make the flight. But as I stepped out of the taxi at the airport, I realized that I had not changed shoes after the hike. I was wearing fur-lined hiking boots more suitable for New England (or Alaska) than Florida.

As I ran to my plane, I realized that it would look ridiculous to show up in these boots. I could see the television footage emphasizing that Paula's campaign was being run by a Yankee who didn't even realize that it's hot in Florida in February.

I called Eileen to share my predicament, but all I got for the call were howls of laughter. No help there.

My plane landed at 8 p.m. on Sunday of President's Day weekend, long after shoe stores had closed. I asked my taxi driver as we drove toward my hotel if he knew of any stores that might be open at that hour that sold shoes.

"Thems as wants to buy shoes usually does it durin' the day," he drawled in reply. No help there either.

But, as I checked into the Holiday Inn, I spied the valet vacuuming the floor. I looked down and he wore a pair of dignified black shoes. City shoes. Florida shoes even.

Inspired, I asked him if I could buy his shoes. "I only got this pair," he said.

"Yes, but when does your shift end?"

"At midnight."

So we struck a deal. I agreed to pay him $100 for his black shoes (probably worth about $40 when new) if he came to my room at midnight.

"What'll I wear home?" he asked.

"Would you please consider going home in just your socks this one time? I would really appreciate it."

He considered my offer for a minute and then agreed. At midnight, he gave me his shoes and went home barefoot.

I imagined what he would tell his wife. Did he lose his shoes in a card game? Were they under a girl's bed somewhere? Was he losing his memory this early in life?

I borrowed black socks from Paula's husband. And a new "Dick" story entered our family lore. Paula kidded me about it for years. But there was no media coverage.

43. Just Checking

Paula was a piece of work. She was the first woman ever elected to the Senate on her own in American history. (All women up until then had succeeded to office after the death of their fathers or husbands. Paula made it on her own in 1980.)

Before there was Nancy Reagan or Sarah Palin or Michele Bachmann, there was Paula Hawkins. She made the mold for a conservative, pro-life, vocal, active female candidate...and U.S. Senator.

Disliked by the Florida establishment for her vocal role in fighting the utility companies, she ran a low budget campaign. Very low budget.

We shot our main ad in a supermarket aisle and, instead of a teleprompter—that we couldn't afford—the script was on a roll of Bounty paper towels that I unrolled as she read each line. Sometimes she faltered, but, as the ad says, "Bounty is the quicker picker upper."

Paula was the original feisty Republican. In the Senate, it was fun to watch her take on the mighty and powerful. It was sometimes less fun to work for her.

Like when she grew jealous of the time I spent with other clients. She wanted to be first. So I got a pager (in the pre-cell phone era) and gave Paula the number. I promised to return her call within an hour, unless I was on a plane. But, if she added 911 to her message, I would call immediately if I could get to a phone.

No sooner had I left her office than I got a 911 page from her. Already? I thought. But I told my taxi driver to pull over at the nearest pay phone so I could call her. She picked up the phone and, in response to my question "What's up?" She replied, "Just checking."

Paula established a great record as Senator. She was the first politician to elevate the problem of missing children to national significance and, through her efforts, she got the Missing Children's Act through Congress and signed by President Reagan in 1982. That led to photos of missing kids appearing on milk cartons.

But I felt her greatest achievement was in virtually drying up the supply of quaaludes on U.S. streets. On learning that most of our "ludes"—as kids called them—came from factories in China, she arranged a trip to Beijing and wangled a meeting the top leaders. They promised to close down the factories if Paula could provide evidence of quaalude production. On her return to Washington, she got it from the FBI and sent it to China.

Amazingly, they kept their word and stopped making the stuff. It soon almost dried up on our streets.

When she ran for re-election in 1986, I was determined to run an ad explaining the triumph. I asked Paula which Chinese official she had met with and she answered, "The top guy—Deng Xiaoping." The ad explained that the meeting resulted in the quaalude ban. It worked. Paula soared up in the polls.

But then the newspapers began sniffing around the story behind the ad and it came out that she had not met with Deng on her visit to China but with a lower ranking official. When I pressed Paula for details, she said, "Oh, well, they all dressed the same." Oh? A big gaffe, but the fact of her huge achievement remained.

But she did lose the election.

44. How Senator Phil Gramm Really Wanted to Marry Sophia Loren

It was 1992 and Tommy Hartnett, a former Congressman from South Carolina, shifted uneasily in his chair facing Texas Senator Phil Gramm. We all knew why Tommy was here. Phil was the chairman of the Republican Senate Campaign Committee and he was trying to recruit Tommy to run against the longtime incumbent Democrat, Senator Fritz Hollings, whose credentials stretched back to the Watergate era.

Tommy should have been flattered, but he knew that Phil had earlier met with the guy he really wanted to make the race—the Governor of South Carolina: Carroll A. Campbell, Jr. Now, after Campbell had already turned him down, he sought out Hartnett, hoping he would run.

As the meeting opened, Hartnett made it clear that while he was pleased by Senator Gramm's attention, he was well aware that he was not Gramm's first choice.

That triggered a story from Phil Gramm's prolific repertoire.

Gramm leaned back in his desk chair and drawled, slowly stretching out his words: "Ah-Ah-Ahm gonna tell you somethin' that I have nevuh told anyone else before." He quickly added "and I would appreciate your discretion."

We pulled closer to hear the secret.

"My-y-y-y wife Wendy was NOT my furst choice." He looked at us both for a reaction. "Sopheaa Lowren was mah furst choice. But she wasn't available and I have had thirty years of a wonderful marriage to Wendy."

Tommy made the race and finished only three points behind Hollings, the closest race Senator Hollings ever had (out of six).

45. The Key Turning Point for Clinton's Presidency: Our Meeting in May 1995

A tension had gripped the White House ever since my work with the president became known throughout the building and to the public in April 1995. Until then, it had been our little secret from November 1994 until March 1995. During those five months, I operated under a code name "Charlie". Only the president and his two personal aides—Nancy Hernreich and Betty Curry—knew who I was. I chose the name Charlie after Charlie Black, a top Republican consultant and my mentor.

Even in the leak-prone world of Washington, we kept the secret. I would call Clinton during meetings and, I was told, he would excuse himself to take a call from "Charlie."

It was all very heady, but I couldn't get much done. In the White House, having the president on your side is sometimes not enough. Without the cooperation of his staff, it was hard to do what I wanted.

I would draft a speech for the president that broke sharply from the Democratic Party orthodoxy of solid opposition to the Gingrich program and, at the last minute, the liberal staff would include one sentence attacking the GOP and that would be the headline the next day.

To deal with the problem, the president decided to let Vice President Al Gore, Chief of Staff Leon Panetta, Deputy Chief Harold Ickes, Director of Communications Don Baer, and George Stephanopoulos in on the arrangement. From there, my role was immediately leaked to the media and made the front page of the NY Times.

Until my arrival, the president's staff had been in total denial after the Democrats lost both houses of Congress in 1994.

Nothing really had happened, they contended. Just wait for the next election and we will rally the troops, bolster the turnout, and sweep back into power.

I thought that was nonsense. I argued that the President had to move to the center and co-opt key Republican themes and make them his own.

The first step was the line "the era of big government is over" that I had written into the president's 1995 State of the Union speech to Congress. Now he had to back it up.

The Republicans were calling for massive cuts in government spending. My polling showed that their proposed reductions in Medicare, Medicaid, education and the environment were particularly unpalatable to voters.

The president's staff seized on the data and said we should oppose all the GOP cuts, standing firm for a continuation of the liberal-left policies.

Their position concealed an unpleasant truth: Neither party was sincere in wanting a balanced budget.

The Democrats didn't really care about eliminating the deficit. The true believers on the president's staff wanted to keep government spending high and rising, which would inevitably grow the government. They pretended that the only way to balance the budget was to slice Medicare, Medicaid, education and the environment. But this was phony. You could (and we did) balance it by cutting everything else and leaving the big four (plus Social Security) alone.

The Republicans also didn't really care about balancing the budget. They wanted to slice spending in the four big programs and justify the cuts by saying they were the only way to achieve balance.

Both sides were hiding the truth: You could eliminate the deficit and leave the key programs untouched.

The unanimity of the establishment consensus about lying to the people was exposed when the president's proposal to cut the deficit but leave key programs alone was rejected in the Senate by a vote of 99-0. The only thing the parties could agree on was to hold Medicare, Medicaid, education, and environment hostage to their real desires to raise (Democrats) or lower (Republicans) spending in general.

So I proposed that the president give a speech on national, network, primetime television calling their bluff and saying we *could* balance the budget but leave these core priorities untouched, a speech that would strip both parties of their disguises and reveal their true motivations.

The liberals on Clinton's staff went nuts. They gloomily predicted certain defeat for the president when he ran for re-election if he gave such a speech. But with the support of Vice President Al Gore and Deputy Chief of Staff Erskine Bowles, I argued that President Clinton had to give the speech and outline a third way between and above both parties dogma—a position I called "triangulation."

The showdown came in a key White House meeting in late May 1995. My father, who was 85 at the time, had to undergo surgery that morning at

115

Mt. Sinai Hospital in New York City. I visited him before I left for Washington and he cheered me on. When I landed in DC. I called the hospital and learned the surgery went well. I even spoke to my Dad in the recovery room. I was greatly relieved.

But it had been a scary few hours. And the thought of a contentious meeting at the White House was unpleasant. I remember thinking as I sat on the plane on the tarmac at DC's National Airport: "If my father, at 85, can fight so hard in the hospital, I can fight equally hard at this meeting."

The White House showdown lasted two hours and featured a back-and-forth debate between George Stephanopoulos and me. Then, as if to summarize our case, Gore spoke eloquently of the need for the speech. Finally, the president told Panetta: "Leon, I have to throw long," using a football metaphor.

It was over. The speech was a go.

Clinton spoke on national TV on June 13, 1995, and called for a balanced budget that "reflects our priorities and protects the things we care about the most."

I stood in the Oval Office as the president spoke with a glow of triumph in my heart.

In 1997, after the election, Clinton and Republican leaders Trent Lott and Newt Gingrich negotiated an agreement to balance the budget in seven years. They didn't have to wait that long. The deficit was gone the very next year and the Clinton Administration had three more years of balanced budgets.

46. The Last Time The Parties Worked Together

It was one thing to make the speech, but how did Bill Clinton do it? How did he balance the budget and reform welfare, achieving a bi-partisan consensus: something we haven't had since. Instead we've had twenty years of bickering.

It all went back to a meeting I had with Republican Senator Trent Lott at his home in Pascagoula, Mississippi. in November 1994.

Lott woke me up that morning with an urgent phone call: "Come to Pascagoula right away. I'm sending a plane to pick you up."

I had advised Lott on his first race for Senate when he was elected in 1988 and for his re-election in 1994. But why was he calling me now, after the election?

"But, Trent, the election is over. You won," I reminded him. But he still insisted that I come.

When I arrived at his amazing home in Pascagoula, the first thing I noticed was an incredible, huge tree that sheltered his entire front yard (since destroyed by hurricane Katrina). Then, Trent's graceful and elegant wife, Patricia, came out and ushered me onto their back porch overlooking the Gulf of Mexico. Sitting on rocking chairs next to each other and gazing at the Gulf, we chatted about the election. Trent was, of course, excited by the Republican victory in the '94 elections and was chewing over its significance for him.

"I'm thinking of running for Majority Whip," he ventured. (The second highest position in the Senate leadership.) It was unusual for someone just entering his second term to seek such a high post, but Trent was very good at transcending tradition...and counting votes.

After we reviewed the political situation, we counted the likely votes and concluded that he should run and could win. The new Republican majority in the Senate was sick of the RINO (Republican In Name Only) policies the party had followed while in the minority and saw Trent as the kind of dynamic leader they needed—a counterpart to the new upstart Republican speaker of the House, Newt Gingrich.

Then, I had a surprise of my own to tell him. "Clinton wants me back advising him and I'm going to accept."

How would it work, Trent asked, with me working in the White House if he became leader of the Senate Republicans? Both were distant dreams that November 1994 afternoon, but the prospect was tantalizing.

"Let's pass everything," I answered.

And then it happened.

By the spring of 1996, President Clinton had given me an increasing role in his campaign and in formulating many aspects of his domestic program. And Lott had just replaced Senate Majority Leader Bob Dole, who had resigned to run for president.

I called Trent and we discussed what to do. "Let's pass everything," I repeated, this time for real.

June 1996 was a rare time in Washington. It was the political equivalent of a solar eclipse. The planets were all aligned perfectly for massive legislative accomplishments. The two parties worked together as they haven't since.

The Republicans were still licking their wounds from their two government shutdowns in November and December 1995, which the public blamed on them. Their ratings were down sharply. And Bill Clinton was working to recover from his defeat in the 1994 elections.

Both sides needed legislative achievements to bolster their cases in the 1996 election—Clinton as president and the GOP for a control of Congress. Neither side would say it out loud, but the Dems were willing to let Republicans keep Congress if they could re-elect Clinton. And, likewise, the Republicans were willing to undermine Bob Dole, their candidate for president, by handing Clinton a substantial achievement—if that would help them keep Congress.

So, working with Trent on the one hand and Clinton on the other, we passed everything: welfare reform, portability of health insurance from job to job, a rise in the minimum wage, and we laid the foundations for the 1997 deal that produced three years of budget surpluses.

The key to our success lay in getting both Clinton and Lott to see themselves as incumbents before they were Democrats and Republicans. They had to understand that they would sink or swim together, regardless of the fate of their parties.

If the voters felt Washington was working, they would re-elect both a Democratic president and a Republican Senate majority. They weren't interested in apportioning blame for failure. They wanted success and would reward all incumbents for achieving it…or punish failure in both parties.

So Trent, the president, and I thrashed out the details of welfare reform, going back and forth with proposals and possible deals. We spoke constantly. The formal channel for negotiations between Chief of Staff Leon Panetta and the House and Senate committees mattered little. Our back channel was where everything got done.

One day, George Stephanopoulos, the Clinton aide left over from the 1992 days, warned me against working too closely with Republican Trent Lott. "I'm not free-lancing, George," I told him. "The president knows

118

everything I'm doing and wants me to do it." That shut him up! (But didn't stop him from leaking about it.)

George (and his buddy Rahm Emanuel) were champion leakers. Once I told the president, after a confidential matter ended up in the media, that I had only told George and Rahm. "You *only* told George and Rahm. You *only* told George and Rahm" he said, his voice dripping in sarcasm. "Why didn't you just issue a fucking press release???"

My meetings with Trent were secret and hidden from the public, the media, the White House staff, the Congressional Democratic leadership, and his fellow Republicans. His staff would sneak me into the Capitol building, up the back stairs, and into his Majority Leader's office. I kept the president closely informed about every detail, usually in late night phone calls.

He would call me "Mr. Prime Minister" and I would call him "His Majesty's Opposition." We had great fun.

It was bipartisanship at its best. Their joint goal was to work together and get major results for the American people. And they did.

I ran a shuttle between them. After Trent and I would meet, I would debrief the President on the up-to-the-minute details of the welfare and budget bills. Then I would carry his views back to Lott. Frequently, I would propose compromises or other measures to bridge the differences between them.

For example, Clinton fiercely objected to the cuts in benefits to legal immigrants that Trent was pushing. (Illegals were already excluded.) "Why shouldn't a hard-working laborer who gets hurt on the job and is disabled get benefits if he's here legally and contributed to Social Security?" the president would demand heatedly.

But Trent wouldn't budge. "You keep moving the goal posts," he protested.

But they were both open to compromise.

The solution that I proposed was a bit unorthodox: Clinton should sign the welfare reform bill as it stood, but, as he did so, decry the cuts in benefits to legal immigrants and call on governors to press Congress to reverse them next year. "You mean I should attack the bill even as I sign it?" he asked in a late-night phone call.

"Damn right," I answered. "Politically, it is the only way you *can* sign it."

And it worked. The President got what he wanted. And ultimately, the Republicans did, too. The following year, after welfare reform was implemented, Republican governors raised hell about the cuts in benefits to legal immigrants since they had to make up the money with state funds. The cuts were then repealed by the Republican Congress.

I remember during the negotiations that Trent and I were discussing what cuts we should make in welfare. "How about restoring money for diapers and baby food that the Republicans had cut out of the bill?" I asked.

"I'm for allowing anything an adult can't use or eat," Trent replied.

Eventually, they compromised. Both men needed a deal to bring to the voters, so they made it work. Both kept their power: the president was reelected and the Republicans kept Congress.

We joked with the Washington establishment about our collaboration when Trent spoke at the Gridiron Dinner with the President sitting at his side in 1996. The event was traditionally a time to roast the nation's leaders.

Trent and I put on a little skit he had cooked up. It began when Trent began to read his speech. He sounded like a liberal and sent the audience buzzing.

"It's high time that we adequately funded day care in this country," the Republican Leader began. "We need a higher minimum wage. We have to increase our spending…"

I stood up from my seat in the audience and, putting my cell phone to my ear, called Trent while he was standing at the podium giving his speech. Trent's phone rang and he answered it: "Not now Dick, I'm giving a speech," he said.

"I know, I'm in the audience," I answered loudly so everyone could hear. "You have the wrong speech! You are giving Clinton's speech. I must have given you the wrong one!"

Trent mumbled his apologies to the audience and turned to the president and handed him a copy of his "speech."

The audience howled. So did Trent, the president, and I.

That was the last time Washington worked as it should.

47. What is Triangulation?

I was flattered when longtime *New York Times* columnist Bill Safire called me in late 2007 as he was writing *Safire's Political Dictionary*. He wanted to get a definition of the word "triangulation."

I had coined the term when I worked for President Clinton because I thought that it was a good metaphor for how his agenda could stand in the space between the two parties, but above them at the same time, at the apex an isosceles triangle. (One where both vertical sides are the same length) .

Of course, I didn't invent the word—it's been around for a thousand or more years. Its classical definition—from the realm of geometry and surveying—is the use of "triangles to determine the distances and relative positions of points spread over a territory."[17]

Triangulation was used most commonly in maritime navigation to help sailors locate their geographic position by using stars.

But I developed a political use of the word to denote a third political position apart from and above the political parties and their agendas.

Triangulation is not just a way to split the difference between the parties and compromise, leaving each with half a loaf. It was designed to create a new third way, combining the best of the left and the right and leaving the bad parts behind.

Each party approached each issue with a full agenda. To fight crime—a goal they shared equally—the left wanted strict gun controls, but also demanded restrictions on police behavior—no stop and frisk, no profiling. The right demanded tougher sentences for repeat offenders and the death penalty, but also interpreted the Second Amendment rigidly to ban any regulation of firearms.

Ordinary voters didn't fully agree with either party. They accepted the need for mandatory sentences, but wanted them reduced for non-violent drug offenses. They agreed with the basic right of citizens to bear arms, but would make exceptions to stop felons and fugitives from getting them. They would take the best of each side and leave the rest behind. They would, in my words, triangulate.

As I worked with Clinton—first in Arkansas and then in the White House, we chaffed at the constraints parties would seek to impose on their candidates. For example, he agreed with the left that we needed more social spending, but he saw merit in the conservative view that people had to assume responsibility for themselves.

So, first as governor and then as president, Clinton spawned a whole new genre of transactional policies where government would demand that citizens take responsibility in return for public generosity. You could get partial forgiveness on student loans if you agreed to teach in under-served parts of the country. You'd get welfare assistance, but had to have a job.

I called these couplings the New Social Contract, but Clinton rejected the name as too legalistic and used The New Covenant instead. We were so secular and ill-steeped in religion that neither Clinton nor I realized the offense that this title would give to Evangelicals, borrowing—without permission—Jesus' description of the post-crucifixion pact between man and God.

The idea found tremendous traction, particularly during the campaign of 1992, Running as a "new kind of Democrat," Clinton carved a third way between Carter's policies of handing out government money to all claimants and Reagan's of cutting social spending.. The perceived naivete of Carter's approach and the penury of Reagan's left voters unfulfilled and the New Covenant's give-in-order-to-get approach made sense to voters.

Each party is wed to an agenda on virtually every issue in our politics. I liken it to a restaurant's dinner menu where each dish is paired with another for a set price. It's as if you walked into a restaurant and the waiter told you that if you want the smoked salmon for an appetizer, you have to order the lasagna as a main course and the souffle for desert. You can't order a-la-carte.

And so, in politics, if you are a liberal, and are pro-choice, you have to embrace the other left policies of high taxes and more government regulation.

Triangulation is a way to have the parties work together to achieve reasonable and workable policy objectives through bipartisanship.

That's something that we haven't seen much of in Washington lately.

48. Spied on in Romania by Secret Police

In 2004, Lia Roberts, the Nevada Republican Party Chairman, called to ask for help in her campaign. Not in Nevada. In Romania.

She had fled Romania in 1979 while it was still under the heavy boot of Communist dictator Nicolae Ceaușescu. Settling in Nevada, she became active in local politics and acquired great wealth, but always dreamed of returning to her native land. When she saw the post-Communists (who were not so 'post') running the country again, she was galvanized into action. She decided to return to Romania and run for president

In working on her campaign, Eileen and I got an up- close taste of what it was like to work in a country dominated by the secret police. Although the communists were out of power, the "socialist" government of Ion Iliescu was, essentially, just a continuation of the communist rule under a new euphemism.

Lia was a very attractive candidate -on many levels. She was pretty and articulate. In a country that had been mired in corruption and suffered through the aftermath of the most vicious form of communism under Ceaușescu, a fresh face from the U.S. was welcome. Since Lia had been out of Romania for most of her adult life and especially during the brutal years of the Ceaușescu dictatorship, she was not compromised by the Secret Police as almost everybody else was.

The Communist practice of kompromat (compromising material) that we have heard so much about in the phony anti-Trump Steele dossier was alive and well in Romania. Politicians and journalists were routinely blackmailed and leveraged with evidence of embarrassing or even criminal material that had been gathered about them by the much feared Secret Police—usually by surreptitious listening and taping. It was pervasive.

Romania has had a tough time.

During World War II and its aftermath, Romania suffered more than any other Eastern European satellite. In World War II, Romania lost 500,000 of its 16 million people after siding with Hitler and suffering great losses at Stalingrad. The poor country lost two million more under Ceaușescu's repression. The dictator initiated a strict policy of killing anyone with any intelligence, just for the crime of being smart. He executed professors, grad students, professionals at random. He forced women to give birth and then made millions peddling adoptions for their babies.

But the assassination of Ceaușescu did not outlaw kompromat. The Securitate, as the secret police were known, was alive and well despite the fall of formal communism. And they were determined to preserve the old order, which an outsider like Lia threatened.

We would meet Lia and her staff in one of Bucharest's hotels, renting a suite so we could confer in privacy.

But it turned out that it wasn't too private after all.

The Securitate was listening in.

One morning, Lia came to our hotel room door. When Eileen opened it, she said nothing but put her finger to her lips, signaling us to be quiet. She handed Eileen a piece of paper that said "last night, a friend of mine at the Securitate showed me a transcript of everything we said yesterday and last night in this hotel room. Every single word. We can't talk here, let's leave. Now."

We were shocked and grabbed our coats and followed her out the door. We spotted a coffee shop across the street and the three of us entered and ordered food. The shop was almost empty and we found a table adjoining a horizontal partition that divided the place in two. No one was near us and we were seemingly out of the reach of the Securitate. But, when I got up to use the bathroom, I saw a guy sitting against the other side of the partition writing furiously on his laptop and wearing earphones that were attached to a small listening device. He hadn't even pretended that he came for some breakfast—there was nothing on the table but his electronics.

We wondered if there was any place in the entire city where we could talk in private.

After Lia announced her candidacy, she began to gain in the polls, but that just attracted even more attention from the police. We couldn't trust anyone. The independent newspapers reported that a person who was one of the few people working in the campaign was himself, a former secret Securitate operative.

Eventually, Lia tired of the cat-and-mouse game and returned to America, deciding not to run, after all.

But, as we worked in Romania, we began to see how the communists and the Securitate really operated. Their goal was to "get something" on everybody. They would not rest until they had found everybody's secret so they could control him. Their goal in surveillance was not to find crime so they could punish it, but to find sexual misbehavior, tax cheating, domestic issues or anything to blackmail politicians, journalists, or opinion leaders to assure their loyalty.

That's how the state acquires its power. Not by shooting people or sending them to Siberia, but by blackmailing them.

49. A Taste of Socialism in Romania

A recent poll by Gallup revealed that 60% of Democrats have a favorable opinion of Socialism while only 47% felt favorably about capitalism.[18] They are wrong. Very, very wrong. They have no idea what changes Socialism would bring. These findings come at a time that candidates like Bernie Sanders and Elizabeth Warren are becoming increasingly outspoken about their socialism.

Our time in Eastern Europe gave Eileen and me a real understanding of the creed. There, fresh from their experience behind the iron curtain, all those who worked in the private sector voted against the socialists and for the pro-free market parties. But the socialists depended entirely on the votes of those who didn't work in the private sector— pensioners, students, stay-at-home mothers, the unemployed and public employees—everybody else. Every vote they got came from people who depended on the government to live.

Those who paid taxes voted for one party and those that consumed the money voted for the other.

In fact, when the socialists won an election in post-Soviet Eastern Europe, the first thing they would do is lower the retirement age. They wanted to increase the number of pensioners—voters dependent on their handouts. But, didn't that reduce the pensions for each family? Sure it did, but the socialists wanted their dependent pensioners to be a little hungry. It was the way to keep them loyal and motivated to vote for them.

Particularly in Romania, we encountered stories of life under socialism at every turn. The most dramatic was when we learned about the state of health care.

In the Socialist Romania of the '70s and '80s, the government boasted about offering free health care. Free, but awful. Hospitals were so woefully understaffed that each patient had to share his bed with a total stranger—not king or queen sized beds, but single beds normally just about enough for one person. Apart from separating the genders, there was no system. It was just double occupancy all around.

We were repeatedly told stories about fathers who had heart attacks and found themselves sharing a bed with a patient with a broken leg. Or a wife who had a gall bladder operation and shared a bed with a woman who had a knee surgery. In Socialist Romania you couldn't get any "free" health care unless you paid for it! You had to "tip" the doctors, nurses, and orderlies. No bribe, no care. The same with "free" schools. You had to "tip" the teacher if you wanted your child to be taught anything. Without these payments, your kid might as well be staring at a wall all day.

Before we travelled in Eastern Europe, we had thought that communists stayed in power through terror, torture, exile, and execution. But our time there, particularly in Romania where we got to see socialism up close, made us realize that this view was outdated. In recent decades, they attempt to exercise power through blackmail. It is government by intimidation. As some benighted countries in Eastern Europe vote the ex-communists into power, the regimes keep people loyal by having something to hold over their heads. Their tyranny was based on shame.

Kompromat was king. Former communist political leaders won't rest until they have something on their opponents and even their colleagues and allies.

In Romania, we spent time with a party leader who straddled the socialist/free market divide. I remember telling him that one of his young followers was exceptionally capable and had a bright future. He beamed with pride and told me that he had said to the young man's father than he would look out for him. "Now," he told the dad, "I am his father."

Some father! A few weeks later, we overheard him telling an aide to work on getting dirt on the young man. "We need to get something on him," he said matter of factly. It was not that he was rebelling or a potential dissident or that he had a shady thing in his past. It was that this was a young man on the rise and his "mentor" needed something to hold over his head to control him.

It's nothing personal. Just insurance.

The socialists deliberately pass laws and levy taxes they know nobody can obey or pay and then use "tax evasion" as a cudgel to prevent dissent. For every citizen, there is a file maintained by the secret police with kompromat to keep them in line.

I'll pass on Socialism.

50. Flying First Class Socialist Style

To get from Bucharest, Romania, to Cismea, Moldova, a still communist country 300 miles away, seemed like it would be an easy flight. But, even when there is no corruption involved, the value system of a socialist society is weird to those who live in free market countries.

When we booked the flight, we were told there was no first class seats for sale on the plane. So, we were surprised when we boarded and were seated at the front of the aircraft in what were clearly first class seats. Correction: There *were* available first class seats on the plane, just none for *sale*.

We were probably given first class because we were foreigners. The bureaucrats were the ones who decided who got the perk. You couldn't just book first class and pay for it. The bureaucrats made the decision about where passengers would sit.

Devotees of socialism will celebrate this equality. Many "progressives" would prefer a system of government fiat to private purchase on the open market. The government, they reason, is at least elected but nobody voted for the business tycoons. But, on the other hand, if you didn't like the government's decision, you were stuck. In free market countries, you can always go on another airline.

But it is unnerving to delegate the power to award first class seats to bureaucrats who follow government policy. Do they make dissidents ride on the wings?

On the return trip, we again requested first class seats. As we waited at the gate, we could see the agents going over a manifest and assigning seats. Others, too, had requested the upgraded seats. But no one would know their seat status until the last minute.

As they called the names, we saw that we had made it. No rational reason. No explanation.

When you cannot use the price mechanism to determine priorities or who goes first, the choice falls to bureaucrats. And when power and privilege are not open to all who can work hard and earn it, there is no incentive to go the extra mile, work the additional hour.

Without incentive, people don't work and we reach a situation like that which gripped Eastern Europe and Russia by the time communism fell. The government passed out money, but there was nothing to buy. The shelves of the markets were empty because nobody made a profit by stocking them with goods. With nothing to sell, money was useless, nobody worked, and the cycle repeated itself. Rationing power and privilege by money has this advantage over doing it by government fiat: It incentivizes work and lets the economy function, giving everyone a shot at the top.

Welcome to socialism.

51. A Candlelight Rally for Freedom with 100,000 People in Moldova

When we arrived in Moldova, it was a freezing cold night but, even though it was Valentine's Day, one hundred thousand people, stretched as far as the eye could see, all holding candles against the night darkness, huddled together, demonstrating for freedom.

It was an inspiring sight.

American rock music belted out from the huge amplifiers and the spirit of rebellion was thick in the air. These people who lived in a country the world had seemed to leave behind were determined to throw off communism and get their liberty.

Moldova might be the most unlucky nation in the world. It is the only surviving victim of the Nazi-Soviet Pact of 1939—the alliance between Hitler and Stalin that lasted for two years until Germany invaded Russia. Under the terms of the treaty, Moldova, formerly part of Romania, was "given" to the Soviet Union where it stayed until it got independence in 1991.

The minute Moldova was freed from the Soviet Union, the local communists moved in—without bothering with the fig leaf of renaming themselves "social democrats"—and took over, propelled by the votes of the millions of ethnic Russians who had been ordered to migrate there over the years of Soviet control.

That made Moldova the only Eastern European country that chose, in elections, to keep the old line communists in power.

Conditions went from bad to worse. About a million of Moldova's almost four million people have fled the country since 1991. And a recent poll showed that an additional third would like to leave if they could.

But the communists held power with an iron grip. They owned the news media and used it shamelessly for propaganda and denied any coverage to opposition parties. The pro-democracy advocates couldn't even pay for advertising. With this control over information flow—and a full measure of voter fraud—the communists stayed in power.

But now, in 2005, the Moldovan people were rising against communism, at long last. I was working for the Christian Democratic People's Party, the only anti-communist party in the country and, that night, was slated to speak at this rally.

The translator introduced me as President Clinton's former advisor. It seemed that I was about the only American who had ever come there to talk about freedom. The ovation still rings in my ears.

Eileen and I had met with the pro-democracy political party candidates, but there was not much they could do to campaign; the communists had so effectively tied their hands.

"The free people of the world stand with you!" I said, beginning my speech. "Throw off the shackles of Communism and live in freedom!" The ovation was deafening.

The next day, we went to a meeting with the American Ambassador, Heather M. Hodges. We expected a sympathetic reception and a condemnation of communist rule. Were we surprised! Hodges defended the communists at every turn.

Frustrated beyond belief, I asked, "Is it not the policy of the United States to oppose communism?"

"Not if democratically elected," she shot back.

I was incredulous. "Democratically elected?" I challenged her. "With a controlled media, no press coverage allowed, and no access to paid television advertising? You call that democratic?"

It became clear that the answer was, in effect, "no." It was not American policy to oppose communism.

I'll bet this is changing under Trump!

But the question loomed: How can you wage a campaign when the government blocked you from all communication with the voters?

I suggested comic books. My idea was to publish colorful, funny comic books that volunteers could leave at the door of every Moldovan voter once a week.

One strip featured a robber attempting to hold up a bank. But the teller won't give him the money. "You don't have a gun," she says. "I don't need one," the robber answers, "I am the president's son."

This unorthodox form of political communication worked nicely.

As Fredo Arias King, a democracy advocate who introduced me to the party wrote, "I recall vividly you recommending the comic-book approach, since the party was essentially banned from TV and other mass media. They deployed hundreds of supporters to distribute all over the country these comic-book leaflets critical of the regime and its corruption."

Fredo, a Mexican who helped me in my work with Vicente Fox, published a periodical called Democratsia, focusing on the fight for freedom in Eastern Europe. Fluent in Russian and Czech, he has been my guide in finding good pro-democracy candidates in Eastern Europe.

The election results shocked the communists. While the Christian Democrats did not win anything close to a majority, they did amass a sufficient vote share to bargain with the government and get significant democratic reforms.

52. Donna Shalala Suggests How I Could "Make Something" of Myself

My father served on the Board of Directors of Citizens Union, a prominent good government watchdog group in New York City. Also on the Board was Donna Shalala, who became well-known as the only woman on the Municipal Assistance Corporation, which was charged with saving New York City from bankruptcy and overseeing its finances in 1975.

One day in 1976, my Dad ran into Donna in a subway station near City Hall. They began talking about me and Donna said that she thought that I had great potential and "could really make something of myself…if I got an advanced degree."

I never did. Donna went on to do great things. She became President of Hunter College, Chancellor of the University of Wisconsin, and, eventually President of the University of Miami. Bill Clinton appointed her as Secretary of Health and Human Services. One day, as I was leaving the Oval Office, I met her as she was waiting to go into a Cabinet meeting. We chatted for a few minutes and she congratulated me on the work I was doing for the President. (No mention of a graduate school degree!)

In 2018, at 77, Donna was elected to Congress for the first time. She has, apparently, made something of herself!

53. All Scandals Lead to Hillary

So much of my White House work with Bill Clinton was spent putting out fires and scandals. They came in a seemingly endless procession: Whitewater, Travelgate, the Rose Law Firm, the billing records, the FBI files, the Futures Market windfall, Paula Jones, Vince Foster's suicide, Troopergate. (That's to say nothing of those that came later in his presidency: Monica, White House gifts, removal of furniture from the White House, FALN pardons, Pardons-for-fees to Hillary's family.)

After a while, I realized that all these scandals had one big thread in common: Hillary Clinton was always at the core of the misconduct.

Some she directly caused:

- It was her edict that led to the unjust firing of the White House Travel Office staff so she could replace them with her cronies and allies so they could make millions.
- She was responsible for the Clinton family purchase of land in the Whitewater development that led to a major scandal that triggered the appointment of a Special Prosecutor. It was one of her many get rich quick schemes.
- In the course of the Whitewater development, she was the attorney for a fraudulent land sale using a phony purchaser to mislead federal regulators…and then "lost" the billing records of the transaction.
- Vince Foster, her former law partner and close friend, was in charge of cleaning up her scandals and preventing full disclosure. Immediately after his death, Hillary sent close friends into his office to remove documents that were never made public.

131

While she was First Lady of Arkansas, Hillary was given special treatment in a brokerage account that she used to purchase high risk cattle futures. She had no experience in this complicated field. But that was not an impediment. Despite being a greenhorn, she was not required to make the minimum investment required. And somehow she was not subject to margin calls when her account was in the red.

After insisting that she learned how to trade and manage the account from the Wall Street Journal, she finally admitted that James Blair, an Arkansas lobbyist for the poultry industry, actually made the trades on her behalf.

Amazingly, within ten months, her meager $1,000 investment grew to $100,000 through unusual and special trading. Some wondered if it was bribery.

Even Bill's sex scandals were aggravated by Hillary.

The Clinton's White House years were really one continuous scandal, all with Hillary as the enabler.

It began when Bill arranged to have Paula Jones escorted to his hotel room by a state trooper at a Little Rock speech. She was working at the registration desk downstairs. Jones claimed that he exposed himself and propositioned her.

Paula went public with her charges when the *American Spectator*, a conservative magazine, published reports that Clinton often used State troopers to proposition women.

When Hillary heard of the charge—and Paula's story—she ordered all hands on deck to defend against them.

Defend and attack. Clinton allies took to the airwaves to humiliate Jones. Perhaps the worst comment was made by James Carville who snidely said of Ms. Jones, "Drag a hundred dollar bill through a trailer park and you never know what you'll find."[19]That comment did not help the President.

Despite the facts of the case, Clinton's talented lawyer, Bob Bennett, was reportedly able to make a deal with Jones to drop the suit. Despite Carville's revolting statement, she wanted no money or even an admission or apology. She only wanted to clear her name of the charge that she knowingly went to Bill's room for sex.

Hillary, amazingly, vetoed the settlement because it would verify the trooper allegation. (Which was true!)

The Jones suit went ahead.

Eventually, it led to the deposition of Bill Clinton and his infamous denial—under oath—of an affair with 22-year-old intern Monica Lewinsky. That led to impeachment, Bill's disbarment, and a fine of almost a million dollars. All because Hillary wouldn't take the deal.

Recently, Hillary insisted that the affair between the President of the United States and the young Monica Lewinsky was NOT an abuse of power. Why not? According to Hillary, it was because the 22 year-old Monica was "an adult."

Hilary still doesn't get it.

(Hillary's later scandals—removing furniture from the White House, her brother's pay for pardons, Benghazi, the Clinton Foundation, and her private e-mail server all happened after I left. But she kept up the improper conduct.)

I recall realizing how central Hillary was to all the scandals—and her ethical tone deafness. It was really then, in 1996, that I came to formulate my view that she was unfit to hold public office.

54. Darkness in Warsaw

In 2007, Eileen and I were in Warsaw, consulting with the Law and Justice Party—the colorful and charismatic conservatives who came into power in 2005. Jarosław Kaczyński (pronounced Ca-jinx-skey) was the Prime Minister of Poland from 2005–2007, while his twin brother Lech Kaczyński was President from 2005–2010. The two brothers founded the party in 1981.

Originally the leaders of Solidarity with Lech Walesa, they later parted ways from him.

Sadly, President Kaczyński was killed while en route to lay a wreath at a memorial at Katyn Forest to honor the Polish officers who were massacred there by the Soviet Union during World War II. For decades, Russia blamed Hitler for the atrocity, but it turned out Stalin was responsible. His goal was to kill off the leadership of the Polish military and society to make them easier to conquer.

President Kaczynski had been determined to move Poland's political orientation toward the west and away from Russia. So there are understandable doubts about the cause of the crash, which killed 92 leading Polish diplomats, and political and government leaders.

Did Putin have a hand in the air crash that conveniently wiped out one of the most pro-American presidents on Earth? I have always thought it likely.

One night, Eileen and I had dinner with the president's twin brother -- Prime Minister Jarosław Kaczyński -- at his palatial official residence. Seated around a large round table with four or five other people, he spoke emotionally about the horrific Polish losses during its World War II occupation by the Nazis.

Almost six million Poles were exterminated. Only Russia had greater losses among the allies.

His sadness about that unfathomable tragedy seems to motivate his well-known Euroscepticism—his concerns about European integration.

When we left his residence, we went back to the hotel and researched the losses that small but brave nation endured. The reminder of the Warsaw Ghetto was heartbreaking. But just as bad was the uprising of 1944 when the Polish resistance rose against their German occupiers as the Russian Army approached Warsaw. Although Radio Moscow had encouraged the revolt, the Soviet Army sat outside Warsaw for 63 days and didn't lift a finger as 16,000 Polish resistance fighters were slaughtered in the City. The Russians even refused to cooperate with Allied relief flights that wanted to land behind their lines. Another 150,000-200,000 civilians were killed or executed by the Nazis in reprisals. As in Katyn Forest, the Soviets wanted to make Poland easier to subdue after the war by letting the Germans kill off the entire resistance.

Our last day in Warsaw was about two weeks before Christmas and we had about an hour to kill before we had to leave for the airport. It was just before dark on a freezing cold night, but we decided to take a walk anyway. We had been inside all day and it would be a long plane ride.

Within a few minutes, we unexpectedly witnessed an unforgettable and moving sight.

Our hotel, the Bristol, was about a block away from the Royal Castle at the base of the Old Town, an area that had been beautifully and painstakingly restored after its complete destruction during the war. It was a cornucopia of great restaurants, shops, galleries, and beautiful buildings.

At that time of year, the streets and the colorful buildings were sparkling with Christmas lights and decorations.

It was December 13ᵗʰ, but, at that moment, the date was not particularly significant to us. That would change.

As we headed towards the Square in front of the Castle, we noticed a large crowd of people. There were beautiful Christmas lights on the front of the red brick building and the crowd sang Christmas hymns to the music of a pianist. It looked like a Christmas ceremony was about to start. We stopped to watch and listen.

But suddenly, it was pitch black and utterly silent. We wondered if there had been a citywide power outage. All the lights in the Old Town and for as far as we could see were out. The music stopped. It was completely quiet and we were in total darkness.

What happened, we wondered?

After about a minute of stillness, all the people in the crowd began simultaneously lighting the tall white candles they had been holding in their hands. Beautiful music echoed from the loudspeakers in the square. The glimmering candles, the music, and the old buildings were breath taking.

What was going on?

Then a speaker slowly took the podium. Silent at first, he stared out at the noiseless crowd. It was an emotional moment, even before he uttered a word. We knew something unusual, something important, was happening.

What was it?

Although he was speaking in Polish, we quickly understood that it was the anniversary of that awful day, December 13, 1981, when the Polish communist government imposed martial law. For the next eighteen months, the communist military was in charge of all law-enforcement in the country and strictly controlled political and economic life. The reason for this crackdown was the rising threat to the Kremlin of the opposition Solidarity movement, led by the brilliant, fearless, and dynamic Lech Walesa with the assistance of the Kaczyński brothers and other brave patriots. Solidarity had been openly resisting the communist government for almost a year.

The martial law declaration changed life in Poland and anyone who lived through it never forgot that day and what it meant. Several people we met had recounted their recollections—even as children—of that horrible moment when the announcement was made on radio and TV by the Polish General Wojciech Jaruzelski.

135

Suddenly, they had told us, everything was different. Civil liberties were seriously curtailed and a curfew was imposed. Backed by tanks, the communist government outlawed Solidarity, the labor union led by Walesa, that had openly agitated for freedom. Walesa was jailed as were Jarosław and Lech Kaczyński, along with all the anti-government, pro-democracy leaders.

Tanks and soldiers flooded the streets, national borders were sealed, airports closed, and highway access to the main cities restricted. Phone lines were disconnected, mail searched and censored, and classes at schools and universities suspended. By the time martial law was lifted eighteen months later, more than ninety people had been killed and thousands thrown into prison.

Some government crackdown on Solidarity had been expected. Some feared a Russian invasion. As Solidarity defied the communist regime before martial law was declared, the world waited in tension as the Soviet Union (pre-Gorbachev) massed troops on the Polish border. But then General Jaruzelski pre-empted them by his own massive crackdown, using Polish police and troops.

In an article for *The New York* Times on the first anniversary of martial law in Poland, political scientist Arnold Beichman tried to describe the abomination of martial law:

[It is] "...a system that prohibits personal freedom and punishes citizens who insist on such freedom—a system run by a single party, the sole repository of truth, which brooks no dissent from that truth... What else shall we call a government that rules by terror, secret police and the midnight knock on the door; that maintains concentration camps and "psychiatric'" hospitals; that practices racial and religious discrimination against national minorities; that bars free elections and opposition parties..."[20]

But the Solidarity forces never gave up the resistance. By December 1983, martial law was over.

It took a while to dismantle the communist government. But, in December 1990, Lech Walesa was elected President of Poland in the first free elections. He served until 1995, when Lech Kaczyński succeeded him, appointing his brother as Prime Minister.

We had the honor of meeting Lech Walesa in Rome in 2014, at one of the events surrounding the canonization of the two Popes, John XXIII and John Paul II, the first Polish Pope and a relentless fighter of Communism in Poland.

Walesa spoke at a small dinner where I also briefly spoke.

His speech focused on another assault on freedom then underway, this time in Ukraine where Russian troops had invaded, again using proxies— Ukrainians of Russian ethnicity. Walesa emphasized the importance of constant resistance in the streets of Kiev after the Russians annexed Crimea and helped the rebels in Ukraine. His point was that the battle for freedom must be waged through mass demonstrations, constant protest, and thorough vigilance.

Like the Kaczyńskis, he never forgot the misery and repression under martial law.

December 13, 1981, was a horrific day in history. But, eventually, with the strength of the Polish people, the moral intervention of Pope John Paul II, and the moral and economic support of President Ronald Reagan and Prime Minister Margaret Thatcher, the communists could not sustain their control. But the scars remained.

So, the lights in Poland went off for five minutes while the entire country remembered how the light of freedom was extinguished that day twenty-six years earlier. And like then, they came on again and Poland was back on the path to freedom.

55. Poland Goes Toe-To-Toe with Germany...Again

One of the reasons I was so enthusiastic about working for the Kaczyński brothers was how Lech, when he was president of Poland, had faced down German Chancellor Angela Merkel a few years earlier.

Kaczyński was in Berlin for a meeting with the German head of state. And she mouse-trapped him in public. Standing in front of the TV cameras and media, she asked him, without prior notice or consultation: "Mr. President, we have a problem and I wonder if you can help? Poland has almost as many seats in the European Parliament as Germany does, but Germany has more than twice Poland's population. Don't you feel some adjustment would be in order?"

Kaczyński was furious that she had confronted him in public with no notice or preparation. So he said: "I have a good idea Madam Chancellor. Would you like to hear it?"

Merkle nodded and moved closer. "Why don't you give Poland credit for the people we lost in World War II?"

(Six-and-a-half-million Poles died in the war, about a fifth of its pre-war population.)

A hush fell over the German media as Merkel struggled to regain her footing.

56. Another Dark Night in Warsaw

One Sunday night in Warsaw, Eileen and I attended a wonderful Chopin piano concert at the stunning former royal "Palace on the Isle" in Lazienki Park, the largest in the city.

The Palace had been the summer home of King Stanislaus in the eighteenth century.

During the intermission, we mingled with some other people in the audience who recommended that we walk through the park to get to the restaurant where we had reservations for dinner after the concert. The restaurant was apparently just beyond the far end of the beautiful park.

It was just beginning to get dark and, for about ten minutes, we enjoyed walking through the paths that were surrounded by beautiful gardens and shrubs. Lovely antique lanterns lit our route.

Then suddenly the lights went out—all of them. It was completely dark, pitch black and very difficult to see anything at all. There was no moon. There was no light.

We were disoriented and not even sure we were still going in the right direction. We looked around and saw some light to our right. Walking slowly, we headed toward the distant light.

Soon we came to a huge, ornate black metal gate about 20 feet wide and 10–12 feet tall. We walked towards it, but as we approached it, we realized that it was locked. Really locked. It didn't budge when we tried to shake it.

On the other side of the gate was a traffic circle that was the source of the light. Lots of taxis were driving around it. They seemed so close, so we put our arms through the gate and frantically waved, trying to catch the attention of a driver.

That didn't work.

We started thinking of our options. Almost an hour had passed since we had left the concert. We had no idea where we were or of how to get where we were going. The park was obviously closed and we were apparently locked inside. What next?

Clearly, we couldn't climb over the fence. And although there might have been other exits, we had no idea where they were or how to get to them. It could be a long night.

Then we saw a man walking along outside the gate. We called out to him and he stopped and stared in at us through the bars of the gate. We felt like animals in a zoo. Unfortunately, we didn't speak Polish and he didn't speak English. We tried to rattle the gate and he shook his head and pointed to a small structure beside it. From the back, it looked like a guard house.

The Polish good Samaritan signaled that he would be back and walked toward it. In a few minutes, he returned with another young man in uniform. He pointed to us as he spoke to the man, obviously explaining our plight. But the guard immediately began shaking his head "NO." He would not—or perhaps could not—unlock the gate. At that point, the good Samaritan shrugged his shoulders and left.

Now we truly wondered if we would be spending the night in the park—and we weren't too happy about it.

The guard was still at the gate, Suddenly I had an idea. I remembered that I had the hotel number in my cell phone. I called it and got a concierge who spoke English. I quickly explained our predicament. I got the guard to take the cell phone and asked the desk clerk to explain that we were Americans and that we needed to get out of the park. Immediately!

The guard told him that there was no way he could open the enormous gate; it was on a timer.

We were back to square one and the prospect of sleeping in the park was looming large. We weren't happy.

But, as we looked at the building beyond the guard shack, we could see that it was familiar. It was the residence of the Prime Minister, my client, with whom we had had dinner a few nights before.

So I called back the hotel and asked my new friend at the desk to call the residence of the Prime Minister and ask whoever answered to call me right away. Within a few minutes, my phone rang, breaking the silence in the park. He asked me to hold while he found someone who spoke English.

He told us to stay put. (Not that we had a choice.) A few minutes later, he called back and told us to return to the gate. He promised that the guard would tell us how to find an exit from the park that was open and that he would translate on my phone.

We were told to walk to another exit, which was down some rickety stone steps and up another narrow rock staircase. We moved slowly in the dark and finally saw the guard on the other side of a much smaller gate—with street lights visible beyond it.

He let us out and we high fived each other and the guard.

We hailed a taxi for the remaining short distance to the restaurant and immediately ordered a drink to celebrate our freedom. The atmosphere was beautiful; the dining room felt like a large greenhouse with huge tropical trees and other huge plants.

We were just glad to be out of the park, out of the dark and into the light.

57. A Room Full of Irish Talent

For many summers, Eileen and I rented a charming cottage overlooking the sea in the tiny town of Culdaff, Ireland. It's on the Innishowen Peninsula, the northernmost part of the Irish Republic in beautiful County Donegal. The area is breathtakingly gorgeous and not very touristy. In fact, Culdaff has less than 250 people!

We'd stay for two or three weeks and spend our days driving through the dramatic mountain scenery and gasping at the wild shoreline where waves crashed against the rocks and cliffs. We explored the elegant National Trust homes and gardens, searched out restaurants, walked on the wide sandy beaches, and visited with the owner of the house who had become a close friend. We also loved to see columnist and FoxNews contributor Cal Thomas and his beautiful, brilliant, and spirited wife Ray, who had a home right nearby.

It's a heavenly place.

There were a number of very good restaurants nearby and on one Saturday night we went to the neighboring town of Carndonough, known as "Carn," to have dinner at a tiny restaurant called Corncrakes. It was run by two women and one of them looked exactly like photos we'd seen of Eileen's grandmother when she was young. That happens in Ireland. Faces look very familiar.

When we went to Ireland for the first time in September 1977, we visited Eileen's father's family. We drove from Dublin to the family's dairy farm in Leitrim and knocked on the door. An elderly aunt answered and stared at Eileen. "Well, I've seen that face before," she said.

That night, we chatted with one of the restaurant owners and enjoyed a delicious salmon dinner. The place was almost empty with only two tables in use. As we were finishing our dinner, a vaguely familiar looking man with jet black hair came over to our table and introduced himself. He was John Hume, the brilliant and widely admired Irish politician who shared the Nobel Peace Prize in 1996 with David Trimble in recognition of their "efforts to find a peaceful solution to the conflict in Northern Ireland."[21]

Hume is widely recognized as the long-time intellectual architect of the peace process, and, according to *The New York Times*, "is widely credited with being the single most important influence for peace in Northern Ireland… [who] spoke out against violence for thirty years."[22]

We were honored to meet him and his wife and we discussed Irish—and American—politics for about ten minutes. Then he introduced us to the couple at the remaining table who were starting to leave the restaurant: the famous Irish author and playwright, Brian Friel and his wife. Friel was a prolific modern Irish writer and many of his plays were produced in Ireland and New York. Among them were *Philadelphia Here I Come* and *Dancing at Lughnasa*, the winner of a Tony Award and the Drama Critics Award. That play was later made into a film starring Meryl Streep. Friel also wrote about the state of Irish politics.

Both Hume and Friel lived in neighboring Greencastle. We were so thrilled to meet them both and struck by the amazing Irish talent assembled in that tiny restaurant. Both men addressed Irish politics and its shortcomings in their work—each in his own way.

We'll never forget that night.

The Corncrake closed, but over the years, we occasionally ran into John Hume at Kealy's Restaurant in Greencastle. He was unfailingly charming, funny, and bright—a tribute to Ireland.

141

58. Eileen Figures Out A Secret

In January 1996, all of Washington was buzzing about a new best-selling book, *Primary Colors: A Novel of Politics,* that told the inside story of the 1992 Clinton campaign. For nine weeks, the book sat on top of the New York Times best seller list at #1. What captured everyone's imagination was that the author was simply identified as "Anonymous."

Who was it? Was it a man or a woman? Suspicions flew all around as everyone seemed to be looking over their shoulders.

Whoever it was, the author was remarkably familiar with the inner workings of the campaign, accurately describing private conversations and the internal conflicts that roiled the campaign. Its portrayal of how Hillary reacted to the Gennifer Flowers scandal was especially on target.

All the late night talk shows vied with one another to guess who the author was, but none of them got it right.

In the White House, the suspicion was especially thick as people would look around the room at meetings and wonder who was the hidden source. Once Bill himself brought up the subject at one of our strategy meetings, ruminating on who the author might be. After the meeting, I went up to him and, privately, told him that Eileen was convinced Anonymous was Joe Klein, a former journalist with Newsweek and then a consultant to CBS News.

I told Bill that Joe had joined us for lunch at our hotel that day and that Eileen was in the middle of reading the book. During the lunch, she observed the similarity between the words and phrases in the book and Joe's similar speaking style. After he left, she told me that she believed he was Anonymous. Bill thought about it. Shaking his head, he said, "Hmmm….that's possible."

Nobody else had guessed that it was Joe, although subsequently, a Vassar professor used a computer analysis to identify Klein.[23]

59. Bill Weld Teaches Me the Classics

One of my favorite clients was Bill Weld, who I advised in his election as governor of Massachusetts in 1990. After he took office, I met him regularly and continued to advise him on political strategy as he approached his re-election race in 1994. Educated, brilliant, witty, and engaging, Weld's IQ was competitive with Bill Clinton's, Gore's, and Newt's.

At one meeting, I urged him to stand firm against the Massachusetts Legislature's perennial efforts to raise taxes. Weld vetoed their bill and helped roll back the state's reputation as "tax-a-chusetts."

"Stand like Horatio at the gate," I advised, drawing on my Columbia education. But Weld, a Harvard man, gently corrected me, passing me a note that read: "Entre nous, it's Horatius at the gate or Horatio at the bridge."

As it turns out, I was, indeed, wrong. Horatio stood not at the gate but at the bridge (as Weld had corrected me) where, according to an ancient Roman legend, he stopped the invading Etruscans from crossing the Tiber River.

Horatius, on the other hand, stood at the Gate. In the words of poet Thomas Babington McCaulay:
"Then out spake brave Horatius,
The Captain of the Gate:
To every man upon this earth
Death cometh soon or late.
And how can man die better
Than facing fearful odds,
For the ashes of his fathers,
And the temples of his gods."[24]

— **Thomas Babington Macaulay, Lays of Ancient Rome**

One doesn't usually get corrected by the average American politician for misuse of metaphors from classical literature. But there is nothing about Bill Weld that is average.

60. The Candidate for Governor of Mississippi Who Was Accused of Sex with Three Gay, Black, Transvestite Prostitutes—and Won!

It was September 1983 and right there on television were three black, gay men dressed as women claiming to have had sex—for money—with the

Democratic nominee for governor, my client, Mississippi Attorney General Bill Allain. He had won the Democratic primary and runoff and was coasting to an easy November victory. There was still no real Republican Party in Mississippi. But the GOP had dug up these "men" to attack my candidate. Remember, this was 40 years before the LBGTQ movement made transvestites more acceptable. And it was in Mississippi. "Oh shit! There goes the election," we all thought.

The candidate's three accusers were holed up in a motel room in Louisiana, under guard. The Republicans claimed that they had passed lie detector tests.

Allain's vote share fell 30 points when the allegation surfaced. I rushed to his headquarters in Jackson.

But how to fight back?

Well, start with what we know. Back then, Mississippians didn't much like gays. But they liked transvestites even less. And they won't elect a governor who paid them money for sex.

But we had to go deeper and understand their attitudes toward homosexuality in general.

To get the answers, I conducted a survey. But I didn't dare do it in Mississippi. If word got out that we were testing responses, it would have made things far worse. So I polled Arkansas voters figuring they were like their next door neighbors in Mississippi. That way, it wouldn't get back to the press that we were polling.

The results gave us a path back. Apparently, voters in 1983 did not believe there was such a thing as bi-sexuality. You were either gay or straight. One or the other. So we persuaded Allain's former wife to go on television and she say that she knew, for a fact, that these charges could not possibly be true "against my former husband." After all the Allains had children together.

Then, having denied the allegation, we proceeded to the second step: Shoot the alligator. We traced the money behind the Republican ads and found out that the utility companies had put it up in retaliation for Attorney General Allain's regulatory zeal against them. That sapped all credibility from the attack and I thought we were home free.

Against all odds, we won the election. Allain served four scandal-free years as governor. But my troubles were only beginning.

The week after the election, I met with my Arkansas client, Governor Bill Clinton. I proudly recounted the Allain saga, telling him about my poll in Arkansas.

"That was your poll? Your poll?" the governor shrieked at me. "Your poll?" he continued. "Everybody has been asking me about it!" He enumerated their comments. Sex?, hookers?, transvestites? Everyone is wondering if it's me!"

61. Gov. Edwin Edwards (Louisiana) and the "Silver Zipper"

Bill Clinton wasn't the only one. Edwin Edwards, the governor of next-door Louisiana had amassed quite a reputation for womanizing.

On the day I arrived in Baton Rouge at the Governor's Mansion for a breakfast poll briefing, I faced a bit of a quandary: How to explain my poll results to the governor? The situation grew more complex when we convened our meeting and I saw that Governor Edwards' wife was in attendance.

Before the meeting got under way, I asked the Governor for a private word. We went into the next room, out of earshot, and I told the governor "we asked voters in our poll 'what words or phrases' would you use to describe Governor Edwards to a friend." I explained that it was an open ended question, so the respondents supplied their own answers rather than just saying yes or no.

"Well," I explained, "16% of the respondents used the phrase 'silver zipper.'"

I waited for Edwards' reaction. But he wasn't upset or embarrassed and even seemed intrigued. "You break them results down by all kinds of demographics, right, boy?" he drawled.

"Gender, race, age, income and so forth?"

"Yes, sir."

The governor drew closer. "Can you tell me how many women between, say 16 and 25, called me that?"

The rest of the poll briefing was just as interesting.

The night before, in New Orleans, Eileen and I went carousing around the Latin Quarter listening to really good jazz. The next morning I was a bit hung over and mentioned it to the governor.

He laughed and I asked him a question Eileen had posed to me in New Orleans: "What are you going to do with the beautiful decorative gas lighting now that it was illegal?"

"Illegal? What you mean, boy?"

"The new energy conservation law makes decorative gas lighting illegal," I replied.

The governor was totally puzzled. "What law is that?" He turned to his counsel and other members of his cabinet arrayed around the table and pressed "any of you heard of that law?"

Nobody had. "What law you talkin' 'bout boy?"

The federal energy conservation statute just signed by President Carter."

A look of vast relief flooded the governor's face. "Oh," he explained to his cabinet "he's just talking about a federal law. Only a federal law. Don't worry about it. Just a federal law." He turned again to me and asked, "What's that got to do with us down here in Louisiana?"

62. My Brief Stint as an Upholsterer

Sometimes even the most talented of secretaries gets it wrong. When I called the office of former Mississippi Lt. Governor Evelyn Gandy in December in the early '80s to introduce myself, her secretary got my name and occupation wrong.

Miss Gandy, as she was universally known, had served as State Treasurer, Insurance Commissioner, and Lt Governor—elected positions all—over the course of a public career that stretched back to 1960. A venerable figure in Mississippi politics, she was a sweet old lady who ran for office without a trace of modern feminism.

Her secretary, perhaps accustomed to handling her personal errands, buzzed her and said that her "upholsterer" was on the phone. (Pollster had morphed into upholsterer.) Miss Gandy picked up and proceeded to ask about her slip covers when I interrupted her and corrected her assistant's mistake, thereby ending my new career in home decorating.

But Miss Gandy was an elegant Southern lady to the core. Before she let me get off the phone, she spent quite a while asking about my plans for Christmas and closed by wishing me "and my entire family the very best for a happy and health holiday season and a wonderful and prosperous new year."

63. What on Earth Has Astronaut Jack Schmitt Ever Done?

A problem in modern politics: How do you run against an astronaut who walked on the moon? Answer: gently.

In 1982, I worked for Jeff Bingaman, the Attorney General of New Mexico, when he ran against Harrison "Jack" Schmitt for the Senate. Schmitt, elected in 1976, was a hero in New Mexico.

His distinction was to have been the twelfth and second youngest person to set foot on the Moon. And he became the second-to-last human to step off the Moon as he boarded the Lunar Module right before commander Eugene Cernan.

Unfortunately, his record in the Senate was less distinguished. A typical go-along, get-along Senator, his only claim to fame was to serve on the Science, Technology, and Space Subcommittee.

But you don't run negative ads against a hero. So we came up with the slogan: "What on Earth has Jack Schmitt ever done?"

We had to proceed carefully, so we ran a totally new kind of negative ad: One that I would recommend to all candidates—an impartial negative.

Here's how it went:

"Should we drill for oil in our national parks and wilderness areas? Jack Schmitt says we should because we need the oil. Jeff Bingaman says no matter how much we may need the oil, we need to protect our heritage more."

"Two good men are running for the Senate, but they disagree on drilling in our parks. On election day, vote for the one that agrees with you."

Back in those days, we didn't have to put the candidate on saying he agreed with the message. So the ad was, almost anonymous. Its very impartiality lent it force.

In the polling after we ran the commercial, voters ascribed all sorts of evil motivations to Schmitt's position—he was paid off by the oil industry, he didn't care about the environment, etc.—but we hadn't said that. The voters said it to themselves. Our ad was just a catalyst.

It bounced us into the lead and we won 54-46. Jeff went on to serve five terms in the Senate.

In negative advertising, the ferocity of the ad and its credibility are inversely related. A mild, impartial ad like this one has great credibility while one dripping with blood will be received more skeptically.

64. How Clinton Survived the Monica Scandal

On Friday, January 17, 1997, my pager went off summoning me to call the White House. I had been expecting the page for a few hours, ever since I read the newspaper accounts of President Clinton's affair with a 22-year-old intern, Monica Lewinsky. Although I was not officially working for Clinton since August 1996, we were in frequent touch and he regularly asked for advice.

When I called back, he came straight to the point, although in his usual legally circumspect and abstruse style. "Ever since I got here—to the White House I mean—I've had to shut my body down sexually. But I screwed up with this girl. I didn't do what they say I did, but I think I may have done so much that I cannot prove my innocence."

Wow. Try understanding that! I had no idea what he meant. And, in a situation like that, you don't ask. (About six months later, on the set of the Hannity Show, I realized that he was distinguishing oral sex from intercourse, but I didn't realize it back then.)

But even though I did not know the facts, I sure knew how to deflect a scandal. It's like how you handle a forest fire. You try to get ahead of it and head it off.

"Maybe you can tell the truth," I suggested. "Remember, Nixon was impeached because of the coverup, not because of the scandal."

"You think so?" he prodded hopefully.

"Yes, I do," I said, my enthusiasm returning. "The American people have a vast capacity for forgiveness. If you play it straight it might work."

"Might work" sounded a little weak to me as it was coming out of my mouth, so I added "Do you want me to take a poll and find out?"

Polling. Our standard solution to getting out of trouble. Our paddle to get out of shit's creek. Clinton gratefully accepted my offer.

The next day, I called back with the results. "They will forgive the adultery, but not the lying."

"So what do I do?" he asked.

"Don't lie. Avoid the question. Plead privacy, and let them down gently. Let them understand gradually that the charges are true. No hard denials. No aggressive rebuttals."

I used a baseball metaphor comparing my advice to that given to rookie shortstops in baseball. "Soft hands."

I knew Clinton had the subtlety to pull it off.

But Hillary didn't. The next thing I knew, Bill was saying emphatically, with Hillary at his side, "I did not have sexual relations with that women…Miss Lewinsky…"

Just what I had advised against.

My theory is that after he told Hillary, she insisted on a firm, solid denial. As First Lady, her status stemmed from the validity of their marriage. If it was a fraud, or an "arrangement," then so was she.

My bet is that she told Bill: "You go out there and deny it in no uncertain terms and I'll defend you." The implication would have been clear—If you don't, I'm gone. After all, the Clinton M.O. had always been that 'it's his word against hers.' But that was before DNA.

Then, Bill managed to hang on, win an acquittal in the Senate, and stay in office.

How did he hang on? Throughout the scandal, his job approval hovered around 65%. His personal favorability tanked down to the low 40s. They did not like or approve of the man, but, as president, Americans felt he was doing a good job.

How did we do it? How did we keep his approval ratings up? Our strategy was based on the idea that "public values defeat private scandal."

We divided Americans into three age groups. Older people had a firm moral compass and Bill Clinton repeatedly violated it. No forgiveness there.

Baby Boomers didn't care one way or the other. Their own morality was so relative and relaxed that they didn't really give a damn what the president did in his private life.

It was young parents who were the swing group. They did not have the moral compass of the elderly or the live-and-let-live attitude of their

149

Boomer parents. Rather, they had a very practical attitude toward morality. Promiscuity wasn't wrong, it was just stupid—with the risk of AIDS and the complications of infidelity. Drug use wasn't immoral, it was just insanely dangerous.

Above all, they cared about raising good children. The president's morals didn't matter as much as those of their own children.

If Bill Clinton embraced policies to help them be good parents, they would support him even if they were turned off by his personal conduct.

Hence, our "values" agenda. Clinton took the lead in fighting teen drug abuse and smoking, extending family and medical leave, reforming welfare, widening day care, raising school standards, fighting teen gangs, promoting curfews and school uniforms, screening school bus drivers for sexual misconduct, maintaining drug free zones around schools, and so forth. Everything to help them become good parents raising good kids.

It didn't matter if the president was moral, just as long as he helped you to raise good kids.

That's how he survived.

And, then, as the scandal wore on, Clinton's Republican accusers overplayed their hand. As testimony about the president's conduct became more explicit, young parents turned away in disgust. In a focus group, a 30-something Mom said, "I don't want my ten-year-old daughter to learn about oral sex on the evening news."

So the scandal backfired on the Republicans since it seemed that they were the ones keeping it in public view. Voters didn't so much blame Clinton for his misconduct as the Republicans for making an issue of it and putting it in their faces on the nightly news.

Clinton succeeded in staying in office and the GOP did not even gain seats in the 1998 midterm elections.

65. Bill Uses the Baseball Strike to Divert Attention from His Affairs

In early March 1995, Pulitzer Prize winning author David Maraniss published the first credible biography of Bill Clinton entitled *First In His Class*. As advance word of what was in it leaked out, the book rattled

Clintons' world as few others have done. He had a copy of the manuscript and read parts to me.

In it, he cited Bill's Chief of Staff Betsey Wright as saying that Bill used Arkansas State Troopers to solicit women. This charge, verified by Betsey—who was Hillary's point person in keeping tabs on Bill—triggered chaos in the Clinton household. No-one was speaking to Bill.

Because I had a good relationship with Betsey, Bill asked me to call her and try to get a retraction of what she had told Maraniss. She was traveling, but I tracked her down hours later and worked out a lukewarm non-denial denial.

But the denial wouldn't be adequate to stop the bleeding after the book came out.

So Bill and I developed a strategy to distract the media from the Maraniss book. On January 26, 1995, six weeks before the book's official publication date, as review copies were circulating and leaking to the press, the president decided to intervene in the major league baseball strike that had been raging since August 11, 1994. He ordered that both players and owners resume bargaining. He demanded that they settle the strike by February 7th.

Of course, he had no power to stop the strike (he was unwilling to invoke the Taft-Hartley Law that would give him that power), so his deadline came and went with no resolution. It did, however, serve to force a moderate concession from the owners.

But Clinton's intervention led to a settlement of the strike. On March 27th the president got the National Labor Relations Board to file an unfair labor practices complaint against the baseball owners and US District Court Judge and future Supreme Court Justice Sonia Sotomayor supported it. The next day, the baseball players voted to return to work.

Clinton's headline grabbing intervention served its political purpose as well. Maraniss' book did not get the publicity the president had feared, although the rift in his family did not heal.

66. Clinton's Fear of What the Arkansas State Police Might Know about Him

The fallout from the Maraniss book, *First In His Class,* continued to roil the Clinton household for months. Not only did it incite Hillary to turn on her husband with a vengeance after the book told of Bill's use of state troopers to solicit women, but also it led Hillary to break off her relationship with me in a rage because I had spilled the beans on her desire to build a swimming pool at the Governor's Mansion in Little Rock.

But there was a third explosion, also caused by the book. Shortly after it was published, I got a fierce, angry call from President Clinton as I was having dinner with Eileen and her brother Paul and his wife Jean. We were dining in a New Jersey restaurant near their Florham Park home when my pager went off. It was the president. And he was fuming—excoriating me because I had told Maraniss stories of my work with the president, including our collaboration in the campaign to defeat Congressman Jim Guy Tucker in the 1978 election for the Senate.

As noted, Tucker was the other brilliant, young, handsome, charming, charismatic figure in Arkansas politics. Clinton saw him as a mortal threat. He didn't care who won the Senate seat, he was wanted Tucker to lose to get him out of the way.

So, as I've described, the future governor and I sat together throughout the campaign writing the negative ads against Tucker that led to his defeat. I spent relatively little time helping Clinton get elected governor. That was pretty much a given. The hard part was beating Jim Guy Tucker, which we did.

Back then, negative ads were rare. But when Eileen found that Tucker's attendance record in Congress was terrible—he had taken time off from Congress to run for Senate—we ran ads attacking him.

Pryor won. But Tucker recovered from his defeat and ran for governor in 1982 against...Bill Clinton. The Tucker v Clinton rematch was vicious with negatives flying both ways, but again, Clinton won.

Afterwards, Tucker and Clinton kissed and made up. In fact, when Clinton ran for president in 1992, he handed the governorship to his Lieutenant Governor, Jim Guy Tucker.

(Eventually, Tucker was himself implicated and convicted as part of the Whitewater scandal that engulfed the Clintons.)

In the interview with Maraniss, I recounted how Bill and I had worked together in 1978, to craft the ads, the issues, and the speeches that elected Pryor to the Senate and defeated Tucker. Maraniss published the story and now Clinton was livid.

"What the hell are you mad about?" I asked trying to recover after he had unleashed a tirade cursing at me for having told Maraniss about the 1978 election. "You ran against Tucker for governor in 1982," I recounted, "and thrashed him soundly with negative ads. Why do you think he'd hold the '78 campaign against you?"

"He didn't know about '78 until you talked to Maraniss!!!" Clinton shouted back into the phone.

"What do you care? He's governor and you're president. How can he hurt you now?"

Shocked that I would be naive enough to ask such a dumb question, Clinton raised his pitch to a sarcastic height and said, as if he were correcting the most stupid comment he had ever heard. "He controls the State Police!" With that, he hung up the phone.

Poor Bill Clinton. He had been accused in an article in the American Spectator, a conservative magazine, of using state troopers to solicit women for him. He denied it vehemently, but now, if Tucker became angry with him, there was every prospect that he would get the troopers, who now worked for him, to confirm the stories.

Bill Clinton lived much of his political career in a state of high anxiety and fear. As he tried to juggle his complex personal life, his public image, his electoral majority, and his various affairs, he was a man haunted by threats both real and conjured.

67. What It's Like to Be on Hillary's Shit List

The same Maraniss book that got Bill in trouble with Hillary landed me in the dog house too. When I gave Maraniss an interview for his book, I told him about the time Hillary wanted to install a swimming pool at the Arkansas Governor's Mansion for Chelsea to use.

At first she wanted the government to pay for it. I cringed when she told me that. Then she decided that she was going to pay for it by raising the money from friends and supporters (no tax money). I told her that "would be even worse. The media would insist on disclosure of who provided the funds and crucify you with what they would say were conflicts of interest."

"Why can't we give our daughter a swimming pool like other kids have?" she insisted.

"You can, if you pay for it," I replied.

Then she launched into her familiar monologue about all the sacrifices she and Bill had made to take low paying jobs while serving the people of Arkansas.

I stood my ground. "Next time you fly out, look down and count the number of swimming pools. That's how many votes you'll get."

When Maraniss' book came out, Hillary's doors slammed shut.

She stopped talking to me. Not a word. Wouldn't return my phone calls, cancelled our meetings. She just disappeared. Dropped off the ends of the Earth.

I got the message.

When Hillary is mad at someone, they no longer exist. They are out of her universe, out of her thinking. That goes for Bill, too.

Once you cross her, she never lets you back in...until she needs you.

Bill, even as president, would dwell in Hillary Purgatory for long periods of time before she would acknowledge his existence again.

During the Hillary blackout, Bill asked me to send her weekly memos of advice—which I did. She often followed my counsel but never, ever spoke to me.

Finally, I asked Bill about the cold shoulder. "I've worked with you two long enough," I said, "to know that one doesn't last long around you if Hillary doesn't want it." I asked, "Can you do anything to get me back in her good graces?"

"She reads your memos and follows your advice."

Bill held up his hands defensively and, with a rueful smile said, "Don't ask me. I am definitely not the person to help you get back with her. Not right now." After the Maraniss book, she stopped speaking to him, too.

She was particularly outraged, he told me, over Maraniss' charge, seemingly confirmed by his Chief of Staff Betsey Wright, that he used the State Police to solicit women for sex.

Bill was in the dog house. "Even Chelsea's mad at me," he confided.

March, April, May, and no contact from Hillary.

In the meantime, my relationship with Hillary sprouted a new connection. My mother had died (in 1993) and my father, in a romantic story worthy of publication, re-married his high school and college prom date, Blanche Funke, with whom he had broken up sixty years earlier to marry my mother. As it happened, Blanche's closest friend was Florence Thomases, the mother of Susan Thomases, one of Hillary's closest friends.

I went to see Susan to say hello and renew my relationship with her. (I joked that we were practically related now but I couldn't figure out how.)

In the middle of the meeting, Susan interrupted to take a call, obviously by pre-arrangement. It was Hillary. When Susan mentioned who she was with, she handed me the phone. Hillary and I chatted about everything except why we had been estranged. That was strictly "don't ask...don't tell."

Our relationship quickly warmed up again, like old times. In fact, she had reached out to me because she wanted my help in getting her close friend, Ann Lewis, former head of Planned Parenthood and Barney Frank's sister, an appointment as White House Communications Director. The job fell within my unofficial orbit, so she—the wife of the president—may have felt she had to come to me to get it done. I wondered about that. Couldn't she just talk to Bill?

I had a problem with Hillary's request. I liked Ann, but I enjoyed a very close relationship with Don Baer, who held the job. So I suggested that maybe Ann should be the Communications Director of the campaign, not the White House. That satisfied Hillary, fine.

The battles within the White House for power and turf continued as Leon Panetta, George Stephanopoulos, and Harold Ickes—the top three on the president's staff worked to get rid of me.

The president and the vice president were my allies and, oddly, now Hillary, my term in purgatory over, joined their ranks.

I only had the president, the vice president, and the first lady on my side against the united opposition of the liberal White House staff. Sounds good, but in the day-to-day functioning of the White House, it often meant being out-gunned and cut off from information.

Hillary, for her part, felt cut off, too. The "boys," as she put it, had little use for her either. She formed a "girls club" of many of her talented long-time friends and allies. She even invited me to a meeting once so I could get to know Ann Lewis better.

We met in the White House solarium, where the "club" seemed to meet weekly. I was the only man in the room until Bill walked in to keep an appointment to see me half an hour after my girls club meeting. I moved to leave to begin my talk with the president, but Hillary and Bill both insisted that I stay and finish the girls club meeting.

Hillary and I formed a closer alliance after my sentence in purgatory.

68. The First Candidate to Reject PAC Money: Warren Rudman in 1980

Senator Bernie Sanders made national headlines in the 2016 campaign by refusing to take campaign contributions from corporate PACs—the special interest money that has so corrupted our system.

But former Senator Warren Rudman (R-NH) beat him to it. He was the first one, when he ran for Senate against incumbent John Durkin in New Hampshire in 1980, to refuse PAC funds.

Eileen had sensitized me to the increasing power of political action committees that had just been authorized by the campaign finance law passed in the aftermath of Watergate. The Rudman campaign was the first time anyone attacked his opponent for taking their contributions.

Rudman, one of my first Republican clients, was running against incumbent Democratic Senator John Durkin. It was hard to find issues to use against him. But we found that Durkin was taking lots of money from PACs.

New Hampshire voters were especially sensitive to out-of-state PAC campaign money, worried that liberal campaign contributions from neighboring Massachusetts could swamp the politics of their conservative state.

The issue caught on and Rudman used it to topple Durkin and move into the Senate.

Media guru Tony Schwartz worked with my Columbia buddy Frank Baraff and me on the campaign.

Tony was an expert in using the candidate's or announcer's intonation in an ad to trigger memories among the audience. For example, he did ads for Bufferin and coached the announcer to say "come to bufferin" using the same loving, maternal inflection he would use to say "come to Momma." While the words remained "come to bufferin," the reading triggered the more emotional reaction.

Tony used his genius in the ad for Warren Rudman. The script read: "When the special interests offer me campaign contributions," Rudman said "I tell them to take their money someplace else."

But, the way Tony coached Warren to read the script—with a derisive sneer—it sounded like he was telling the PACs to "shove it." (And he was.)

We thought that the Rudman win would kindle a national uprising against PAC money, but nothing much happened. California governor Jerry Brown tried to use the issue to defeat Bill Clinton in the Democratic primaries of 1992, but failed. It wasn't until Bernie attacked PAC money almost forty years after Rudman that it attracted the national attention it deserves.

69. How I Avoided Being Lynched in Boston

I am and always have been a maniacal Yankee fan. 1978 was a great year to root for them. My team came from way behind in August and September and forced the Red Sox into a one game playoff since New York and Boston were tied at season's end.

Famously a Yankee with no reputation for power won the game with a home run. He is still known in Boston as "Bucky (Effing) Dent."

The best Red Sox player was future Hall of Famer Carl Yastrzemski (aka Yaz). Carl not only played for the Sox, but he was a good friend of my client Ed King who was running for Massachusetts governor that year against the incumbent Mike Dukakis in the Democratic Primary.

On the night of our primary victory, Yaz was sitting on the bed in our campaign hotel room while downstairs the victory party raged. He had kicked off his shoes and was sitting in his socks.

Those days I used to wear zippered up boots with big heels, a particular fashion for those of us who are 5-6 in height. I was standing just in front of Yaz when someone brushed past me and I rocked backwards. To stop from falling, I had to bring my foot down hard one quarter inch from Yaz' little toe.

Had I broken it, had this New Yorker broken Yaz' toe, knocking him out of baseball for the month, and thus costing Boston the pennant, I never would have gotten out of town alive.

Luck.

157

70. Vote.com

Eileen and I realized the potential of the Internet very, very early on. In 1999, we wrote a book entitled *Vote.com: How Big-Money Lobbyists are Losing Influence, and the Internet is Giving Power to the People.*

In the book, we predicted:

- That the Internet would allow mass fundraising from small donors.
- That online digital communications would replace TV advertising.
- That democratic revolutions abroad would spring from the communications permitted over the Internet.
- That the speed of political campaigns would increase exponentially as the back-and-forth dialogue took place online.
- That money would no longer determine who won elections since the Internet is free and candidates and their supporters can freely spread their message.
- That voter interest and turnout would increase dramatically as the Internet increased focus on politics.
- That the direct democracy that was possible over the Internet would increasingly take power from legislative bodies and give it back to the people through referenda and ballot initiatives.

With the intellectual input and generous financial backing of our friends and fellow believers Steve Bozeman and Dick Scruggs, we set up an early internet company called **vote.com** in late December 1999. We purchased the name **vote.com** for $250,000 from a person who didn't use the internet or faxes. We had to fed ex the documents to him. We don't know if it's true, but we were told that the term vote originally stood for "vegetarians of the earth."

But now, it stood for a venture in direct democracy.

At that time, according to Pew Research, only 41% of American adults used the internet.[25] The early users—like those today—were passionate about their ideas and eager to be heard. We gave them a platform to express their opinions and try to influence decisions on government, corporations, the media, and wherever else decisions that affected their lives were made.

Each day we would post a new vote on a controversial topic. This was way before online opinion questions came to be ubiquitous. It was non-partisan and neutral. We did not advocate a point of view.

For example, if we were doing it now, we might have a question like:
SHOULD THE MIGRANT CARAVANS BE ADMITTED TO THE U.S.?

The voter could choose yes or no. Once a user voted, we would then send an e-mail, with their e-mail address, to the White House, to their congressman and senators, and Homeland Security, telling them how they voted on the issue. Then the online voters would often get a response sent to their e-mail.

It was an online lobbying opportunity that allowed voters to have easy access to their elected officials.

We worked hard to build up our base of users. They trickled in slowly until 2000 when Governor Howard Dean of Vermont proposed gay civil unions. Within a few days, 325,000 supporters jammed our website to vote "yes." The outpouring of support then triggered an equal and opposite response when another group of 300,000 opponents voted "no." With a database that now reached to almost 700,000 users, we were a going concern.

Each day we would e-mail our list, telling them what the vote was for that day. Tens of thousands more joined in. Eventually, our list of active users exceeded one million.

After a while, we expanded into additional daily votes—adding issues on the environment, entertainment, education, technology, law, sports, movies, and gay issues. People loved to be heard.

We fiercely guarded the privacy of our users. The only data we collected were e-mail addresses and zip codes. (So that we could identify the correct member of Congress to send e-mails.) We never sold our data—or even rented it.

Soon we decided to expand to other countries. We set up **vote.com** websites in Argentina, Japan, France, and the U.K. In Japan, Hitachi joined us and invested in **vote.com.jp**. One big issue that led to lots of users in the U.K. was whether fox hunting should be prohibited. There was a lot of controversy about that!

So, we had plenty of interest and users, but no ability to monetize the site.

Our defect was the timing of our launch. We started right in the middle of the internet bubble. Internet advertising was in its infancy and, even though we had massive amounts of traffic, we could not monetize it.

Another problem was that Congress worked hard to block our e-mails. They really didn't want to hear from people. Neither did the White House. Eventually, we stopped sending individual e-mails and sent a petition on the vote with the list of e-voters and zip codes.

We had some bureaucratic issues in foreign countries, too. For example, after we had been operating **vote.com.fr** in France for over a year, the internet regulator notified us that we could not use the word "vote" in a domain name.

So much for the French site! They claimed that word belonged to the state.

After several years, we reluctantly closed the site.

But our belief in direct democracy didn't go with it.

We are especially grateful for the people we worked with us on developing the **vote.com** site—Dick Scruggs, Steve and Laurie Bozeman, Boris Kyselstein, Frank Baraff, David Steinberg, Paul McGann, Joel Morton, Mary McGann, Casey Bozeman, and Vivek Chandra, Tom Gallagher, and Elizabeth Jacoby. And in Argentina the late Miguel Sal and the late Jorge Estrada, Goucher in the U.K., Giles Delafon in France, Kumi Yokoe and Hitachi in Japan, and to all of the other wonderful people who worked on the site once we got started.

Don't stop believing!

71. Censored by China

In 1999, I wrote a book, *Vote.com,* that predicted the Internet would take over politics. I forecast that money would be raised online for political campaigns from hundreds of thousands of donors, only a click away. That was unheard of at the time, when only 36% of Americans had access to the Internet. Now, with just about 80% online, it has taken over a large segment of politics.

Another prophecy was that online ads would increasingly replace television commercials, vastly increasing the amount of information available to the average voter and raising to lightning speed, literally, its dissemination. We're not there yet, but the amount of political ads and information on the Internet is overwhelming.

On the international front, I speculated that the Internet would spur democracy and produce an "online Tiananmen Square" in China and other authoritarian regimes when the governments could not control the flow of information.

Writing that was a mistake. Later that year, I was invited by the United Bank of Switzerland (UBS) to speak at a conference in Hong Kong on the growing political role of the Internet. We arranged to ship 500 copies of the book *Vote.com* to the event to distribute to the attendees.

But they never got there. We frantically checked with the shipping service, the hotel, the post office, everybody. We were able to confirm that the books had arrived in China by DHS. But there were no books to be had.

It turned out that the Chinese censors had read my book and didn't much like it. They probably noticed the reference to Tiananmen Square. They seized the book and wouldn't allow it to be used at our forum.

Thankfully, the Chinese people are getting the message anyway and are figuring out how to use the Internet to oppose the regime – or at least to go around it and get the truth on their own.

72. Is Hillary Anti-Semitic?

Hillary was always a bit awkward about my Jewishness. At the beginning, she seemed to be overly conscious of my ethnicity.

I would usually begin my regular visits with the Clintons by joining them for breakfast at the Arkansas Governor's mansion. Eliza Jane Ashley, their skilled and wonderful cook—who always had a big smile—would offer me a formidable breakfast. Inmates from the State Prison worked in the Mansion and served the meals.

But, Hillary wondered, would I eat bacon or pork? I made clear that—even though I was Jewish—I loved bacon, perhaps too much so. From then on, at every breakfast, my plate was piled high with heaps of tasty bacon.

When Hillary would occasionally invite me to stay for dinner, she would frequently get a worried expression on her face and say, "Oh, Dick, I'm sorry, I just realized we are having ham. Is that OK with you?" It seemed like they were always eating ham or pork or bacon. And Hillary would ask me he same question every time. It started to seem weird. I even kidded her about it.

At first, I thought that these examples of Southern awkwardness around Jews were cute. But then I remembered that she wasn't southern; she was from Illinois. Well, I thought, rural suburban Chicago, so maybe she too hadn't been around many Jews.

But, in 1984, I saw the ugly side of her uneasiness with Jews. I sat at the Mansion's breakfast table in the evening negotiating my fee for consulting in the 1984 governor's race. I was determined to get a raise and suggested a high figure.

Neither Clinton liked to pay consultants, so it was always an unpleasant conversation when we discussed fees. I believe it had to do with their view that Bill was paid so little as Governor and they were "sacrificing" to serve in public office. Hillary believed that she had given up a lucrative career in Washington, D.C.. But the truth is that right before she decided to move to Arkansas, she had failed the D.C. Bar Exam and was not likely to be offered a job in any law firm.

And in all of their whining about their "sacrifices," they never mentioned the free rent in the luxurious and elegantly furnished Governor's Mansion, along with free utilities, household and babysitting help, insurance, cars, telephones, and an entertainment budget. So it was not much of a sacrifice after all.

But that night, both Clintons recoiled in horror at the idea of paying a larger fee. I stuck to my guns and said that was a deal breaker.

Them was fighting words for the Clintons. As noted, I had helped Bill get elected in 1978 and, in 1979—when he was governor—he fired me and tried to seek another term without me in 1980. He lost. Hired me back in time for the 1982 election. And won. So my implying that I might leave were words that carried a lot of baggage with them.

Bill got agitated and, red in the face, said, "Don't Mau Mau me." (The Mau Maus were a guerrilla group in Kenya that violently agitated for independence, pressuring the colonial British regime at every turn.)

Hillary was even angrier and blurted out: "Money. That's all you people care about is money."

Wow. That was a low blow.

162

What did she mean? Stiffening, I said acidly, "I assume that by 'you people' you mean political consultants?" But I believed that she had meant Jews.

We resolved the fee issue, but I felt like I was visiting another planet. While I became a Catholic in 1997, I grew up ethnically Jewish and still identify with my heritage.. If a census taker asks, I would list my religion as Catholic and my ethnicity as Jewish.

My brush with Hillary's Jewish stereotypes may have been the first time—but by no means the last time—that my warm relationship with Hillary Clinton cooled a bit.

73. Shadow Boxing with the Next President of Argentina

We were shooting an ad, but we were really shooting blanks. My candidate for president of Argentina, Fernando de la Rua, was reading the script as if in a trance. No expression. No feeling. Really, he was just mumbling it. Zero energy. Zero charisma.

De la Rua, the Mayor of Buenos Aires, had a deserved reputation for being boring. His stable, honest, unexciting, competent rule stood in sharp contrast to the flamboyance and corruption of Argentina's president Carlos Menem.

Handsome, witty, and dashing, Menem was always seen squiring beautiful women around town in his Mercedes. But his source of wealth was troubling: He stole the money. Not just thousands or hundreds of thousands, but tens of millions (if not hundreds). Voters had become sick and tired of his shenanigans and having a boring president began to look good to them.

So we decided to do an ad where he would be staring out the window of his office as Mayor, looking out on the beautiful Plaza de Mayo, one of the most famous in the city. It faced the Pink House, the Argentine equivalent of the White House (where Evita was filmed on the balcony).

As de la Rua looked out, and pigeons flew below, he was supposed to say, "*Boring*? People say I am *boring*? Is it *boring* not to be corrupt? *Boring* not to steal the people's money? Am I *boring* because I don't have a Mercedes and respect my family? Boring?..."

But de la Rua was just going through the lines, reading the script as if it were the least interesting thing he could say.

His reading was, well, boring.

"Could we speak privately for a moment?" I asked. His aides showed us both into a small room adjoining the Mayor's office and we closed the door behind us.

As soon as the doors shut, I shocked the 63-year-old Mayor by pretending to box with him. On my toes, Mohammed Ali style, I circled him, throwing imaginary punches and returning to my crouch. "Come on, come on, box with me." I taunted him. "Put up your dukes." "Come on. Show me what you got."

Faced with the spectacle of me circling him and pretending to box, de la Rua had no option but to get in the mood and join the fray. For several minutes, we boxed, circled, danced, feinted—everything except actually punching. We had a ball.

When we finished, de la Rua emerged from our room, red-faced and a bit out of breath, but with his adrenalin and energy levels up. Way up. He turned toward the camera and delivered the performance of his life!

The ad—Aburrido (boring)—became famous and they still talk about it in Argentine political lore. De la Rua won and took office in 2000.

For his part, Menem was convicted of his crimes after he left office and sentenced to years of house arrest. But he served his time living with his mistress of the moment, Miss Universe! Home arrest at its best!

74. How Shakira Toppled Argentina

The Colombian singing sensation—Shakira—was a latter-day Helen of Troy. Her face did not launch a thousand ships as Christopher Marlowe said Helen's had (in his sixteenth century play Dr. Faustus), but it was enough to ultimately lead to the resignation of Argentina's president—my client Fernando de la Rua.

I began to work for de la Rua in 1998. Then the Mayor of Buenos Aires, he was challenging the Peronists for the presidency the next year. A wonderfully decent and honest man, with a solid record as Mayor, he had one fault: He couldn't make up his mind. He would mull over a decision, never coming to a conclusion. He would never resolve his quandary, but would move on to stewing over something else. He never decided anything. It was maddening.

164

I was about to quit his campaign when he pleaded with me: "Oh Dick, please stay. Don't leave. Antonio will soon be here. Then things will be better." Antonio de la Rua, his son, was a 23-year-old newly minted attorney who looked like a stereotypical Latin rock star: tall, black hair, and soulful brown eyes. Every woman wanted to pack him up and take him home.

But he was also brilliant. A born politician. Decisive where his father was not. Sure footed when the old man was tentative. I loved working with him. Antonio and I made a great team.

The candidate trusted Antonio completely. No longer would I have to wait weeks before he approved an ad. "Is it OK with Antonio?" he'd ask. If it was, he'd shoot the ad, often reading it for the first time on the teleprompter as he was delivering it.

Under Antonio, the trains ran on time. And Fernando won. He was president. Antonio was at his side in the Pink House (their White House) and functioned as de facto president even as he had been the de facto candidate. Everything was running smoothly.

Then came Shakira.

Six months into Fernando's term, Antonio visited the Argentine Andes for a vacation and stayed at the fabulous Llao Llao Resort (pronounced shao shao) in Bariloche. There, he relaxed and soaked in the incredible mountain and lake vistas. But then he saw the lovely Shakira, who was vacationing there, too.

From that moment on, he could think of nothing else but Shakira. Shakira. Shakira. And, suddenly, poor Fernando was on his own. Antonio went back to the Bahamas with Shakira, commuting back and forth to Miami and rarely even visited Buenos Aires. In fairness to him, he had his own life to lead.

It was no good advising the president, his indecision had returned and he watched—tossed and tormented—as the International Monetary Fund (IMF) closed in, demanding steep spending cuts in return for a bailout. The cuts alienated the provincial governments that had enjoyed Peronist largesse and things began to fall apart.

I met with President de la Rua a few days before he resigned in the middle of his term. Haggard, aging fast, and shopworn, he put his arm around me and said, "Oh Dick, Dick, Dick you have come, but maybe you are too late."

I was and he had to resign.

An honest man who did his best to rule a sometimes ungovernable country.

Antonio went on to have great success. He helped to launch Shakira in the American market and nurtured her talent to full bloom.

The romance, too, blossomed for eleven years, ending in 2010.

We had the pleasure of meeting Antonio and Shakira in the Bahamas. She is lovely, talented, bright, and unassuming. Although a very petite woman, she has a large and warm presence and a hearty laugh. It's easy to understand why Antonio was so enchanted.

But Argentina, it's OK to weep.

75. Living Like a King in Buenos Aires

Eileen and I both enjoyed working for de la Rua. She advised him on how to campaign through the internet, then coming increasingly into use in Argentina. We quickly grew to love Buenos Aires and the friends we met in the campaign.

We still go back whenever we can.

For over two years before the election—and a year after it—we spent at least one week a month in Argentina's magnificent capital city. And for several months before the November 1999 election, we lived there full time.

We loved it! And we lived like kings!

We had an apartment in the prime area of Buenos Aries, one of the most beautiful cities in the world. It was on the twelfth floor, with two sides of floor-to-ceiling glass spanning about seventy-five feet in either direction. One side faced the downtown skyline, while the other looked down on the beautiful formal gardens of the U.S. Ambassador's residence. Beyond that was the gorgeous Rosadell (Rose) garden and park.

Even though my work for de la Rua was not really a secret, I kept a low key profile. But our friend Miguel Sal joked that when our apartment lights were on, the whole city could see us. It looked, he said, "like the presidential suite at Caesar's Palace."

We had a lot of fun in B.A.. Our colleagues there became good friends, many lasting to this day, twenty years later. It was one of my first foreign campaigns after I left Clinton. I didn't know they wouldn't all be this nice.

Argentine hours and schedules took some getting used to. We would be invited to a campaign meeting starting at 8 p.m. and capped by a dinner that didn't start until 10. You had to eat before… and take a pre-dinner nap.

We loved the wonderful restaurants in B.A. and went to a different one almost every night.

But, on one trip to Buenos Aires, we decided to throw a dinner party at "our" apartment. We invited the candidate's son and campaign manager Antonio de la Rua, who, as I've explained, ran his father's career until Shakira stole him away. Antonio is a striking man with a great sense of humor. Eileen's sister, Maureen Maxwell, and her husband Joe who were visiting us, enjoying a vacation in beautiful Buenos Aires, also joined us.

The guest list also included Jorge Estrada and his wife Nancy. Jorge, a native of Colombia living in Argentina, had first summoned me there to help elect de la Rua. We became lasting, close friends until his tragic death in 2015. Also there was Carlos Souto and Miguel Sal, who were working on the campaign's message and media. Miguel later moved to Italy where he became a world famous branding expert and architect. We stayed close until his death. (As noted, this book is dedicated to the memory of Jorge Estrada and Miguel Sal.)

We still feel the loss of those dear, dear friends.

We all had a great time, laughing and joking and drinking great Argentine wine. We ate slightly earlier than the customary ten to eleven o'clock dinner hour, but the last guest left at about two o'clock and we did our best to celebrate this wonderful city and these close, new, delightful friends.

Eileen served a delicious dinner of mussels, clams, and other seafood. We had enjoyed shopping for the fish in the local markets and the experience of entertaining in a new, luxurious apartment provided its own intoxication.

But, then it was time for all to go home (except Maureen and Joe who were staying with us). We all helped cleanup and left the garbage bags near the back door service entrance. We would figure out where to take them in the morning.

We were leaving for New York the next day and, in the morning, I tried to take the garbage bags out the back door. But the service door was locked and we didn't have a key. We had never tried to open it. We checked with the doorman, but he had no key either.

So I tried to take the garbage down in the passenger elevator to the horror of the doorman who would not let me carry it through the apartment building lobby.

We didn't know what to do. We clearly couldn't leave the garbage in the apartment. The discarded muscle and clam shells would stink by the time we returned in three weeks.

We were stuck.

But then I remembered Carlos Souto. He had been at the party and he lived on fifth floor of the same building. I meekly went to his apartment and rang the bell. Could he take care of the garbage? He smiled graciously and said he would.

When you invite someone to dinner, they always ask if they can do anything. But we never thought to ask if Carlos would arrange for the garbage removal. But he did and a disaster was averted.

When I was honored this year to be inducted into the inaugural class of The Washington Academy Hall of Fame for Latin American Political Consultants, Carlos turned out to be the master of ceremonies. We enjoyed a good laugh about the seafood garbage.

76. Why Did We Get A Free Trip To Greece? We Have No Idea

I answered my phone and it was a high school classmate who I had not seen nor spoken to since, well, high school. We hadn't been particularly close back then and it was quite a surprise that he called.

"Would you be willing to come to Greece, all expenses paid?" he asked. "My client wants to meet with you. He will pay your first class airfare for you and your wife, five days in a luxury hotel, and all your meals. Everything."

Hard offer to refuse.

"Who is your client?" I asked. He named someone I didn't know who he said was a Greek businessman, active in media.

"Why does he want me to come?" I pushed.

"We want to show you Greece. Have you ever been?"

"No and I'd love to. But do you want me to speak to a group or write something?"

168

"No, just come to Athens.."

"Is he thinking of running for office?"

"We'll talk in Athens. Can you come next week"

We could and we left for Athens.

We stepped off the plane into a fantasy world. Limos whisked us to the Grand Brittania hotel, one of the most luxurious in Athens. We met the Greek business man, a suave, elegantly dressed, cultured man we'll call Ari.

Ari wouldn't let us pay for anything. Nothing.

We had dinner the first night in the hotel's fabulous roof top restaurant looking directly at the Acropolis, brilliantly lit against the night sky.

There is no building in the world as beautiful as the Parthenon. I'm never sure why it moves me, but I can't get enough of it. Its lines are so perfect, its architecture so clean. It was hard to pay attention to the excellent Greek food—seafood right out of the ocean with only olive oil on it that tasted like candy—because we kept staring at the Parthenon.

The next day, they took us around Athens, answering questions with the aplomb of a tour guide. We had lunch at their favorite waterfront restaurant and chose our fish from a basket of a variety of freshly caught fish. We climbed up to the top of the Acropolis and spent hours exploring the Parthenon and the other buildings.

They quizzed us on US politics. I reminisced about the Clinton Administration, which I had left some years earlier. We talked about George W. Bush, then president, the war on terror, the war in Iraq, Afghanistan. Every major current events topic.

The one thing we did not talk about was why the hell they had invited us.

We kept waiting for the hook, the question, the offer behind their incredible hospitality.

We met Ari's wife and family. My high school buddy and another couple joined us for a weekend jaunt—all expenses paid (you know the drill) to the enchanting island of Mykonos, where we stayed in a white hotel perched on a cliff overlooking the incredibly blue Med and sky.

I was so moved, I wrote a short poem:

The white town goes down to the water's edge
And its coiled streets slither into the sea.
And I stand upon the ledge
And the view comes up to capture me.

The pigeons warble and the wild birds sing
Desperate for the night to end at last
Eager to know what the day will bring
On the isle where the future is just like the past.

They loved the poem and reveled in our appreciation of the beautiful island.

We had a wonderful lunch and fantastic dinner looking out at the windmills in the water,. We talked about everything except the elephant in the street that was growing larger by the day.

Why were we here?

Ari described his business. Media, security, electronics. Nothing that had to do with politics. Nothing that might involve me.

Still no request.

Then we went on a short boat trip to Delos, a small island off Mykonos, that is famous in Greek mythology for being the birthplace of Zeus's twins, Apollo and Artemis. Abandoned about 68 BC, it was an important sanctuary for Apollo worshipers for hundreds of years. Incredible ruins of homes and sculptures dating back as far as 300 BC. Rows of intact stone lions lined the main road to the ruins. We saw mosaic tile floors with seemingly modern three dimensional designs that were thousands of years old.

Then we returned to Athens and they took us to the airport. We kissed good-bye and we thanked them for an incredible time..

We boarded our plane and returned home. We never heard from them again.

We still don't know why we were invited. They never answered our e-mails. We still haven't a clue.

But we are grateful for the wonderful introduction to Greece.

77. The Hungarian Fortune Teller

Eileen and I were proud to work for Victor Orban's campaign for Prime Minister of Hungary. Orban was the legendary student leader who fearlessly stood up to the Communists and went on to govern the country.

170

Perhaps because my grandparents on my mother's side were Hungarian and my Mom was fluent in that very difficult language, I felt that I was on a personal mission.

Eileen and I loved our time in Budapest and explored the quaint streets, wonderful restaurants, museums, churches waterfront, and shops. The people were friendly and curious about the U.S.

And Orban was such an extraordinary candidate. For his entire adult life, he had been a hero in Eastern Europe. In 1989, at the age of twenty-six, he delivered an impassioned and courageous anti-Communist speech to hundreds of thousands of people at Hero's Square, the imposing plaza in the center of the City that commemorated those who had died for the cause of Hungarian freedom.

Orban was speaking as a student representative at the historic and long-delayed funeral for Imre Nagy, the Hungarian Prime Minister who led the uprising against the Soviets in 1956. Nagy was brutally executed and thrown in an unmarked prison grave by the Communists. The ceremony celebrated his reburial with his fellow Hungarian freedom fighters.

As the last speaker of the day, Orban, had followed other well-known dissidents who spoke loftily, but carefully, about the need for democracy.

Then came Orban. "Ruszkik haza!"—"Russians go home!"—he shouted, taunting the thousands of Soviet troops, demanding that they leave Hungary.

It was a dramatic moment. Apparently people in the Square expected him to be shot down or arrested. Amazingly, he was allowed to finish. He had proven his point: You could defy evil—and survive!

(Eileen and I got a full dose of the evil of communist rule when we visited the House of Terror Museum in Budapest, housed in the very building used first by the Gestapo and then by the Hungarian Communist Secret Police. The circular building was constructed around an interior courtyard that had a huge, monstrous, Soviet T-34 tank sitting there, reminding everyone of who had been the boss back then!)

When the Communist government fell several months later, Orban founded a new political party, Fidesz, and was elected to Parliament in Hungary's first democratic elections in 1990. Fidesz was a centrist, anti-Communist, pro-family, nationalist, pro-market economy party that had attracted young people and toppled the status quo.

Orban's charisma and ideas had drawn first-time voters flocking to the polls. He advocated popular programs for his constituency: loans for first homes, technical training, and part-time work for mothers. At thirty-five, he was elected Prime Minister. But, four years later, Fidesz, narrowly lost the next election in a surprising defeat by the Socialist MSP Party, the newly contrived name for the former Communist Party.

As Orban battled to overcome the post-communist party, he hired me to consult on his campaign. He was brilliant, charismatic, handsome, sophisticated, and Oxford educated. He surrounded himself with the best and the brightest staff and consultants in Hungary.

But his local Hungarian pollster was not as fluent or forthcoming. When we met, he would mumble "three ahead" or "two behind" in the day's tracking poll. He never analyzed why we were up or down or gave any demographic breakdowns. I was climbing the walls. How could I consult without polling data beyond the simple head-to-head?

One day, Eileen and I were meeting with him when his cell phone rang and he began excitedly speaking Hungarian. His voice rose and it was clear that he was tremendously aroused by what he had heard. "Had he just gotten good numbers?" we wondered.

When he hung up, he turned to the ubiquitous translator, "He just got a very important call with good news," the translator told us. "A witch that he knows…"

Eileen interrupted. "A witch?"

The translator struggled for a better way to explain: "Well, it was a fortune teller. And she told him that we are going to win this time. Definitely. And last time, she knew that we would lose."

Great, we thought. So much for the science of survey research...

We went back to the hotel, barely able to stop laughing.

Now, as Prime Minister, Orban has defied the European Union by keeping immigrants and refugees from Muslim countries out of Hungary. With a population of only nine million—and a low birth rate—he has legitimate fears that his small country might be taken over by foreigners, changing its culture drastically.

The EU is totally committed to open borders and has threatened to sanction Hungary for straying from its dictates. But, instead of submitting,

Victor has doubled down on his program, leading Poland, Slovenia, Denmark, Sweden, Italy—and even Britain—to follow his lead.

78. How Clinton Meddled in the Russian Election and Saved Boris Yeltsin

Mexico was not the only new democracy I worked in. Through a strange twist of events, I also found myself working to re-elect Boris Yeltsin as president of Russia in 1996.

The saga began a few days after Bill Clinton was elected president, when the infamous Roger Stone called me with a message for the new president from Roger's client, former president Richard Nixon. Roger, who had aided the disgraced former chief executive in his political recovery said Nixon wanted to speak to Clinton. Could I arrange it?

I called the president-elect to relay the message and he asked, "Should I speak to him?"

"Sure," I replied. "You can." I meant that, as a Democrat, he could speak to Nixon where Republicans might fear to, lest the disgraced president's taint rub off on them.

So the call happened.

Nixon's message was simple: Don't lose Russia. Nixon was presciently worried that the new Gorbachev policy of glasnost (openness) and perestroika (restructuring the economic system) wouldn't last and that the old Communist hardliners would make another bid for power.

Nixon worried that the new Russian leader Mikhail Gorbachev, was at best transitory and, at worst, a ploy to lull America to sleep. He cautioned against relaxing our guard in the cold war.

Nixon's frame of reference was 1952 when he used the question "who lost China?" to undermine Truman and elect the Eisenhower/Nixon ticket. Everyone was shocked at the ease with which Mao Zedong had taken over China for the communists and, Nixon warned, it would be worse should Russia return to Marxism now.

Clinton took the advice to heart. For him, henceforth, the key to domestic politics was to carry California (then a swing state) and, in foreign policy, not to "lose" Russia.

So it was a worried president who called me in October 1995 after his summit meeting with Russian president Boris Yeltsin at the FDR homestead in Hyde Park, New York.

Apparently, it had been a good meeting. (He said "it was the first time Yeltsin was sober when I met with him.")

But Clinton was worried, as Nixon warned, that he would lose Russia. Yeltsin had to run for re-election eight months later in June 1996. And the embattled Russian leader was facing Gennady Zyuganov, the Communist candidate who wanted to bring back the days of Leonid Brezhnev if not those of Joseph Stalin. He essentially wanted to win at the ballot box what the communists had failed to get by their unsuccessful coup d'etat in 1991.

"Yeltsin's job approval is 17% and he still thinks he can win," Clinton marveled. "You're at 40 and you think you can win," I parried. Clinton chuckled grimly.

Turning serious, the president said, "We've got to get him elected."

I proposed that he ask Yeltsin to hire my former business partner Dick Dresner to do his polling. Dick had agreed that he would show me the data each week and I could bring it to the president. That way, Clinton could advise Boris on what to do. When it came to campaigning and politics, Clinton was Yeltsin's guru. Having lived under a dictatorship, the Russian president was a distinct amateur when it came to elections and he looked up to Clinton.

So Boris hired Dresner.

After my weekly strategy meetings with President Clinton, I would stay behind, as instructed, to discuss foreign affairs.

President Clinton drew a clear line delineating the role he wanted me to play in domestic and foreign issues. On the former, I could get into anything I wanted. On foreign policy he said, "You can give me advice on anything you want to, but only in private, never in front of any third person." He was doubtless worried that word would get around that polling was influencing his foreign policy, which clearly it was. I obeyed his instructions strictly and when my consulting team and I finished our weekly meetings with the president, vice president, and the staff, I always stayed behind, alone, to discuss foreign issues with the president one-on-one.

I polled constantly on public attitudes toward each aspect of our foreign policy, but kept it strictly between the president and me.

During the Russia elections, Clinton would eagerly await the results of Dresner's polls. Then, he would wait impatiently until it was daytime in Moscow to call the Russian leader directly on the "hot line" to discuss the findings and recommend changes in his campaign. (The "hot line" was a phone connection originally installed to connect the two leaders instantly and directly to avoid a nuclear war.)

Yeltsin had not been campaigning much and was way behind Zyuganov in the polls. He really did not know how to run for president. Nobody had done it in Russia for at least seventy-nine years, if then.

At Bill's urging, Boris set out on a vigorous campaign swing throughout his vast country, highlighting his local achievements at each stop. The American president worked over the hot line on persuading Yeltsin to run the television ads we and Dresner had created. Soon, Yeltsin began closing the gap with Zyuganov.

Campaigning in the places and in the way Clinton suggested, Yeltsin's numbers improved and he ultimately defeated the Communist by 35-32 in the first round and 54-46 in the runoff.

The then Deputy National Security Advisor Sandy Berger got wind of my work with Clinton on electing Yeltsin. "Are you showing the president Dresner's polls for Yeltsin?" he asked me one day. I told him that I was. "Well, don't. He'll talk about Dresner's figures one day and it will come out," Sandy warned.

I asked the president about it and he said, "Keep giving me the numbers, but tell Sandy you've stopped."

In light of this history, it's interesting and amusing to read now about the charge that Russia meddled in the 2016 U.S. election campaign. In 1996, we not only meddled, we ran Yeltsin's campaign!

That wasn't the first time the U.S. worked to influence foreign elections. It is important to put our efforts in perspective. In the big stick era of Theodore Roosevelt, we used our military force to oust governments we did not like. Particularly in Latin America, we "reinterpreted" the Monroe Doctrine to allow the U.S. military to intervene to stave off foreign colonization in the Western Hemisphere. When a banana republic looked likely to default on its debts necessitating an invasion by some European power to collect them, Roosevelt would send in the Marines, seize the customs house, and collect enough revenue to repay the creditors.

Under Eisenhower, Kennedy, Johnson, and Nixon, we stopped invading and used the CIA to foment revolutions—in countries like Guatemala, Chile, and Congo—to oust governments we did not like. In democratic systems, we subsidized anti-Communist parties, particularly in Italy and France, to elect the parties we wanted.

Clinton was just using political advice to achieve what the Marines used to do—get the foreign governments we wanted elected.

79. Russia's Short-Lived Democracy

During the summer of 2016, Eileen and I travelled to Moscow with our niece Norah. I had been invited by the Russian dissidents to address the "Other Russia" conference where the opposition to Vladimir Putin tried to organize a political party.

The effort, led by chess champion Garry Kasparov, was timed to coincide with the meeting, in St. Petersburg, of the G-8 summit conference. Since Russia had just been admitted to the G-8, the conference leaders hoped Putin would be reluctant to use police to harass and arrest them during the summit.

They were wrong.

It was quite a conference. The speaker scheduled before me was unavailable to address the gathering since he had been waylaid by thugs outside his hotel and beaten up. He was in the hospital.

When I arrived, the building was surrounded by SWAT teams with police dogs. As I entered the hall, I saw four participants being arrested by the cops and carried out by their arms and legs. It took four days to locate them. Hundreds more were "detained."

Seeing the mayhem, I retreated to my hotel, concerned about Eileen and Norah. It was not the time to give a rousing speech for freedom in Moscow.

Later that week, I met with a friend, a fellow American political consultant, who worked for the International Republican Institute (IRI), an NGO funded by the Republican Party to promote democracy abroad (the Democrats have one of their own). We had worked on U.S. campaigns together and he was deeply concerned by the end of democracy in Russia.

He warned me that our conversation would be monitored by government agents. We decided to meet in the hotel lobby—in plain sight—but not to speak. We each brought our laptops and silently wrote messages to one another. As soon as he finished writing a message, he would physically pass his laptop to me. I would read the note and quickly erase it. Then I would write out a reply and pass the laptop back to him.

I had been involved in the democracy movement in Russia before. In the late '90s, a neophyte Russian political consulting firm was formed called "Machiavelli Associates." They invited me to travel to Moscow for their grand launching. They translated my 1998 book, *The New Prince: Machiavelli Updated for the 21st Century,* into Russian. They launched the book—and their firm—at a high profile media event in Moscow at which I spoke.

I returned several times to Moscow to help them elect a slate of pro-democracy candidates to the Russian Duma. I would spend two days during each visit meeting with their candidates, one at a time, and coaching them on their campaigns. I would write their ads and campaign literature during our meetings.

I remember, in particular, one woman who was a heart doctor running for a seat in the Duma. There were 500,000 people in her district. My slogan for her was: "She used to listen to one beating heart. Now she listens to half a million."

I worked for eleven candidates, all of whom won.

The excitement of democracy was palpable. Eileen and I marveled as we watched kids playing stickball off the Kremlin walls in perfect freedom. I went to Red Square at night and stood next to a Russian soldier who was on guard. I saw a rainbow over the painted domes of St. Basil's and motioned to the guard to look at it. We both marveled in silence.

Freedom was visible right there on the sidewalk. Cafes buzzed. One restaurant we went to was filled with Soviet kitch (posters from the Khrushchev and Brezhnev eras).

But those days are long gone. A decade long flirtation with freedom has come to a close. Putin shut the door.

I had a tip off that this might happen. I asked, in my polling, which "would you rather have, economic security or political freedom?" Security won out overwhelmingly. (Nobody realized that you can't have one without the other.)

I also asked, "If you saw someone with great wealth, would you be more likely to think that he got rich by hard work and good investments or that he got his money by corruption and criminal activity?" By 2:1, the Russian people embraced the cynical view.

Russia is a society dominated by envy. Nobody wants to see anyone else succeed. Someone told me, that in Russian TV quiz shows the audience always roots for the contestant to fail.

I learned a funny story. Ivan died when his house caught on fire. In heaven, St. Peter granted him one wish. He replied: "My neighbor Sergi? I want his house to burn down, too."

The U.S. has jealousy. Russia has envy. Psychologist Nancy Friday wrote about the distinction in her book, *Jealousy. They're different:* Envy is a negative emotion while jealousy is positive. The jealous person wants what you have. The envious one just doesn't want you to have it.[26]

An envious society cannot long sustain a democracy. The rage of the classes that feel left out will destroy it from within.

That's beginning to happen in Russia.

80. Netanyahu Tells Me: "It's 1938"

I've always been a huge supporter of Israel. I was born to Jewish parents who raised me to be culturally Jewish. The UN resolution approving the partition of the British Trans-Jordan territory and creating Israel was passed on November 29, 1947, one day after my birth, so my parents celebrated the birth of Israel at the same time that they celebrated mine.

They traveled to Israel often, invested in and promoted Israel bonds, and discussed the politics of Israel with me constantly. My mother wrote a biography of Gold Meir, *Shalom Golda.*

(In her interview with Golda as she was writing her book, my Mom noted that the Israeli Prime Minister lit up a cigarette. A lifelong smoker, she asked Golda about it. "I've lost the opportunity to die young," the 73-year-old Prime Minister replied.)

I have avidly followed the difficult path Israel has had to tread and I've done whatever I could to help it. I was deeply moved and honored when I was invited to participate in an event honoring "seventy at seventy"—seventy non-Israelis who have been particularly supportive of the Jewish State, then celebrating its seventieth year. The fact that I turned seventy myself the same year Israel did made it even more poignant.

When Benjamin Netanyahu (Bibi) asked to meet with me, I was blown away. He wasn't the Prime Minister of Israel yet, but I could see that he was heading there and I felt that he would be perfect for the job.

I looked forward to talking with him. Eileen and I arrived at the Carlyle Hotel in New York for our meeting and introduced ourselves to Bibi and his wife, Sara.

There was no small talk. Bibi got right down to business.

Without missing a beat, he leaned closer to us and said, "It's 1938."

That was all he needed to say. Our historical memory did the rest. 1938 was, of course, the year that Hitler decided to implement the "final solution to the Jewish problem," (i.e., the extermination of the race).

There had been evident and overt anti-Semitism in Hitler's Germany until then, but it was in 1938 that the Nazis closed in and began to exterminate six million Jews.

Bibi elaborated. "If Iran gets nuclear weapons, all it would take is one hit on a major Israeli city to kill almost as many as the Nazis did. 1938 was the last real chance to avert the holocaust and now we have the last real chance to stop Iran from getting the bomb."

I have never forgotten Bibi's prophecy. It rang in my ears ever since. It is still indeed, 1938.

Thank the Lord that we now have a president who takes the danger seriously and is determined to stop Iran from getting the means to destroy Israel.

81. Adventures in French

I did poorly in French class in high school, so my parents hired a tutor to help me through the complexities of the language. My problem was that I didn't see the point in learning a foreign language. "Everybody speaks English," I had heard my parents say as they travelled extensively abroad. So why bother learning French?

But then my tutor showed me a story that could only be said in French about a boy out on a date with a girl. His mother came along, too. The French story read: "La mere etait la. Et bien la." The literal translation was: "The mother was there. Very well there." But, as the literal translation shows, there is really no way to say it in English. Only in French. I was fascinated to learn of a concept that could only be expressed in a foreign language. An idea that could only be really said in French! The thought—that some things could only be said in the original language—captured my imagination and motivated me to learn the language.

So, I worked hard at mastering it. I thought I had. I did well in college French. But a few experiences unnerved me and broke my self-confidence.

In 1981, I was hired to advise Gaullist Party leader and Mayor of Paris Jacques Chirac in his national election. I quickly refreshed my French and hired another tutor to get up to speed.

The highlight of my involvement in the Chirac campaign came when I was able to help design a poster attacking our leftist opponents featuring—French fashion—a naked woman (back only) with a logo that read "Sous le socialisme, je n'ai plus rien." (Under socialism, I have nothing left.)

From then on, I was a French talking machine. Eileen and I have travelled to France more than forty times on vacation and I delighted in showing off my language skills. (In retrospect, I realize that everyone who appreciated my French was getting a tip from me—whether in a hotel or a restaurant—or was just being polite. That may explain their enthusiasm for my skills.)

My first dose of reality came when Canal Plus, the main French TV station wanted to interview me. I asked that the interview be in French. All seemed to go well until they asked for a second interview a few weeks later and, this time, they said delicately, "we would prefer it to be entirely in English."

So much for my getting up to speed.

In 1996, I met with a man who spoke Arabic, so we needed a translator. When my friend switched to French, midway in the interview, I did, too. Our translator who had been reliably translating my words into Arabic, didn't miss a beat. Quickly realizing how deficient my French was, he continued translating, this time converting my bad French into good French!

Damn.

As Mark Twain once wrote in *The Innocents Abroad*: "In Paris they just simply opened their eyes and stared when we spoke to them in French! We never did succeed in making those idiots understand their own language."[27]

82. The Bankers Strike in Paris

Things can get pretty ridiculous pretty fast in Paris. Someone is always on strike and the main streets are often lined with hundreds of participants in a "manifestation." (demonstration) One morning, we emerged from our hotel on the Left Bank to see a horde of well-dressed men in suits marching up the Boulevard Ste. Germain holding up picket signs.

We looked closely. They were bankers on strike. Because banks are tightly regulated by the government, the bankers were protesting changes in regulations and demanding higher pay. Where in the U.S. or Britain, an angry letter from their lawyer or, at worst, a petition might be filed, in France it called for a strike.

Nor was the strike gentlemanly. Taking their cue from generations of street protests in Paris—some of which toppled governments—the bankers chanted slogans, sang the Marseilles, and protested "tyranny" and "abuse of human rights." A real demonstration.

Amused, I called President Clinton that evening as he wrestled with the Republican government shutdown—their version of a strike. I thought a bulletin from Paris that the French had similar difficulties might cheer him up. It did. He marveled at the idea of bankers marching under their banners, shirts buttoned down and ties neatly clasped to their shirts. We shared a good laugh.

83. Conning the Pollster in Spain

One of the great things about working abroad is that you get new perspectives that help you in American politics. In Spain, I came to realize how dramatically political correctness biases polling. We see this now in Trump's showing in the polls, constantly understating his actual vote share. I first saw it in Spain in the election of 2008.

I've long been fascinated by politics in Spain, especially after my daughter Gabrielle spent a year of college there taking courses—in Spanish—and working for a political consulting firm. I wondered if she would follow me into political consulting, but her considerable talents took her elsewhere.

My candidate, in 2008, was Mariano Rajoy, who became the Prime Minister of Spain a few years later. In the 2008 election, which he lost, he was the center-right candidate against the incumbent Socialist Party. The polling showed him far behind. Even as we caught up, through a good and vigorous campaign, the final polls still showed us seven points back.

"It will be a tie election. We might win or lose, but it will be close," my Spanish colleague told me.

"A seven point deficit isn't close," I replied.

"It's not seven points," he maintained. "In Spain, the conservative always polls seven points worse than he does in the actual voting."

I asked why and he explained that the residue of bitterness from the Spanish Civil War of the 1930s and the regime of the dictator Franco (who ruled until his death in 1975) was so intense that conservatives dared not tell pollsters that they were going to support the center-right candidate. It was political correctness carried to its extreme.

You could vote for the conservative, but it was so against the prevailing fashion that you didn't dare admit it in public.

The Socialist Prime Minister Jose Luis Zapatero knew how deeply the Franco era polarized Spain even thirty-three years after his death. Indeed, shortly before the election, he tried to revive the bitter memory of Franco's atrocities by renaming hundreds of streets, parks, boulevards, and avenues, stripping away their Franco-era names and replacing them with those of anti-Franco figures.

As the returns trickled in, it became clear that the race was, indeed, close and that the right was running seven points ahead of what the polling predicted. By the end of the night, Rajoy lost by less than a point.

As I scrutinized the U.S. polls in the 2016 election, all of which predicted a Hillary win, I thought of the Spanish example. When the media makes a vote for the left candidate fashionable and support of the right candidate, well, gauche, it is often able to program how people will tell pollsters they will vote.

Does that kind of media coverage, making a vote for Trump unfashionable, influence millions of impressionable voters? Is that why Hillary chose to run, not just against Trump, but against his voters too, calling them "deplorable?' Who, after all, wants to do cast a vote that would be seen by society as "deplorable?"

Of course, the Spanish election also demonstrated the great flaw in basing one's electoral strategy on image perceptions and fashion. The voters may refuse to tell polling firms that they will vote for the center-right candidate, but, when in the polling booth with a secret ballot, they often vote for him anyway.

Hillary can tell you that.

84. Coastal Elites Have No Idea What is Happening in America

If you don't understand how little attention the mainstream media pays to what is happening in the 90% of America outside of New York, Washington, and Los Angeles, listen to this story:

As I got deeper into Clinton's 1995–1996 campaign for re-election, it was clear to me that the media would never report our message correctly. Their world view was so completely dominated by the party divisions in Washington that they couldn't understand, much less cover, anything else.

Before I went to work for Clinton in the White House in 1995, he governed as a straight Democrat. It was Democrats vs. Republicans—a zero sum game. His gain was the GOP's loss. By definition.

But I urged a different approach: triangulation.

But the media would never cover that idea. If Clinton gave a speech that was 90% triangulation and 10% a traditional partisan attack on cuts to the school lunch program, the headlines inevitably ran: Clinton Raps GOP on School Lunch Cuts. The media wanted a fight.

So Clinton and I despaired of getting our view heard by the media.

In Arkansas, Clinton and I had made extensive use of advertising to drive home our message while he was governor. Of course, we'd run ads—like everybody else did—around election day, but we would also run ads in between to drive home a point about Clinton's program or to try to force the Legislature to pass a bill. At the time, this was unique in the country.

So I took a page from what we did in Arkansas to get Clinton's program out: Advertise our message, paying for it to reach the public unfiltered or diluted by the media.

To advertise in mid–1995 for an election in November 1996 was unheard of. "People will say I'm desperate," the president complained.

"You are," I countered. He was down 17 points in the polls against Bob Dole. His job approval hovered below 40%, and, of course, he had lost both houses of Congress in 1994.

183

"But if people think I'm desperate, they won't give me money to run these ads," he replied.

"OK," I conceded, "we'll keep it a secret."

"A secret?" the president asked. "How much media will you buy?

"About $40 million over five months," I told him.

"And you're gonna keep that secret?"

"Yes sir."

"How?"

"We won't advertise in New York, Washington, or Los Angeles," I explained. "The media will never realize that we are advertising. Everybody in the media lives in one of those three cities and never know what's happening in the rest of the country."

I got my approval and the president's poll numbers rose constantly. Six months later, he led Dole by twelve points and his job approval was over 60%.

Over the next six months, the president was locked in a constant battle with the Republicans in Congress. We refused to approve their cuts and they wouldn't pass a budget without them.

For twenty-seven days, spanning two periods in December 1995 and January 1996, most of the government had to close its doors.

There had been nothing comparable in American history. The federal government had never shut down for more than one day at a time and, in each case, it reopened almost immediately.

Each day, the president and the GOP leaders—Bob Dole and Newt Gingrich—went out before the media and pushed their messages and President Clinton would hold his own media events pushing his view.

The polling showed that ours was getting through, but the Republicans' was not. Eventually, Gingrich and Dole surrendered.

But the secret reason we won was advertising. Every day for six months, we had been pounding the message that there was a third way—not free spending like the liberals wanted and not draconian cuts like the conservatives preached. We said we could balance the budget along with keeping our "values." That meant overall cuts—some quite drastic—but not in Social Security, Medicare, Medicaid, education, or the environment. The third way—triangulation.

Nothing could better illustrate the extent to which "flyover country" doesn't matter to political society in New York, Washington, or Los Angeles. Here we were running ads that directly related to the national crisis that had the entire country focused on Washington. Two government shutdowns, one lasting six days and the second lasting twenty-one had been going on and the media never covered our ads about them.

And there was not a single front page story or TV mention of the ads. (Allison Mitchell, of the New York Times, caught on, but her story was buried on page 24 and nobody noticed!)

In fact, it was not until the election was over and my memoir about it (*Behind the Oval Office*) was published in January 1997 that anybody realized what we had done. Neither the Republicans nor Dole nor the media understood why our numbers kept moving up. We only advertised in 90% of the country, so our secret was safe from the coastal elites!

The media not only didn't jam our message, it didn't even notice our ads. The *New York Times* ran an article that the president and I chortled about. It said that the average voter in Ohio saw things our way. They told the *Times* reporter that they supported Clinton's program using almost the exact same wording as our ads. But nobody caught on. We didn't advertise in NY, DC, or LA. Just in the rest of America.

85. Lost in Translation

I speak pretty good English, enough French, and a smattering of Spanish. But in Japanese, I'm out of luck.

Translating the words back and forth is easy. It's the meaning and context that really trip you up. I found out the hard way after I was hired to advise a candidate in Japan who was running for Prime Minister.

Despite the language barrier, I charged ahead anyway, writing television ads in my best U.S. advertising style.

The campaign had decided to zero in on corruption as our best issue. A banking scandal had been roiling Japan (before it came to our shores.) So I addressed it head on and wrote out an ad on my laptop:

"Bad loans have almost bankrupted Japan. Companies closed. Billions lost. Some people have lost their jobs, their homes. But what about the bankers who made the bad loans? They are still there! Still making loans. Can we trust their judgement? Haven't we learned our lesson? The

Democratic Party says 'why take the chance?' Replace the bankers who let us down. Restore our banks and our economy."

A good thirty second spot.

My Japanese clients loved it. They appreciated the hard hitting style and promised to film the ad and run it heavily.

When I returned two weeks later (a 14-hour flight each way every two weeks. So much fun!) I asked them to show me the finished ad.

But when they played it, the ad went on and on. I had written a thirty second ad, but suddenly it had more than doubled in length.

"What does it say?" I asked.

"Just what you wrote," my client's communications director answered.

"But it seems much longer. Can you give me a translation?"

"A literal one, word for word?"

Here's what my ad had morphed into:

"Some of the loans our banks have recently made may have turned out to have been a bit ill-advised. The Democratic Party thinks that some of the bankers who made these loans could benefit from a period of new training and contemplation. We don't want them to repeat any mistakes that may have been made…"

And so forth.

"That's not what I wrote," I complained. "It has no edge to it."

"It's exactly what you wrote," he shot back. "If we literally translated what you wrote, it would be very discordant to Japanese viewers. It would be like using the F word on television in the U.S.

"Oh! OK."

86. Neither "Yes" nor "No" Exist in Japanese

After our banker corruption spot ran, we switched to an attack on global warming.

The Kyoto Conference had just adjourned with a world-wide declaration to address the problem and rein in carbon emissions. Well, almost world-wide. China refused to sign, but that was no big problem in Japan.

Clinton signed, but, typically, he hedged his bets and refused to submit it to the Republican-controlled Congress (where it would have died). Our opponents, in the Liberal Democratic Party (LDP) wouldn't commit to

186

enforcing the treaty without American participation. But my clients were still gung-ho for it.

Because the treaty had been negotiated in Kyoto, the former capital of Japan, the nation's prestige was on the line. So we decided to make it a big issue.

Again, my American style came out as I wrote copy for another ad:

"If America says no, should Japan go ahead with the Kyoto Accords anyway? The LDP says "no." But the Democratic Party says "yes." Protecting our planet is too important not to act."

Blunt and straightforward. But not in Japanese.

Again the translation droned on far beyond the length of the original draft, but I was used to that by now.

What really surprised me was that the words "yes" and "no" were in the ad in English.

Puzzled, I asked "why don't you run the ad in Japanese?"

"That is Japanese," my client answered.

"But 'yes' and 'no' are English".

"In Japan, too" he replied.

He then patiently explained to me that there were no words in the Japanese language for yes or no – they simply used the English words.

"Hi," he said, "doesn't really mean yes. It means uh-huh. I hear what you are saying. It's more of a neutral comment than an affirmation."

"And no?" I pressed.

"There is no word for that. Just 'euw' like a baby says when he doesn't like the food his mother is spooning out to him. It's not polite. You'd never use it in an ad."

True enough. When I wondered how they polled public opinion without using "yes" or "no," my Japanese friend explained that they did not ask people to answer yes or no. Instead they phrased the question this way: "Do you think that this idea is a good one that should be adopted? (that meant yes) or do you believe it should receive further reflection and consideration (that meant no)?

The omission in Japanese vocabulary reflected the nation's sense of etiquette. To reject an idea by simply saying "no" would be impolite. The softer language was the proper way to turn something down.

87. My Pillow and I Arrive in Brazil

My friend and frequent partner Luis Rosales had been building me up for weeks to try to induce a Brazilian candidate to hire me for his race for president. Luis, an Argentinian, had worked with me in elections in South and Central America and as far away as in Kenya. He often went ahead of me and tried to drum up business.

His descriptions of my abilities were sometimes a bit exaggerated. In this case, he had extolled me as a "genius" in my profession. Stoked by Luis' hyperbole, the candidate and his staff gathered anxiously at the airport gate for a glimpse as I got off the plane.

I emerged from the jet bridge—after a twelve hour flight—clutching my pillow, wrapped in a brightly flowered pillowcase. It wasn't a small pillow, but a king size bed pillow that I used to curl up with to sleep on long tedious flights.

Luis hastened to assure them that I, like many geniuses, was eccentric and not to worry that I was carrying a pillow as I got off the plane. "You know, all geniuses are a little crazy," he assured them.

Even though they say that the first impression is the key to any relationship, I got the client, despite my pillow.

88. An E-Mail from Turkey

Eileen and I loved Istanbul. In our three visits there, the chance to see Christianity and Islam living in peace right next to each other was inspiring. (Past tense, unfortunately as Turkish president Tayyip Erdogan has moved his country into Iran's Islamist orbit.)

As we were touring the Blue Mosque, the magnificent structure in the heart of the City and listening to the moving call for prayer that booms from all the City's minarets every day, we found ourselves, as always, surrounded by men who wanted to be our tour guides. A western couple unescorted in the tourist area is a bit like walking with a cute puppy in the park. People swarm around you. It's like you are a taxicab with your light on.

We selected one of the horde begging for our patronage and off we went, tour guide in the lead. Over the days of our trip, we bonded with him, learning about his family and his life in Turkey.

So I was surprised, several years after our trip, when my e-mail inbox had a letter from him. "You are very famous here," he began. "But not everyone agrees with you." He enclosed several Turkish newspapers featuring my photo and, I gathered, uncomplimentary remarks in Turkish in the body of the story.

I had appeared on FoxNews' Hannity Show that week when the subject turned to Bush's invasion of Iraq. The specific question was whether Turkey would allow our troops access through their territory to attack Iraqi dictator Saddam Hussein from the north.

I spouted off "of course they will." I cited the $19 billion loan from the International Monetary Fund (IMF) to Turkey (about half American money) to stabilize the sinking Turkish currency   the lira. "We bought and paid for Turkey. Of course, they will let our troops through."

Apparently, they get Fox News in Turkey.

The next day, I was denounced on the floor of parliament and the newspapers all featured that a "Top Clinton advisor" had said Turkey would have to let our troops through. The fact that it was true lent further force to the story. My flippant, off the cuff comments had sparked an international incident.

Sometimes, it's hard to realize how widely your remarks in a TV studio are broadcast. And even harder to understand that my background in working with Clinton would lend authority to my predictions (in this case, undeserved—Turkey did not let our troops through.)

When I told Fox News CEO Roger Ailes about the e-mail from Turkey, he laughed it off. "We got a call from someone named Suleyman who wanted your home address. We naturally gave it to him." Nothing like having a network that watches your back!

89. Advising Clinton on How to Overcome the Gennifer Flowers Scandal

Eileen and I were asleep in our Paris hotel room when the phone rang at about 7 a.m. in mid-January 1992. It was Bill Clinton. "I stayed up as late as I could so I wouldn't wake you," he began, alluding to the six-hour time difference between New Hampshire, where he was campaigning, and Paris, where he knew I was vacationing.

As the '92 presidential primaries unfolded, Clinton was hit with two key charges as he entered the critical New Hampshire primary: That he had evaded the draft (likely true) and that he had a longtime affair with Jennifer Flowers (he's admitted as much now, but back then he still denied it).

And now he was calling for advice.

"You have two negatives to handle: Flowers and the draft. Flowers won't kill you, but the draft will."

"The draft has me worried," he conceded and then launched into a long explanation of how innocent he was of draft evasion.

I had heard all that before and cut him off mid-sentence. "That explanation won't work. You can't answer the draft accusation. Nobody will buy your story. The only way to avoid getting killed is to hype the Flowers story so it gets all the media coverage and the draft is pushed off the front page."

The idea of actually drawing attention to Jennifer Flowers' likely true tale of a twelve-year affair with Bill was, to say the least, surprising. "People won't vote against you over Flowers. It's not 1988 and you're not Gary Hart," I said referring to how Colorado Senator Gary Hart's affair with Donna Rice had sunk his presidential campaign back. "America has moved on," I said.

And, in the ensuing weeks, Clinton ducked questions about the draft, but he and Hillary agreed to appear on 60 Minutes to discuss their marriage and Flowers' charges. The draft evasion story was buried and played no further role in the campaign. If the draft evasion charge had been more widely covered, I do not think Clinton would ever have been elected president, particularly since he was running against George H.W. Bush, a World War II hero.

At first, however, the Flowers scandal appeared to cripple Clinton. He had expected to win the New Hampshire primary or, at least, to finish second behind Congressman Paul Tsongas from neighboring Massachusetts. After the bludgeoning of the scandal, he finished third.

But, as I had predicted, the Flowers affair soon faded from the headlines and Clinton moved into the subsequent primaries in the South still alive and kicking on his way to the nomination.

There was an amusing sequel to this story. Right before he went on 60 Minutes, Clinton called me to ask what he should say.

"You should say that you are sorry you have caused pain in your marriage and will try to improve as a person, but point out that FDR was not always faithful to Eleanor, Eisenhower was not always faithful to Mamie, Kennedy was not always faithful to Jackie, and Johnson was not always faithful to Lady Bird, and that you hope you can be as great a president as they were."

Bill chuckled and replied, "That's good. That's cool. But if I said that, I'd have to find a new place to live."

90. "Bill Forgot We Slept Together"

Bill Clinton's photographic memory is legendary. Frequently, he would refer me to a passage in a book he was reading and, without consulting the volume, would close his eyes and recount exactly what page it was on and where on the page it appeared.

But his memory for the written word did not extend to other, more intimate, areas.

I remember speaking to a top person on Clinton's Arkansas staff about the accusations of womanizing. She, in turn, repeated to me a story about her roommate who was talking with Bill in 1988 as he assessed whether or not to run for president. Responding angrily to the charges of his promiscuity, he said, loudly, "This is all bullshit. I don't know these women. I never met them. I don't do this sort of thing!"

Later, back in their apartment, she told the staffer that she was so taken in by the fervor and apparent sincerity of his denial that "I actually think he forgot that we had slept together."

brilliant daughter Sarah Huckabee Sanders. I remember an eleven-year-old Sarah hanging around, listening in, as I briefed her father on my polls. And it is wonderful to see her walk the tight rope every day as Trump's press secretary. She never falls or even falters. Her Dad's daughter.

91. Beating Dukakis…Again

After my battles with Mike Dukakis in Massachusetts, I was shocked when he won the Democratic nomination for president in 1988. By then, I had become a full time Republican consultant, but the Party was still suspicious of me. Lee Atwater, Bush's longtime consultant was the exception. A maverick himself, he welcomed me and was interested in my experiences with Dukakis.

Early in the 1988 Bush v Dukakis campaign, the Democrat led by 17 points in the national polling. Bush seemed headed for a monstrous defeat. And Dukakis appeared bound for the White House.

As Bush fell farther and farther behind, I felt that there was a better way to defeat Dukakis. Since I had run the campaign in 1978 that defeated him for governor, I felt I had a lot of insights for the Bush people. I tried to reach out to Lee Atwater, Bush's long time campaign manager.

I asked my close friend and political mentor Charlie Black, Lee's business partner, to introduce me.

When I met with Lee, he quizzed me about the campaign against Dukakis in Massachusetts and was interested in how Dukakis responded to criticism. "I think you're running against Dukakis the wrong way," I advised Lee. "You're attacking him over issues where he will deny your charges. Like saying he's soft on defense or will raise taxes. He will disagree. And because his credibility ratings are higher than Bush's, people will believe his rebuttals more than your charges."

I suggested that they needed to change course. "Instead," I counseled, "run against Dukakis by charging him with positions he will agree to. Like capital punishment, for instance. He will agree that he is against the death penalty and will openly and repeatedly defend that position. If he doesn't, he'll lose his base of support among Harvard intellectuals. And he will never take a chance that he will lose his liberal base."

I pointed out that there were many positions Dukakis would defend and, I said, hit him on those. "Dukakis will defend his opposition to school prayer, the pledge of allegiance in schools, and his support for furloughs for prisoners with life sentences. He believes in that stuff and will defend it."

"Hit him on negatives where he will stipulate to the facts," I urged.

Atwater agreed and the campaign pivoted to these negatives. The first ad we did in following the new strategy (produced by Roger Ailes) contrasted Bush's support for saying the pledge in school with Dukakis' opposition.

True to form and as predicted, Dukakis vehemently proclaimed his opposition to requiring the pledge.

Then a bigger issue arose.

A conservative independent attacked Dukakis for granting a weekend furlough to an inmate named Willie Horton who was serving a life sentence for robbing a gas station and killing the 17-year-old attendant, stabbing him nineteen times and then stuffing his body into a trash can.

As governor, Dukakis ordered a program for furloughs and extended it to those incarcerated for life. The Legislature objected and passed a law banning furloughs for lifers saying that, with no death penalty, there was no incentive for them to return to jail. Dukakis vetoed the bill and then let Horton out on furlough.

While out of prison, Horton twice raped a woman and pistol-whipped and knifed her fiancé before being arrested and returned to prison.

A conservative activist, Floyd Brown, ran a famous ad attacking Dukakis for furloughing Horton. The liberal media attacked the Bush campaign for racism. (Horton was black and his rape victim was white.) The ad scored deeply.

Then, in a debate on October 14, 1988—three weeks before the election—Bernard Shaw of CNN asked Dukakis: "Governor, if Kitty Dukakis (Mike's wife) were raped and murdered, would you favor an irrevocable death penalty for the killer?

Dukakis fell right into the trap answering, "No, I don't, Bernard, and I think you know that I've opposed the death penalty during all of my life. I don't see any evidence that it's a deterrent and I think there are better and more effective ways to deal with violent crime."[28]Not a shred of emotion or concern for his wife in the hypothetical situation. He was finished.

Lee Atwater was astonished at Dukakis' answer. "You said he'd do that." For me, the episode and the Bush campaign proved a bit of a baptism of fire into the GOP and made me an increasing part of the party's strategizing.

(Years later, Dukakis said of his answer to Shaw's question: "I have to tell you, and maybe I'm just still missing it…I didn't think it was that bad."[29]Really, Mike. Think you're missing it huh?

92. To Which U.S. Senator Would You Entrust Your Kids?

Joe Lieberman, the former Democratic Senator from Connecticut who was Al Gore's candidate for vice president, is one of the most moral, ethical, honest, and fair people I have ever known.

193

I was in the Fox News green room with then Senator Fred Thompson (R-Tenn.) and Joe one night as we each awaited our turn to go on Hannity. It was usually fun in the Fox green room where you'd meet a nice assortment of interesting people by chance each night.

I was telling Thompson how highly I thought of Joe and the Connecticut Senator was actually blushing. (How few Senators would still be humble enough to be capable of a blush!)

I said that Joe is probably the one member of the U.S. Senate who most people would choose to entrust their children to if anything happened to them. They'd know their kids would be safe and would learn his values.

As the impact of my declaration was settling on the startled room, Fred, in his inimitable drawl, said, "I think I'd leave mine with Jay Rockefeller!"

93. The Governor of Texas Decorates My Pickup Truck

Mark White, the governor of Texas, had me pegged as a BMW kind of guy. So, he was delighted to learn that this slick New Yorker, his political consultant, had bought a four-by-four TOYOTA pickup truck.

I didn't let on that it was not to haul hay or construction materials, but to bring home tables, chairs, and dishes from garage and yard sales and plants from nurseries in our Connecticut neighborhood. But I did not disabuse the governor of his assumption that I was a convert who had gone "country."

White, who died in 2017, was definitely country—maybe upscale country. We got along well - he was a progressive thinker who started the transformation of Austin into a high tech center.

He was also colorful. He lavished me with praise, calling me "smarter than a tree full o' owls" and criticized his political rival as "dumber than a post." When he looked back over the early months of his four year term (1982–1986), he would refer to the time when "I was only a little bitty governor."

After his defeat in 1986, he noted the bitterness of Texans at the tax increases that had driven him from office. (the low price of oil had forced his hand). But over the years, his popularity returned as people rightly began to credit him with the explosion of IT jobs, particularly in the Austin area. "When the oil dries up, the computers will keep running" was his proudest boast.

He celebrated his return to popularity saying "when I first left office, people waved to me from their cars on the street. They still do. But back then they used only one finger. Now they use all five!"

Once, he was reminiscing about Texas' political history when he said, "John Connally taught us all the difference between innocent and not guilty."

Now, he turned his formidable skills as a country and western expert to decorating my truck.

He began by buying me a gun rack, which he cautioned me to keep empty. (Not because of any gun laws, but because it was cooler that way.) He proudly presented me with pair of red foam rubber dice to hang from my rear view mirror. But he was particularly pleased to give me two bumper stickers. One said "Jesus Loves...Some of Us." The other read "THEY CAN HAVE MY GUN WHEN THEY PRY IT LOOSE FROM MY COLD DEAD FINGERS."

I suitably decorated the truck and presented a photo of it to the Governor, who had it framed. He had converted this particular Yankee to Texan. (He celebrated by naming me an honorary admiral in the Texas Navy—that did not exist).

94. Roger Stone Calls to Make Sure Clinton Will Come to Nixon's Funeral.

I had become close to the bare-knuckled Republican political consultant Roger Stone over the years, but I was surprised to get a call from him in April 1994 as his client, President Nixon, was dying.

As noted, Stone had called me in November 1992, shortly after Clinton was elected, to ask if the president-elect would take Nixon's phone call.

But now, Stone's call had a very specific, if odd, purpose. He said that Nixon wanted to ask President Clinton to attend his funeral.

Ever since Nixon's resignation in 1974, Stone had worked with the former president to restore his tattered reputation. Apparently, Nixon felt that having the honor of the current president—from the opposing party—at his funeral was a big part of the process.

The call reminded me of Huck Finn who, in the *Adventures of Tom Sawyer* by Mark Twain,[30]hid in the balcony to listen to the eulogies at his own funeral, happy to hear how everybody treasured and loved him!

As Roger requested, I asked the president if he would go to the funeral and he said that he was planning to. I relayed the message back to Stone. Nixon's insecurity was so pervasive that he didn't take Clinton's decision for granted.

Wasn't that typical Nixon? To be dying and still so worried about his image that he would ask his aide to assure that the president would attend his funeral?

95. The Brown Paper Envelope that Contained our Plans to Cut the Capital Gains Tax

It was not a tax increase or a cut in spending that was key in Clinton's ability to balance the budget in his second term. It was a tax *cut*.

In 1997, the Congress and Clinton slashed the maximum capital gains rate from 29% to 21%. That reduction led to an *increase* in revenues from $79 billion to $127 billion between 1997 and 2000. And that, in turn, played a big role in bringing the budget into balance.

But Treasury Secretary Bob Rubin, the Administration's go-to guy on the economy, was a classic liberal and fought hard against any cut in capital gains taxes.

To try to win him over to a more moderate position, I visited him in his office in 1996. He was joined by his Deputy Secretary Lawrence Summers.

The irony of the capital gains tax is that it produces no revenue—and actually costs the government money. When the tax is high, investors tend not to sell their stocks, homes, businesses, and other property. Who wants to give hefty slice of one's profit to the government?

So a cut in the capital gains tax stimulates transactions and augments the number of properties paying capital gains tax, although at a lower rate. History shows that the net effect is to boost government revenues.

I pressed Rubin on why we kept the capital gains tax high if it produced no revenue and cutting it could slash the deficit.

"It's a matter of economic and social justice," he replied portentously. "We must not tax investment income less than earned income"—the classic liberal line.

"But people have already paid taxes on the income they earned," I answered. "When you tax the profits they make from investing their after-tax earnings, you are double taxing them."

Liberals and conservatives have used the same arguments over the capital gains tax for decades. We weren't getting anywhere just rehashing them.

Then, Rubin's assistant interrupted to tell him that there was a phone call he had to take. The Treasury Secretary went out of the room, leaving me alone with Summers.

To my surprise, Larry seized on the chance to speak with me alone to push his own proposal on capital gains. "Please don't tell anyone that I told you," he whispered urgently, "but I've run the data and we could cut almost all capital gains on home sales without losing any revenue."

I eagerly asked for details. While Wall Street was pre-occupied with capital gains on stock and other investments, Mr. and Mrs. Homeowner were worried about how much they would have to fork over to Uncle Sam if they sold their home. Was Summers now suggesting that we could cut this aspect of the capital gains tax and it would cost the government nothing?

He was, indeed.

"I'll send you the data in an unmarked envelope later in the day," he whispered hurriedly before Rubin returned to the room. "Just don't tell anyone."

"Can I tell the president?"

"Yes, but ask him to keep it to himself. I can't let Bob [Rubin] know it came from me."

A few hours later, a messenger arrived at my office bearing a plain, unmarked, brown paper envelope with Summers' data inside.

When I saw the president that night, I passed it to him and recounted my meeting at Treasury.

He chuckled at the secrecy and said he'd take care of it and protect Larry.

And that's how the Clinton Administration decided to exempt home sales from the capital gains tax if the gain was less than $250,000 per person, an exemption millions of families rely upon each year.

96. I Am Declared "Persona Non Grata" and Expelled from Kenya

My Argentine friend, Luis Rosales told me about Raila Odinga, running for president of Kenya against the thoroughly corrupt incumbent Mwai Kibaki.

Odinga had played a key role in making Kenya a democracy and he seemed like our kind of candidate. His father was vice-president in Kenya's first post-colonial government. During the subsequent presidency of Daniel arap Moi (1978–2002) and the transition to the democratic constitution of 2010, Raila was a pivotal advocate of human rights and democratic values. A good guy. (He claimed to be a cousin of President Barack Obama.[31]

Now, in 2007, Odinga was seeking to oust Kibaki and end the corruption and authoritarian misrule that had characterized his term in office.

Politics in Africa is heavily influenced by tribe. Odinga is from the Luo tribe (12% of population) while his opponent was from the more dominant Kikuyu tribe (22%). But the record of corruption first in the Moi regime and later in the presidency of Odinga's opponent Kibaki that benefited the Kikuyu tribe (to which both Moi and Kibaki belonged) stirred massive resentment from the other Kenyan tribes and they tended to side with Odinga.

I met Odinga at the inexpensive New Yorker hotel in the City, a notoriously cheap place to stay on the opulent island of Manhattan. The lobby and the lunch area were crowded with hippies and knapsacks.

Raila explained how he was fighting for democracy and human rights against a thoroughly corrupt regime. He engaged Luis and me to handle his campaign.

A few weeks later, we flew to Nairobi, the Kenyan capital, to begin work.

Nairobi looked like an upscale American city dropped into the middle of an African village. Animals vied with Mercedes for space on the street as fashionably dressed women walked by tribesmen in colorful dress.

I was appalled when I learned of the rampant corruption of the incumbent. It reached into billions of U.S. dollars. When Kibaki became president, six years earlier, he pledged that "Corruption will now cease to be a way of life in Kenya." But, in fact, it only increased. After Kibaki was caught stealing $770 million, he fired his anti-corruption czar and sent him into virtual exile.

My arrival in Nairobi was greeted with front page stories in the Kenyan papers and Odinga asked me to be the speaker at a major campaign rally the next day.

The Kenyan people didn't know anything about the full extent of the corruption under the incumbent. Press censorship had seen to that. In my speech, I ticked off a bill of particulars enumerating his scandals to the audience of almost 100,000 people. (who cheered every line)

But President Kibaki was not so happy. When my speech broke in the media—headlining the nightly news and the papers—he signed a decree declaring me "Persona non grata" and ordering my expulsion from the country.

Luis and I were scheduled to depart anyway, but otherwise we would have been arrested and deported.

Meanwhile, we had some time to kill until our flight and we decided to take a tourist safari though the preserve that adjoined the capital city. Touring in an open jeep, watching zebra, antelope, giraffes, elephants, and lions, our guide told us we were perfectly safe. "The lions think you are a car and can't smell you inside. But if you step out of the vehicle, they will smell you and attack," he warned.

Luis was not so sure the lions would not smell us. "Put your arms down, Dick," he cautioned me.

Odinga probably won the election, but there were massive irregularities that exploded into a virtual civil war between the tribes. Hundreds were killed. Ultimately, Odinga and Kibaki agreed to a coalition government—a deal that Kibaki promptly disregarded. Odinga ran again twice but lost each time. He remains a towering figure in Kenyan history.

Am I still persona non grata? I decided never to find out.

97. Wanna See My Sunflowers?

There's nothing more humbling than to be put firmly into your place.
When Eileen and I bought our small house in East Hampton in 1981 we felt like city dwellers unleashed on their first piece of property. It was just an acre, but, to us, it was a farm!

We immediately made plans to plant an extensive vegetable garden. I rototilled the ground to Eileen's specs, all the time fantasizing that I was

Pear Hanza, the Norwegian immigrant from the book *Giants in the Earth*, churning the soil for a new farm in America.

Eileen mapped out the garden with her usual élan and enthusiasm. "The carrots will go there, the lettuce over here, the string beans to the right, the peas on the left." And, she added, "to top it all off, we'll plant sunflowers all around the perimeter."

We rooted for the veggies each day and reported all new sprouts and blooms like excited new parents. But when it came time to harvest our crop and eat it for dinner, we realized that we had planted a little bit of everything. A very little bit. There were carrots, lettuce, celery and everything else, but not enough of each for a single serving, much less a dinner.

Oh well, they looked pretty, especially our pride and joy, the sunflowers.

I love sunflowers. On our trips to Provence in France, I always stop the car beside the sunflower fields.

As the flowers all face the sun, with me standing right there in front of them, they seem to be craning their stems to see over one another, looking like they are fighting to see me.

So I address them: "Gentlemen, Ladies, I am sure you are wondering why I brought you all together here. I have a message for each and every one of you: Sunflower futures are up! Record prices! Your futures are assured! All is wonderful!" The flowers withheld their applause, having no arms or hands, but, if they were adequately equipped, the ovation would have been thunderous.

I thought of my vegetable garden when I was in the Senate Office Building (abbreviated, amusingly, SOB) meeting with my client Senator Mark Andrews, from North Dakota. I couldn't stop bragging about my sunflower garden.

"You'll have to come see mine," he dead-panned.

The next year, when I was in Fargo, North Dakota, for a fund-raiser, I did. While I had a narrow border of sunflowers, perhaps twenty in all, he had 1,000 acres of them that he enjoyed immensely driving me around. Without a word he put me in my place.

Later, I learned that somebody else had a similar experience. A very devout believer in Johnstown, Pennsylvania, died and St. Peter asked if he could arrange something special for him in heaven. The man loved to tell the story of how he had survived the Johnstown flood. He would tell it at any opportunity. Could he tell it here?

"Well," St. Peter said, "as it happens, we are all getting together tonight and I'll put you on to tell the story."

He was so excited that night and, when St. Peter called on him, he puffed with pride. But, before he reached the mike, the saint took him aside and told him "Noah is in the audience."

That's just how I felt.

98. How to Launder Money

Eileen and I were in Freeport, Bahamas, relaxing with a drink at a beautiful outdoor bar overlooking the turquoise water.

We noticed, at the next table, a studious young man, in suit and tie (rare and conspicuous on the island), absorbed in a book. Peering over, we saw the title, "How to Open a Bahaman Bank Account." Obviously, he was learning about how to avoid U.S. taxes by routing financial transactions through off-shore accounts.

The book looked like a beginner's guide. (It might as well have been titled "*Offshore Bank Accounts for Dummies.*")

After about half an hour of intently studying the book, his phone rang and he abruptly put the book down and buried it in his attaché case. Then he got up from the table and walked across the restaurant to greet a well-dressed couple that had just entered. His guests oozed wealth from every pore.

He ushered them over to his table and the meeting began. From what we could overhear (and we were definitely intrigued) he was their lawyer and he was guiding them, with great authority—and, likely for a high fee—on the technical ins and outs of opening a Bahaman bank account, the very subject of the primer we had seen him studying before they arrived.

A good joke for years to come.

99. My Big Campaign for The Co-Op Board

Former House Speaker Tip O'Neill famously said, "All politics is local." That's true, but there is a corollary. All politics is the same.

It doesn't matter if you are running for president or for a very local office in your neighborhood, the way to win is the same. The same principles apply. Find an issue and ride it like a surfboard.

A good example was a campaign that my friend and Stuyvesant High School classmate ran a few years ago. I was a bit surprised to get an e-mail from him asking for my advice on how to get elected to the board of his co-op.

We discussed why he wanted to be on the Board and I asked him about the issues that he and other tenants were concerned about. He mentioned the elevator and told me that a number of tenants were very upset about how unsatisfactorily the Board maintained the elevators. Apparently tenants would swap stories about the times they were stuck in the elevator between floors. The elevator was only one of many grievances, mostly related to a perception that the Board needed new blood to face new issues and problems. But the elevator issue typified the difficulty that the old thinking caused.

The key to the campaign was to encapsulate all the tenant complaints in one slogan. I came up with this:

"Because the Board is stuck in the past, we get stuck in the elevator."

Negative ads in a co-op board election! My friend won—because he tapped into an important issue.

100. Sticker Shock

When Eileen and I bought our first house in Florida, we were excited about living in warm weather in a beautiful house, not too far from the beach—with a yard full of lots of colorful flowers!

We didn't expect to have serious political differences with our neighbors.

Turns out we did, although they were unspoken. We avoided all political debate. In fact, we generally kept to ourselves. And we definitely didn't have anti-Obama signs on our lawn.

But many of them were die-hard Democrats who had migrated from New York City and had been teachers or other civil servants. They didn't like Republicans. Indeed, in New York politics, they most likely hadn't ever met any.

Most were friendly, but a few must have harbored unrestrained resentment over our politics.

One day, during the campaign in 2008, we returned from a trip to Ireland to find that someone had placed an OBAMA sticker on our car!

None of our close neighbors had seen anybody lurking around.

We figured it had to be done in the darkness of night and laughed as we visualized some elderly leftists, dressed in Ninja garb and masks, slithering across the lawn in the dark, reaching up to place the sticker on our car, and sneaking away.

The car was a very old Volvo that we kept for family members to use when they visited. We had already arranged to give it to a close friend's twenty-year old granddaughter.

To her, the Obama sticker was a bonus!

We moved away not long afterwards. It wasn't a good fit for us for lots of reasons!

But, years later, another sticker vandal struck—in another place. In 2016, someone stuck a Hillary sticker on the mailbox at our summer vacation house in the North.

We laughed off the vandalism—after we got over our sticker shock—but, lately, we came to realize that this juvenile acting out was a precursor of what would become the style of the new "progressive" movement of hard Democratic Party leftists who would harass conservatives.

We were its early targets!

It's too early to predict what our next sticker shock might be.

TO BE
CONTINUED...

ACKNOWLEDGEMENTS

Our special thanks go to:

Jim Dugan, our dedicated and talented editor. As usual, he's done an outstanding job.

Clayton Liotta, our friend and collaborator, for his creative advice and cover art, for really making this happen, and for always having our backs.

Fredo Arias King and Luis Rosales, our Latin American friends and colleagues who reminded us of lots of details.

Michael Levine, our longtime friend, for his advice and guidance.

And to Tom Gallagher and Maureen Maxwell, family, friends, and colleagues, who are always there to help us.

Staying in Touch

I hope you will subscribe to my daily videos the ***Lunch Alerts***. If you sign up at *dickmorris.com*, I'll e-mail it to you every morning—for free. I'd love to include you—if you're not already getting them.

ENDNOTES

[1] Polifact, https://www.politifact.com/florida/statements/2010/mar/30/charlie-crist/crist-says-reagan-was-democrat-converting-gop/; Reagan was a lifelong Democrat who switched his party registration to Republican in 1964.

[2] The New York Times

[3] http://www.baltimoresun.com/news/weather/weather-blog/bal-stormpg-0303-photogallery.html

[4] http://www.quotationspage.com/quote/25650.html

[5] https://www.jfklibrary.org/learn/about-jfk/jfk-in-history/john-f-kennedy-and-pt-109

[6] Michael Stern, *Tammany Tiger Finds That Its Cubs Can Bite, The New York Times,* July 11, 1969

[7] https://www.nytimes.com/2013/12/10/us/joseph-napolitan-pioneering-campaign-consultant-dies-at-84.html

[8] https://fred.stlouisfed.org/series/A792RC0A052NBEA

[9] http://www.staugustine.net/blogs/rectify-names-a-blog-on-publishing/e2809cthey-had-learned-nothing-and-forgotten-nothinge2809d-march-11-2013/

[10] https://www.barnesandnoble.com/w/from-hope-to-higher-ground-mike-huckabee/1100390679, Mike Huckabee, *From Hope to Higher Ground,* Center Street; First Edition (January 4, 2007)

[11] http://nation.time.com/2012/11/26/hurricane-sandy-one-month-later/

[12] https://latitude.blogs.nytimes.com/2013/03/15/bergoglio-stood-up-to-kirchner-will-he-to-the-vaticans-bureaucracy/

[13] https://www.gpo.gov/fdsys/pkg/GPO-ICREPORT-MADISON/pdf/GPO-ICREPORT-MADISON-3-3.pdf

[14] https://www.statista.com/statistics/216909/market-share-of-soft-drink-companies-in-mexico/

[15] https://www.ourbigfattraveladventure.com/2018/02/09/medellin-colombia-from-the-worlds-most-dangerous-to-most-innovative-city/

[16] https://www.stuff.co.nz/travel/destinations/south-america/100490552/Medellin-Colombia-How-the-most-dangerous-city-on-Earth-got-a-makeover

[17] https://en.wikipedia.org/wiki/Triangulation

[18] https://www.usatoday.com/story/news/politics/onpolitics/2018/08/14/democrats-prefer-socialism-capitalism-gallup-poll/988558002/

[19] https://en.wikiquote.org/wiki/James_Carville

[20] https://www.nytimes.com/1982/12/12/opinion/poland-s-martial-law.html

[21] https://www.nobelprize.org/prizes/peace/1998/hume/facts/

[22] https://www.nytimes.com/1998/10/17/world/2-ulster-peacemakers-win-the-nobel-prize.html

[23] https://www.washingtonpost.com/archive/politics/1996/07/18/newsweek-writer-anonymous-no-more/817d28bc-2e61-4742-9370-7ae7739947d1/?utm_term=.b8590973a147

[24] https://www.goodreads.com/quotes/21898-then-out-spake-brave-horatius-the-captain-of-the-gate

[25] http://www.pewinternet.org/2014/03/11/world-wide-web-timeline/

[26] Jealousy by Nancy Friday, William Morrow and Company, December 1985)

[27] http://www.twainquotes.com/French.html

[28] http://content.time.com/time/specials/packages/article/0,28804,1844704_1844706_1844712,

[29] ibid

[30] https://www.goodreads.com/book/show/24583.The_Adventures_of_Tom_Sawyer

[31] https://www.telegraph.co.uk/news/worldnews/1574963/Im-Barack-Obamas-cousin-says-Raila-Odinga.html

Made in the USA
Middletown, DE
20 December 2018